Teaching Music in the Urban Classroom, Volume II

A Guide to Leadership, Teacher Education, and Reform

Edited by
Carol Frierson-Campbell

Published in partnership with
National Association for Music Education
Frances S. Ponick, Executive Editor

Rowman & Littlefield E
Lanham, Maryland • Toron
2006

Published in partnership with
National Association for Music Education

Published in the United States of America
by Rowman & Littlefield Education
A Division of Rowman & Littlefield Publishers, Inc.
A wholly owned subsidary of The Rowman & Littlefield Publishing Group, Inc.
4501 Forbes Boulevard, Suite 200, Lanham, Maryland 20706
www.rowmaneducation.com

PO Box 317
Oxford
OX2 9RU, UK

British Library Cataloguing in Publication Information Available

Library of Congress Cataloging-in-Publication Data

Teaching music in the urban classroom : a guide to survival, success, and reform /
[edited by] Carol Frierson-Campbell.
    p.   cm.
"Published in partnership with National Association for Music Education."
Includes bibliographical references.
ISBN-13: 978-1-57886-464-5 (hardcover : alk. paper)
ISBN-10: 1-57886-464-X (hardcover : alk. paper)
ISBN-13: 978-1-57886-465-2 (pbk. : alk. paper)
ISBN-10: 1-57886-465-8 (pbk. : alk. paper)
    1. Music—Instruction and study.   2. Education, Urban—Social aspects.
3. City children—Education.   I. Frierson-Campbell, Carol, 1961–
MT1.T387   2006
780.71—dc22   2005037240

∞ ™ The paper used in this publication meets the minimum
requirements of American National Standard for Information
Sciences—Permanence of Paper for Printed Library Materials, ANSI/
NISO Z39.48-1992. Manufactured in the United States of America.

Part III: Partnerships

Part IV: School Reform

Contents

Foreword

The sounds and sights of America's urban centers are an orchestra unto themselves. What better place to teach music and music education to the multitude of diverse students that attend school there? Many communities across the nation are challenged by demands on resources and time for students, but urban schools generally see those challenges increased because of the sheer number of students, the mixture of issues they confront, and the lack of well-prepared teachers available to teach them. Like every child in America, students in urban schools should have access to a comprehensive, high quality education including the arts as a core subject.

No student at *any* school can thrive without having well prepared, enthusiastic teachers confident in their ability to handle a classroom and passionate about their subject. Research indicates that the student-teaching experiences for most college students do not include an opportunity to practice in urban areas; thus, the attitude and dispositions are often colored by stereotypical assumptions about urban schools and their students. On the contrary, teaching in an urban school can offer the greatest personal and professional rewards. That is not to say that there are not challenges in urban schools, but a good teacher, a great leader, and an appreciation of the students offer more opportunity for moments of discovery and less of defeat.

Teaching Music in the Urban Classroom is not a panacea. No manual on any subject, much less the teaching of music, can provide all of the answers to all of the trials of teaching in the urban classroom. This one is, however, a good first step. Why? Music educators play several roles in their professional lives. These include roles as students, leaders, and partners with other leaders. Sometimes their definitions blur, and the roles vary in sequence and timing. The pace of change in their roles is often accelerated for dedicated teachers in urban school classrooms. The contributors to this book have experienced the thrills and the challenges of urban classrooms. Their passionate commitment to helping others like them by sharing their knowledge and experiences compliments your own passionate commitment to success, both for yourself and for your students. So as you move into the urban classroom, let the music begin!

—Brenda Welburn
Executive Director
The National Association of State Boards of Education

Acknowledgments

This volume is the result of many hours of work on the part of the chapter authors, and of a shared vision on the part of many others. It began for me when Diane Falk Romaine, the music department chair at William Paterson University, invited me to get involved with the New Jersey Teacher Quality Enhancement Consortium, a grant-supported outreach project between the university and three urban school districts in the region. Leslie Agard-Jones, Dean of the College of Education, supported the involvement of music teachers from these districts, and Dean Ofelia Garcia of the College of the Arts and Communication supported the interdisciplinary collaboration between the two colleges. Grant administrators Michael Chirichello, Bob Ross, and Stephanie Koprowski-McGowan provided financial and logistical support for the music education project.

Three things became obvious very quickly: (1) That the challenges faced by music educators in these urban schools were difficult by any standards; (2) that even amidst the challenges, many good musical things were happening in urban schools that deserved attention, and (3) that too few people were paying attention. A conversation with Nick Santoro, then-president of the New Jersey Music Educators Association, led to the creation of an "Urban Issues" position on the board of that organization, and current president Frank Phillips appointed me to that position. Nick also introduced me to the Urban Music Leadership Conference, and eventually to Ardene Shafer, former Assistant Executive Director of Member Services and Publications at MENC. Ardene shared my vision for a book that would re-start the conversation about urban music education at the national level.

This book was first inspired by the music teachers of Paterson, Passaic, and Garfield, New Jersey, who willingly shared their stories and their dedication to teaching music in urban settings. The vision would not have become a reality without the support of MENC. In addition to Ardene,

David Circle—current president—provided support for the book and the "Urban Issues" initiative throughout his presidency. Fran Ponick, Director of Academic and Book Publications, provided incredibly patient advice throughout the editing process. My sincerest thanks go to all of the contributing authors for their ideas, assistance, and patient revision. A special debt of gratitude is owed to Frank Abrahams for his help and advice during the reviewing process. Other friends and colleagues who have provided advice and direction include Mickey Flagg and Susan Conkling. Thanks are also due to graduate students David Hull and Abigail Riccards for help with copy editing. Finally, a special thanks to my husband, Bob Campbell, who still "makes my heart sing!"

Introduction: Perspectives on Music in Urban Schools

Carol Frierson-Campbell

Addressing issues specific to urban schools is not new to the music education profession. In 1967, attendees at MENC's landmark Tanglewood Symposium "sought to reappraise and evaluate basic assumptions about music in the 'educative' forces and institutions of our communities" (Choate, 1968, p. iii). That conversation included luminaries from across the educational, musical, and political spectrum, whose purpose was to set a future direction for music education in "a nation that had only recently reached a fair degree of consensus on civil rights" (Mark, 2000, p. 9). The resulting document is a testimony to complexity of this vision.

Clearly the issues we call "urban" in today's world were part of the discussion. In a blistering speech, David McAllester accused the profession of a kind of blindness in which "the controlling middle class in the United States does not *see* the lower classes and the poor among them" (Choate, 1968, p. 138). McAllester noted that those in "the Establishment" were "profoundly unwilling to face the invisible culture" or to admit that "the invisible culture has a rugged vitality of its own" (p. 138). The declaration reflects this concern: "The music education profession must contribute its skills, proficiencies, and insights toward assisting in the solution of urgent social problems as in the 'inner city' or other areas with culturally deprived individuals" (p. 139).

In 1970, MENC dedicated a full issue of the *Music Educators Journal* to "Facing the Music in Urban Education." Charles Fowler, then editor of the journal, suggested that the profession's cultural shortsightedness was reaching epidemic status. His description, while dated, resonates with many present-day concerns:

> In the ghetto, music teachers find that every ideal they were taught to adhere to seems to be open to attack or, at the least, seriously questioned. Worst of all, the so-called "tried and true" approaches fail to work. Music teachers in the ghetto soon discover an enormous gap. Not a generation gap, but a much more confusing and devastating one—a gap between their middle class values and the particular values held by their students. There is often a vast difference between the teacher's and the student's cultures. The disadvantaged student isn't particularly interested in learning the names of the instruments of the orchestra. He isn't "turned on" by cowboy songs. He won't easily enthuse over studying stringed instruments. He doesn't want our Lincoln Centers. He isn't interested in classical music; in fact he'll tell you with complete certainty how dull it sounds compared to James Brown or Aretha Franklin. The old image, the old ways, and the old music education curriculum are developing cracks. They don't work in the ghetto. Not only that, there is evidence that what happens on the front lines is becoming an epidemic that is certain to spread to the suburbs and beyond. (pp. 9–10)

Perhaps because of the renewal of the nation's highly politicized school reform efforts, urban music education was not a frequent topic for discussion during the 1980s. Perhaps because of the renewal of the nation's highly politicized school reform efforts, urban music education was not a frequent topic for discussion during the 1980s. Fortunately, the effort was renewed at the start of the next decade. I am grateful to co-author Marsha Kindall-Smith for pointing out a particularly pertinent commentary in her chapter: In an essay entitled "Minority Participation in Music Programs," (1993), Warrick Carter exhorted music educators to "work to change the climate of school music to be more welcoming for minority students" (p. 227). Carter's eloquent plea continues to inspire the profession:

> Please, no more hyperbole or philosophical papers; rather, we need Herculean deeds and actions to change the situation. If not, school music programs will continue to miss out on the participation of some of the country's best young musical minds. Young minority musicians will continue to make music, but they will not make music in the schools. (p. 227)

In 1995, June Hinckley, then president of MENC, reiterated the importance of music education for urban students who had lost musical opportunities that had been available to their older brothers and sisters. Hinckley described a population of urban youth who "saw the elimination of music programs as one more expression of a lack of caring on the part of the school leaders and the community at large" (p. 33). As the twenty-first century approached, Hinckley and others hosted the Housewright Symposium to "look at what . . . we as music professionals might do to insure that future generations would continue to experience the deep joy that we know as practicing musicians" (Hinckley, 2000, p. 1). Intending to refocus the conversation that began at Tanglewood, the symposium and resulting document sought to answer questions critical to the future of music education:

- Why do humans value music?
- Why study music?
- How can the skills and knowledge called for in the national standards best be taught?
- How can all people continue to be involved in meaningful music participation?
- How will societal and technological changes affect the teaching of music?
- What should be the relationship between schools and other sources of music learning? (Madsen, 2000)

Paul Lehman's address related to the skills and knowledge question presents a compelling vision of the future of music education. He predicts that the nature of the twenty-first-century music program "will reflect the wide range of diversity that exists in the United States" (2000, p. 95). Further,

Regardless of his or her field of specialization, every music teacher will be able to teach courses open to students lacking the time, background, or interest to participate in the school's select performing groups. Because oral traditions and aural learning are key to most of the musical styles of the world, awareness of these traditions and facility in teaching them will be essential for music educators. (p. 98)

The Housewright Declaration that summarized the event continues to stress the importance of making school music available to all students with this statement: "All persons, regardless of age, cultural heritage, ability, venue, or financial circumstance deserve to participate fully in the best music experiences possible" (Madsen, 2000, p. 219).

As a music educator, I came to the issue of urban music education relatively recently. After 12-plus years of teaching music in the small towns of northern New York State, I took a university teaching position in suburban New Jersey. My experience in urban schools began with my first field observation. On that day I visited two university students—one placed in a high school in a city near the university, and a second in a new elementary school in the town where the university is located. My visit to the urban high school fell on the day after a former student had been murdered in a fight. Guards and police were everywhere in the school, for fear that there would be retribution for the crime. Students' grief hung heavy in the air. A poster had been hung in one hallway for students to place their condolences to the victim's family.

My visit to the music classrooms was an eye-opener. The choir director proudly showed me photographs and news clips from 30 years prior, when the school had been nationally recognized for its state-of-the-art design. Yet on this day it was in lockdown mode. The spacious auditorium, once a performance center for the arts, had become a television studio. The choir director struggled to reach the group of students who did not see the connection between the classical music she taught and the reality of their daily lives.

I went from the urban high school to the suburban elementary school, where the beginning band was rehearsing in the science lab because the new band room had not yet been completed. The only security evident was a buzzer on the front door and a requirement to sign in at the office. The day's most pressing issue was deciding what kind of fish should go in the pond of the newly constructed science room. I returned to the university determined to explore ways that music educators could respond effectively to students in urban environments. It has since become clear to me that contexts traditionally considered "urban"—multiculturalism, interdisciplinarity, assessment, and educational activism—color every aspect of the music education profession.

Toward the end of my public school tenure, I was fortunate to attend a lecture by Dr. James Garbarino, an expert on youth violence. One of his many good points was the idea that "social epidemics" begin in areas of high need and social stress, and eventually move from those borders into the society at large. He noted that people who are not from high-needs areas are often blind to social epidemics because they are "not our problem," but that eventually these issues become universal. My visits to the urban schools in the region where I now live and work brought this idea of "social epidemic" to a new light.

Malcolm Gladwell further illuminates the concept of social epidemics in his book *The Tipping Point*. Gladwell (2000) believes that social epidemics— good ones like urban renewal and bad ones like random violence—"spread just like viruses do" (p. 7). They are "tipped" from inconsequential to epidemic status by incremental changes in the status quo. His thesis is that it is possible to learn to "tip" such changes by understanding how change works. This is why the present conversation is so important. The change needed in urban music education goes beyond placing music at the core of the curriculum. The change needed is that culturally relevant music education must become a *creative force* at the center of urban school reform.

At its most basic level, this change begins in the music classroom. Music teachers are at the forefront of change, of improving the status of music and education in urban schools. But others beyond the classroom—administrators, teacher educators, researchers, and policy makers—control much of what happens in urban music classrooms and schools. Still others—school reformers, advocates for the poor, activists from diverse cultures, and members of the communities served by urban educators—have important insights about the change process that must be acknowledged. While "urban issues" have been at the forefront of the music education conversation for almost 40 years, they have not yet reached the "tipping point" needed to make MENC's mission "to advance music education by encouraging the study and making of music by all" a reality in all urban schools. It is diverse voices, distinct and yet united, that will tip the equation in the direction of change.

The purpose of this book is to bring new voices to this conversation. Authors include graduate students, practicing music teachers from cities large and small, teacher educators and researchers, administrators, and even businesspeople involved in arts-based school reform. We represent a diversity of opinions, but are united in our concern about the role of music in urban education. We met during MENC's 2005 Eastern Division Convention to define what the book would be about. Some felt that we should define *urban* from the get-go, acknowledging the political, cultural, and economic pieces of the puzzle. Others felt we should dispense with philosophizing and politicizing and just talk about getting the job done—reaching kids in urban schools. Ultimately, we decided that our goal would be to stimulate further discourse with the hope of tipping the profession to renewed action. We expect that our readers will like what some authors have to say and disagree with others. We hope you raise your voice to agree, to dissent, or to make points that we have neglected to make. This too is part of the conversation.

EDUCATIONAL LEADERSHIP

> School leadership needs to be a broad concept that is separated from person, role, and a discrete set of individual behaviors. It needs to be embedded in the school community as a whole. Such a broadening of the concept of leadership suggests a shared responsibility for a shared purpose of community.
>
> (Lambert, 1998, p. 5)

Administrative support and educational leadership are critical to the success of music programs in urban schools. Four chapters explore these issues from different vantage points. Jill Warzer describes the reality of music education in a large urban district from the point of view of the arts supervisor. Her compelling narrative points out many pitfalls, but her dogged determination and inspiring results are an example for anyone interested in supporting music education in urban schools. Elizabeth Hazelette shares a music

administrator's perspective for helping novice music teachers learn to navi-
gate urban schools. Elizabeth describes the process that is used in Norfolk,
Virginia, to help new music teachers acclimate and thrive. This three-strand
support system includes a music mentor system, administrative support for
instruction, and a comprehensive new teacher orientation program.

Researcher Michelle Zederayko addresses the issue of school leadership
from the perspective of arts educators. Michelle spent a year investigating
the factors that turned a large urban high school in Canada from failure to
success. Her results indicated that the leadership of the arts teachers, who
had adjusted their schedule and curriculum to include most of the students
in the school, had been critically important for the school's turnaround. She
concludes that many of the leadership skills that create successful arts programs can help in the school reform process. Michele Flagg uses her experience as a public school music teacher in an urban area in New Jersey, to
outline the path from isolation to teacher leadership. According to Michele,
music teachers who build "a collegial and trusting atmosphere with their
colleagues and administrators" are in a pivotal position to fulfill the role of
teacher leader in urban schools.

TEACHER EDUCATION

> Music teacher education programs in colleges and universities must pro-
> vide a well-structured and culturally inclusive core-curriculum represen-
> tative of (a) traditional areas of music study that have undergirded the
> competencies and standards required to complete high-quality degree
> programs, and (b) ethnomusicological perspectives and competencies in
> order to prepare well-trained graduates for the teaching profession. . . .
> Institutions that begin to plan now for this growing social diversity will
> tap the largest talent pool and enjoy a competitive advantage throughout
> the next century.
>
> (Spearman, 2000, p. 167)

An "increased effort to prepare teachers for cultural diversity" is one of
the four most important issues in teacher education across the United States
(Nierman, Zeichner, & Hobbel, 2002, p. 821). Fowler noted this need in the
1970 "Facing the Music" volume of *Music Educators Journal*, and several
authors in this book continue in that vein. In the first chapter of this section,
Marsha Kindall-Smith paints a detailed landscape of cultural responsivity in
teacher education. The issue is still in its infancy in music teacher education,
so Marsha borrows liberally from general education, outlining several
visionary approaches across the country. Music teacher education programs
have much to learn from this chapter.

A related issue is alternative certification. Urban schools increasingly depend on alternatively certified teachers to staff their classrooms. Corinne Mills shares Connecticut's model for training successful candidates, describes additional training provided by the Hartford school district, and suggests ways for universities to reach out to these teachers.

Many innovative models of teacher preparation involve partnerships between schools and colleges. Specifically, the professional development school (PDS) model proposes that public schools and colleges of education should share responsibilities for research, pedagogy, and student achievement at both the collegiate and public school levels (Holmes Group, 1986). This model has influenced preservice teacher education programs around the country to join schools to provide training to teachers and students at both levels. Patrick Jones and Fred Eyrich describe one such approach, where a band director from an urban high school partnered with a college music education program to provide instruction to students at both levels. Donna Emmanuel shares the results of an innovative three-way partnership between an elementary music teacher in an urban school, a music education professor, and an introductory class for novice collegiate music educators. The partnership was structured so that the college students planned the lessons, the professor taught them, and the music teacher critiqued and learned new techniques in the process. Donna found that collaboration, open dialogue, and shared expertise held benefits for all involved.

The partnership described by Cindy Bell and Nathalie Robinson involved an after-school music program for at-risk students. They describe how a university music department and an urban school district partnered to provide undergraduates with hands-on teaching experiences in instrumental music. Utilizing funding from the No Child Left Behind Act, the partners created a successful community of musical learners and teachers. Patrice Madura Ward-Steinman describes a three-way partnership between an arts outreach organization, an urban elementary school, and a music education department from an urban university. These three organizations collaborated to provide preservice music teachers with opportunities to teach in an after-school general music program for at-risk students. Results indicated that these novice teachers reached all of the stated goals for the program and made the experience enjoyable, challenging, and extraordinary for the children. To close the section, we read about a professor and two graduate students from Teachers College, Columbia University, who used their combined ingenuity to create the Musical Heritage Project. This project helped them learn how to "connect what we were studying in class to real neighborhoods and real students." Randall Allsup, Amylia Barnett, and Emily Katz tell the story and share the lessons they learned in the process.

PARTNERSHIPS

It is through the persistent and reflective refinement of the practices of
the partnership—the design and implementation of the instructional
program—that the partners find common ground for their work and the
insights that stimulate their personal growth and development.

(Deasy, 2002, p. 905)

As Mitchell Robinson explains, partnerships can be "powerful vehicles for
improving student learning in music, but can also be frustrating, time consuming and messy." He uses the architectural concept of *tensegrity* to suggest that the inherent tensions that arise in a partnership of diverse opinions
and need are actually a sign of strength rather than weakness. Al Holcomb
describes how an educational partnership between a regional university and
Title I schools in a large southern school district has impacted teacher learning and therefore student achievement in music. Of particular interest is the
use of online portfolios that enabled teachers to learn from critiquing each
other's work.

Herbert Marshall studied three schools where the arts have played an
important part in school reform. A charter school in a southern city utilizes
an arts partnership led by a local university's music department to
strengthen its focus on science and math, project-based learning, and the
arts. Another school, in a northeastern city, utilizes Gardner's Multiple
Intelligences theory to embed music throughout the curriculum and provide
discipline-specific music instruction. The author notes that observing this
school in action taught him more about MI theory than 20 years of reading
about the subject. The successful turnaround of the music department in the
third school is not based on a particular school reform model or on a partnership with an outside organization, but on efforts by the music teachers
to reach out to the student body in ways that met the unique needs of urban
students. These changes resulted in a 349 percent increase in participation in
the music department. As Marshall explains it, this school's partnerships are
internal: "next door and across town."

Boston, Massachusetts, is the legendary birthplace of school music education. Jonathan Rappaport closes this section with the story of a present-day
effort to continue this legacy in spite of an economic downturn that has
taken music out of many Boston schools. The Conservatory Lab Charter
School began as a collaboration between the New England Conservatory of
Music and the Boston school district to create the innovative Learning
through Music curriculum model. This model school offers promising
results for arts-based school reform partnership and school reform.

SCHOOL REFORM

[Reform minded music educators] are the protagonists of change mind-ful of and responsive to the needs of their students and those conditions that create the best opportunities for the development of their students, classrooms, and school. As reforms evolve, their voices are heard, their choices recognized, their knowledge sought and interrogated, and their changes engaged and extended.

(Thiessen and Barrett, 2002, p. 766)

The de facto subtitle to any conversation about urban education is school reform. As Mark so aptly notes, "When the federal government took an active role in school curriculum for the first time, we entered what would be a continuous, ongoing, and never-ending era of school reform" (Mark, 2000, p. 7). While other authors have dealt with parts of this issue, three authors address it specifically. Susan Snyder's experiences constructing and imple-menting arts-infused curricula will challenge anyone interested in under-standing the reform implications of arts integration in urban schools. Beginning with individual music teachers and expanding to include nonmu-sic teachers, school faculties, and eventually entire school districts, Dr. Sny-der suggests that curricular change and therefore school reform should center on the creative processes that are inherent to literacy in the arts. The deeper question, of course, is whether the educational landscape is capable of engaging in the kinds of meaningful change that the arts can provide.

Robert Morrison turns the No Child Left Behind Act on its head, describ-ing negative impacts on some music programs but also pointing out how savvy music educators can use it to serve rather that hurt their programs. He explains that teachers and others who are interested in improving music in urban schools must stay abreast not only of the demands of NCLB, but of its emphasis on accountability in core subjects—of which music is one.

In spite of our ideals, if music educators do not have and take advantage of opportunities to work with each other, with their nonmusic peers, and with those beyond their schools and universities, they will be left out of the professional discussions that define the role of music in urban education. The final chapter in this volume describes a situation where participation in school reform efforts was not expected by, required of, or available to urban music teachers. Contrasting this with Thiessen and Barrett's (2002) vision of "reform-minded music teachers," I suggest that music will remain outside the larger school reform vision unless music educators seek and are given opportunities to join the conversation.

A familiar parable describes a scene in which a person has lost their keys in a dark alley and is searching painstakingly under a lamppost. As James

Garbarino (1999) tells it, an old friend happens by and offers to help in the search for the lost keys. This proves to be a difficult task, so the friend calls in reinforcements. This includes a "campaign" ("Find the keys! Find the keys!"), a "more systematic approach," a "behavioral approach," a "psychoanalytical approach," and finally a "literary-historical approach." The futility of the search becomes clear when the key-seeker confesses that the keys were lost "about a hundred yards up the road," but the light was better under the lamppost (pp. 179–180).

My first encounter with music education in the urban setting left me wondering how I and others in the profession had been left "in the dark" about the realities of urban education and the difficulties involved in addressing the musical needs of urban students. Upon reflection, it seems instead that a long-standing epidemic of social blindness has allowed us *to stay in the light*—that the privilege of our ethnicity, or our economic or educational status, has let us believe that the answers to these difficult problems lie in places where they are easy to see. They do not. If they did, the collective wisdom of the many musician-educators who serve American schools in so many capacities would have solved them long ago.

If music is good for children, then it belongs at the center of education, urban and otherwise. For this to occur, music educators must join forces with others in the corridors and communities in which they work. Administrators, teacher educators, researchers, policy makers, school reformers, advocates for the poor, activists from diverse cultures, and members of urban communities must join their distinct voices together in an effort to bring the transformational power of music to the core of urban education. The tipping point will occur when each of us moves forward individually and collectively to make this difference.

REFERENCES

Carter, Warrick L. (1993). Minority participation in music programs. In M. Mark (Ed.), *Music education: Source readings from ancient Greece to today*, 2nd ed. (pp. 227–228). New York: Routledge.

Choate, R. A. (Ed.). (1968). *Documentary report of the Tanglewood Symposium*. Washington, DC: Music Educators National Conference.

Deasy, R. J. (2002). Introduction: The growing impact of partnerships. In R. Colwell and C. Richardson (Eds.), *The new handbook of research on music teaching and learning* (pp. 905–907). New York: Oxford.

Fowler, C. (Ed.). (1970). Facing the music in urban education [special issue]. *Music Educators Journal*. Washington, DC: Music Educators National Conference.

Garbarino, J. (1999). *Lost boys*. New York: Free Press.

Gladwell, Malcolm. (2000). *The tipping point: How little things can make a big difference*. Boston: Little, Brown, and Company.

Hinckley, J. (1995). Urban music education: Providing for students. *Music Educators Journal*, 82(1), 32–36. Retrieved July 1, 2005, from the Academic Search Premier database.

———. (2000). Introduction. In C. K. Madsen (Ed.), *Vision 2020: The Housewright Symposium on the future of music education* (pp. 1–3). Reston, VA: MENC.

Holmes Group. (1986). *Tomorrow's teachers: A report of the Holmes Group*. East Lansing, MI: Author.

Lambert, L. (1998). *Building leadership capacity in schools*. Alexandria, VA: Association for Supervision and Curriculum Development.

Lehman, P. (2000). How can the skills and knowledge called for in the national standards best be taught? In C. Madsen (Ed.), *Vision 2020: The Housewright Symposium on the future of music education* (pp. 89–107). Reston, VA: MENC.

McAllester, D. (1968). Curriculum must assume a place at the center of music: A minority report. In R. A. Choate (Ed.), *Documentary report of the Tanglewood Symposium* (p. 138). Washington, DC: Music Educators National Conference.

Madsen, C. K. (Ed.). (2000). *Vision 2020: The Housewright Symposium on the future of music education*. Reston, VA: MENC.

Mark, M. M. (2000). MENC from Tanglewood to the present. In C. K. Madsen (Ed.), *Vision 2020: The Housewright Symposium on the future of music education* (pp. 5–22). Reston, VA: MENC.

MENC: The National Association for Music Education. (2002). Strategic plan. Retrieved August 30, 2005, from www.menc.org/information/admin/strategic plan.html.

Spearman, C. E. (2000). How will societal and technological changes affect the teaching of music? In C. K. Madsen (Ed.), *Vision 2020: The Housewright Symposium on the future of music education* (pp. 155–184). Reston, VA: MENC.

Thiessen, D., & Barrett, J. R. (2002). Reform-minded music teachers: A more comprehensive image of teaching for music teacher education. In R. Colwell and C. Richardson (Eds.), *The new handbook of research on music teaching and learning* (pp. 759–785). New York: Oxford.

I

EDUCATIONAL
LEADERSHIP

1

Music Education Administration in an Urban Setting: The Stone Drops Deeper Here

Jill Warzer

On the walls of the cubicle where I work hang two quotations that provide daily guidance and inspiration:

"Aerodynamically, the bumblebee shouldn't be able to fly, but the bumblebee doesn't know, so it keeps on flying anyway." (source unknown)

"Music is not a recreation for the elite, but a source of spiritual strength which all cultured people should endeavor to turn into public property." (Zoltan Kodály)

For the past eight years, I have served as a music curriculum specialist for an urban school system of 184 schools serving nearly 90,000 students. Before taking the position, I had taught music in urban, rural, and suburban schools for more than a decade, and had served as an arts education program administrator at county and statewide levels. I interviewed for this position out of curiosity—wondering what questions would be asked for a music supervisor position. Although I typically like a challenge, it is probably a good thing I didn't know what to expect when I accepted the position—I might have had second thoughts if I could have seen what was ahead. Conversely, I'm not certain anyone could really have described the situation to me in a believable manner. When anyone asks me to describe my job, my stock answer is, "any day can include the sublime, the ridiculous and the tragic, and often all

3

three." When I try to explain to prospective music teachers the challenges they may face, they listen, but I know they won't realize the impact of what I'm saying until they are in the thick of trying to implement their programs.

Music teaching and music program administration in an urban setting are not for the faint of heart. Similar qualities and processes are needed to achieve success, whether by music teachers at the school level or by music supervisors at the district level. Qualities of vision, commitment, persistence, patience, flexibility, imagination, and resourcefulness must be applied to processes of planning, collaboration, organization, assessment, and redirection in order to implement and expand music programs so that they serve *all* children.

THE NORM IS NOT THE NORM

In a typical suburban school system in the United States, there is relative certainty that every school will have a general and instrumental music teacher based on some adopted ratio. At the end of any given school year, it's fairly clear how many new teachers need to be hired for the subsequent year after resignations and retirements are taken into account. Music teachers can be reasonably certain there will be an annual budget at each school for materials, equipment, and supplies, and music supervisors can be reasonably certain there will be a music budget at the district level to fund instrument repair, maintenance, and purchase; pay for buses and adjudicators for music festivals; fund trips to hear the symphony or the local college band; and support professional development workshops. Most suburban districts adopt and purchase textbooks at regular intervals to ensure that there is uniformity among the materials that support curriculum implementation. Many districts also pay registration and travel costs for teachers to attend music conferences or take summer courses. In suburban districts, most families can rent instruments for students who want to participate in band or orchestra, and contribute to funds for uniforms and special trips. I often say to music teachers in our city that even music teachers in upscale suburbs have to sell pizza to support their programs; still, they can reasonably expect that funding to maintain their program will be allocated.

None of these norms exist dependably in the system I work for, and I don't know if they ever will. My colleagues tell me this is common among urban school systems. So why am I here, and why do music teachers who could easily choose to teach anywhere, choose to teach in urban schools? What keeps us going?

AN OPPORTUNITY TO MAKE A DIFFERENCE

It takes dedication to be effective as a teacher or as an education administrator in any system, but particularly in an urban system, where much that is provided as a matter of course in other systems is simply not in place. It is the students that keep us going, and the knowledge that their school music experience has the potential to have a significant, positive influence on their intellectual, emotional, and social development; life choices; and future opportunities. This is true anywhere, but as I say to teacher recruits, "Envision what happens when you drop a stone into a pool and the water ripples out in rings to the perimeter. I am certain you will make a positive difference in the lives of young people as a music educator anywhere, but the stone drops deeper here."

Dontae Winslow is a good example. Dontae started playing the trumpet in a city elementary school and continued through junior high school. Subsequently, he attended our city's high school for the arts, a select program for students who want to pursue the arts as a career. During his high school years, Dontae's mother became involved with drugs, but Dontae's devotion to music and the support of his teachers and school environment carried him through that difficult time. He continued his musical studies at New York University and later completed a master's degree in performance at the Peabody Conservatory of Music. I reached Dontae on his cell phone in Ohio where he was on tour with Queen Latifah, having just completed two years as a fellow with the Thelonius Monk Institute in Los Angeles. "Music was a catharsis for the pain I was experiencing at that time," he explained. "Music was the light at the end of the tunnel, a way to achieve my dreams."

But what if there had been no music program at the schools Dontae attended? In 1992, there were instrumental music programs in 65 out of approximately 130 elementary schools in our city, and in most of the junior high schools. By the time I arrived in 1997, site-based decision making in regards to arts programs had reduced instrumental music programs to 13 in elementary schools, 5 in 27 middle schools, and 10 in 25 high schools. Principals and site-based planning teams typically chose to spend inadequate "resource" subject allocations (art, music, physical education, etc.) for instruction that involved entire classes, so classroom teachers could receive the planning time guaranteed in their contracts. How many students for whom music could have made a significant difference have we missed since then?

How do you restore a comprehensive music program to a large school system in such a challenging environment?

A DREAM AND A SCHEME: THE IMPORTANCE OF LONG-RANGE PLANNING

"You've got to have a dream, if you don't have a dream, How you gonna have a dream come true?"

("Happy Talk," *South Pacific*)

But the dream can't just be the dream of the supervisor, or of individual teachers or parents or community members. In order to make change, a common vision must be articulated and a plan developed for the realization of the dream. I was invited, shortly after joining the school system, to be part of a recently organized advisory committee for fine arts programs (in our system that means fine and performing arts, including dance, theater, and the visual arts) that included system arts administrators, principals, arts teachers, representatives from the school board, higher education institutions, community cultural organizations, businesses, and individual artists. As a newcomer to the community, it seemed important to *listen* to what people were saying and try to get a sense of various people's agendas and ideas. I had previous experience with long-range planning, and realized it might be a useful process to employ, but I knew it would be better if the idea was put forward by the committee chair, as the recognized leader for the advisory committee. I happened to see him at a concert several nights later, and had an opportunity then to discuss a systemic fine arts strategic plan.

We were about three quarters of the way through the next meeting when this same committee chair looked over at me, and said, "Oh yes, the long-range plan." The group agreed, and chose a date for a day-long retreat. During the retreat, the group confirmed a common vision, added to a precrafted core vision statement, and engaged in intensive brainstorming, assisted by an outside facilitator. Over the next several months, I worked with arts administrator colleagues to shape our ideas into a coherent plan with timelines, budget expenditures, and persons responsible for various actions. Our major goals included increasing the number of arts teachers; providing adequate materials, equipment, and supplies; aligning curriculum with state standards; increasing students' access to cultural programs; expanding theater and dance programs; and increasing opportunities for students with special abilities in the fine arts. The plan also included a needs assessment and rationale for plan strategies based on current research. Eventually the plan was adopted by the school board as part of its systemic long-range plan. Our process became a model for arts planning for other districts in our state, and similar plans became a requirement for the receipt of state funding for districts' fine arts initiatives.

Music teachers can engage in a similar process at the school level: setting goals and creating budgets and timelines to improve their programs and involve parents, other teachers, community members, and even students to the greatest extent possible. I encourage music teachers to get involved with their school's improvement team, to make certain music is part of the future planning for the school. I also encourage them to make a budget in priority order and have it on hand at all times, as it is has been said, *Luck is being prepared for opportunity when it comes.*

A PLAN IS NOT ENOUGH: THE CHALLENGES
OF AN URBAN ENVIRONMENT

Implementing the long-range plan in our system has been, and continues to be, a bumpy ride. The most significant factors that impede measured implementation are the socioeconomic factors affecting students and the communities in which they live and the systemic environment of constant change and the uncertainty surrounding that change. Urban school systems live with stresses and challenges similar to those of families living in poverty: Cities typically raise less tax money per capita that can be applied to education than suburban areas, and urban school systems are significantly more dependent on federal and state resources than suburban districts. The federal and state program provisions are dependent upon annual allocations subject to legislative approval, and thus, the vagaries of politics. Federal, state, and local governments often do not confirm budgets on time, so districts dependent on these allocations are handicapped in organizing budgets for the coming fiscal year in a timely manner. Urban districts are often under intense scrutiny by state authorities, and must submit more documentation than other districts before allocations are awarded. Urban districts also have expenses suburban districts do not, from macro to micro scale, such as funding a school police force or replacing copper piping that was stolen for resale from a school's rooftop air conditioner. In addition, there is constant turnover in personnel and reorganization of administrative structures. In the eight years I have worked in this system, there have been four superintendents, four education officers, and eight directors of the curriculum office where my position resides. The curriculum office has been reorganized several times: for the first four years I was part of a fine arts office, which included a supervisor, two music specialists, two visual arts specialists (one of whom also coordinated cultural programs), and a piano technician/equipment manager and an administrative support person. Three years ago we were organized into levels, and I was assigned as elementary music specialist, and two years ago, as the result of a budget crisis, all the positions for fine arts staff were eliminated except one, the one I hold today. I have had to reapply for my job twice. Although it resides in the curriculum office, the parameters of the job description seem to change daily, as a variety of stakeholders call on me to assist with every aspect relating to arts programs.

Teachers at the school level also must deal with uncertainty and change. Approximately one third of students in our system change schools within the system during the school year. Principals are often reassigned from school to school from year to year. This year, 17 of the 23 middle schools have a newly assigned principal. In some schools, students are constantly reassigned from one class to another as their achievement level changes—so the group from Mr. Smith's class that shows up for music class may change from week to week. Classes may be combined with no warning, when a classroom teacher is absent or leaves (of course this is usually right before a performance!) and your first trumpet player all of a sudden vanishes when his grandmother who has been taking care of him is hospitalized and he is sent to live across town with his aunt. Or the radiator in a third-grade classroom blows up, causing a flood, and the third-grade class is reassigned to the music room and the music classes are relegated to the stage in the multipurpose room and compete with the delivery of lunch and physical education.

All of these environmental factors require music administrators and music teachers to be extremely patient and flexible, imaginative, and resourceful. It is important not to take the effects of these circumstances personally, but rather to "keep your eye on the prize," which is creating the best possible music experiences for the greatest number of students using the resources available at any given time.

One might ask, "Of what use is a long-range plan under such circumstances?" The fact is, in the uncertain environment that characterizes urban schools and systems, the existence of a plan can be *the* determining factor in garnering support for program maintenance and expansion. First of all, it represents the interests of an expanded group of stakeholders who care about the music programs, and who will advocate for decision makers and look for resource opportunities. Second, grantors and funders are more likely to provide support when they know their efforts are part of a larger plan that the school system and a diverse group of stakeholders are committed to over a period of time. In addition, the plan provides a rationale and parameters for the school system itself to support the program when funds are available.

For example, I was amazed when one year we were asked (immediately of course) to submit a budget of $200,000 for music program materials and equipment, as some additional state funds had become available. It was never completely clear where that figure came from, but I suspect it had something to do with the recommendation for per-pupil funding in the long-range arts education plan. Fortunately we had recently asked a music technology vendor to make a funding proposal at elementary, middle, and high school levels for keyboard labs, so we were able to draw on those proposals to further a strategy to increase the use of technology in music instruction. (Again, *Luck is being prepared for opportunity when it comes.*) Similarly, when the Fine Arts staff was asked to make recommendations (immediately of course) for where 40 centrally funded additional arts teachers might be placed, we were able to present a rationale for placement based on the long-range plan.

The existence of the long-range plan has helped to garner support from outside the district as well. Examples include $33,000 from the Mr. Holland's Opus Foundation for 17 schools' instrumental music programs as the result of an Annenberg Foundation grant to the MHO Foundation; $50,000 from the Toyota Camry Foundation in conjunction with MENC to provide sets of large, low-pitched xylophones for 24 elementary schools. Our most significant foundation partnership to date began when the VH1 Save the Music Foundation formed a partnership with our city's mayor and the City Council, called the Be Instrumental Initiative, to raise $800,000 in matching funds for a $1.7 million dollar total expenditure. The partnership has allowed us to implement 67 new instrumental music programs in elementary and middle schools over the past six years. Since the VH1 Foundation requires an instrumental music teacher be funded for the schools that receive instruments, at an amount of time appropriate to the size of the school, the school system has also played a significant role in the project. As of 2005–2006 we have reached a significant milestone, with band programs in all of our 23 middle schools. It is possible within the next two years that band programs could be offered in all of the elementary-middle schools as well, meaning that all students entering sixth grade will have the opportunity to be in a band program, something that has not been true in our system for more than 30 years. None of this would have happened without a plan. For more information about long-range strategic planning, see Czar (2005) and Lerner (1999).

KEEPING THE DREAM ALIVE

The challenge for the music administrator, on top of "regular duties" and in addition to coordinating these initiatives, is to keep the long-range plan and the commitments to the partnerships on the agenda of school and city administrators who operate in semicrisis mode most days. This is true for music teachers in schools as well: You must be patient and persistent to try to keep the music program on the school's agenda. You must be organized, and try to keep the daily and the long-range view of what needs to happen in mind at all times. It's important, too, both at the school and system level, not to isolate music as a subject area, but to look for opportunities to collaborate with teachers of other subject areas and involve *all* students in the program. A music supervisor can help music teachers do this by offering professional development opportunities on topics such as integrated curriculum and working with special-needs students. Music supervisors can also collaborate with higher education institutions to help teachers develop action research projects that can provide evidence of the positive impact of music programs in their school and school system. Such evidence can also help to keep the music program on the school and system agenda.

In general, music supervisors in urban districts would do well to become familiar with their teachers' strengths, and empower them to be leaders to the greatest extent possible, involving them in organizing festivals and events, becoming mentors for each other, presenting professional development workshops, engaging in action research, and presenting at conferences outside the system. These types of projects are good opportunities to bring together veteran and newer teachers, to the benefit of all. For example, several years ago in our system, a veteran teacher who was considering retirement found herself working alongside a newer teacher who had a strong interest in Orff Schulwerk. The newer teacher convinced the veteran teacher to attend an Orff conference and they began to work together with Orff pedagogy in their school. The veteran teacher was reinspired, has continued teaching, and recently was certified to conduct Orff workshops. When I became aware of their collaboration and developing expertise, I created opportunities for them to present workshops for other teachers, expanding their capacity for leadership. Similar collaborations with newer teachers can also help veteran teachers begin to use music technology in teaching.

At the same time veteran teachers can help newer teachers to become aware of, and appreciate, the important role that music educators have traditionally played in urban communities, where they are often music directors in churches, and performers or directors in professional and community ensembles. I am very much aware that more than 60% of the music teachers in our system will retire within 10 years, and that the majority of new teachers are coming from outside the city. I want these new teachers to understand what they inherit, and that the music education the young people in our city receive now will likely have a central impact on the future of music in churches and community venues here.

IT TAKES A VILLAGE TO SUPPORT THE MUSIC PROGRAMS

It is important that fine arts administrators regularly attend cultural and community events, as these provide prime opportunities to engage people in conversation about the music programs in the schools and invite them to become involved in appropriate ways. It is critical to attend concerts at schools in the district, or go along on trips when school groups perform in churches or community venues. These types of activities are also useful for music teachers on the school level. None of us can conduct our music program in a vacuum—it's important to engage community organization, business, and parent support. And it's critically important to understand the contribution of music education in the history and future of the community.

The predominant culture in the city I live in is African American. We can claim many artists of note who have made major contributions to American music, in jazz and blues and classical genres. During the past 200 or more years, music has played a central role in church, entertainment, and schools, with many musicians working in all three areas regularly. Several years ago, in February, a gentleman called the fine arts office, accusing us of robbing African American students of their heritage because they weren't learning to play African American music. He was quite obstreperous in his expression, and might have been dismissed as a crank, but I invited him to attend the upcoming student jazz festival and hear for himself. On the day of the festival, a taxi pulled up to the school and the driver got out, pulled out a wheelchair, and helped a distinguished-looking African American gentleman to disembark and maneuver the wheelchair into the school. This was the gentleman of the phone call. He sat through the entire festival—about four hours of music—enthusiastically applauding the students who were indeed learning to carry on the tradition of jazz performance. It turned out that he had been a dancer "'back in the day,'" performing in cabarets and theaters in our city and elsewhere, and had even invented some dances that became popular. Now, however, he suffered from diabetes and was unable to walk. It gave him immense pleasure to hear the young people play the music of his youth, and to know the tradition would continue.

This gentleman still calls periodically, somehow managing to locate me through several changes of phone numbers. It is uncanny how he always seems to call just when I am most discouraged. Most recently, he called me from a nursing home, where he is recovering from a stroke and the effects of a double amputation. "You stay right there, because you are doing the right thing," he tells me. "I feel reassured when I know you are still there."

We are fortunate that an archivist at one of the university libraries discovered a treasure trove of artifacts related to musical life in our city that she has since developed into a traveling exhibit, two websites, and an ongoing oral history project (See Schaaf, 1999; and *Songs and Stories*, 1999). These materials have been added to our city music curriculum, and we have used them to create professional development sessions that enable new music teachers to become aware of the tradition they inherit, and allow veteran teachers to feel like valued contributors to a legacy. Providing a historical context for musical study that is rooted in our city is extremely valuable. Similar resources can probably be found in other cities, and such a project could easily be developed through collaborations between music teachers and local colleges or universities.

Often I receive calls from pastors or parishioners who are looking for a piano accompanist who can play hymns. By this they mean they are looking for someone who can read music, because many young musicians playing in churches today cannot. To me, these queries are warning signs that musical genres and performance styles may be lost because city students are not receiving a comprehensive music education. As the former arts supervisor said to me often: "Do young people know what they like, or do they like what they know?" For young people whose heritage resides in the city, not providing comprehensive music education is a disinheritance as well as a denial of their potential abilities. For other young people in our city, such as the increasing population of new immigrants, music education can provide experiences where students can come together and share languages and cultures and create the music of the future from the creativity of the past.

The urban music administrator has a responsibility to help music teachers understand that the significance of what they do daily in the classroom can have a much larger impact than they might imagine. This understanding can help us get through the days when things seem overwhelming, so we can make it to the day when we go to a concert in a school that previously didn't have a music program, and hear children singing and playing Orff instruments, violins, cellos, and baritone horns, as an auditorium filled with admiring parents, grandparents, and friends listen happily. The happy faces of the students, as they take their bows, give you strength for another day.

REFERENCES

Czar, S. (2005). Virtual arts incubator: Fine arts fund. Cincinnati, OH: Fine Arts Fund. Retrieved September 3, 2005, from www.artsincubator.org/content/planning/index.html.

Lerner, A. L. (1999). A strategic planning primer for higher education. Northridge, CA: College of Business Administration and Economics, California State University. Retrieved September 3, 2005, from www.des.calstate.edu/processmodel.html.

Schaaf, E. (1999). The storm is passing over: The musical life of Maryland's African American communities from emancipation through civil rights. Baltimore, MD: Archives of the Peabody Institute of the Johns Hopkins University. Retrieved September 3, 2005, from webdrive.jhsph.edu/eschaaf/storm/.

Songs and stories: The musical life of Maryland's African American communities. Baltimore, MD: Archives of the Peabody Institute of the Johns Hopkins University. Retrieved September 3, 2005, from webdrive.jhsph.edu/eschaaf/sas/.

2

Surviving the First Year of Teaching Music in an Urban School District: The Music Administrator's Perspective

Elizabeth N. Hazelette

While surviving the first year of teaching music can be a major challenge in any teaching situation, the urban setting creates a host of additional challenges. Urban school districts often struggle with support for arts education as they deal with the requirements of No Child Left Behind and the resultant focus on accreditation and test scores. This can negatively impact arts programs in many ways: a reduction of funding for materials, scheduling irregularities, lack of teaching space, and loss of teaching time. The arts are often considered a frill and not an essential part of teaching the whole child. Unlike most suburban districts, many urban districts offer music as extracurricular or available only to those students who excel in their "core academic" classes. In the most drastic cases, music has been eliminated all together. Principals in urban districts find themselves having to make difficult choices regarding the fate of the music program. Add those issues to the everyday challenges of a first-year music teacher and teaching music in an urban district may feel insurmountable to an inexperienced teacher.

Although student teaching offers a taste of what is to come, the reality of the situation is totally different when new music teachers enter their own classrooms for the first time. Faced with unfamiliar materials, curriculum guides, lesson plans, grading, school policies, and even fund-raising, many new teachers barely know where to begin. They may face such obstacles as eaching from a cart with twenty-five sets of bells and only five mallets, CDs from one series and books from another, and of course, the ever-terrifying new teacher evaluation procedure. Add to that the continued focus on accountability testing and accreditation; the lack of emphasis on music as a critical part of the school curriculum; and issues such as lack of funding, low standards, and expectations, and community/school apathy and you have an overwhelming task. How does a first-year teacher deal with such tremendous challenges? It is critical for the music administrator to be proactive in developing a plan to meet the needs of new teachers in their district.

The greatest need of first-year teachers in urban schools boils down to one word: *support*. The key to building a successful foundation for a first-year teacher in an urban setting is instructional and emotional support. It is essential that they enter the profession well prepared by their college or university; even then, the most well-prepared teacher may find significant struggles without a strong support network. New music teachers who are fortunate to have an arts or music administrator in their district have a built-in support system to help them learn the ropes, especially in that first year. Those without district-level support can still find help from other administrators and from experienced teachers in nearby schools.

Music administrators themselves face a host of challenges. Often being the only advocate for music education in a school system that is focused on accreditation at any expense can be tremendously frustrating. Principals who are charged with reaching their accreditation goals amid reduced funding and increased pressure may not find it particularly important to focus on the music program and can even be outspoken about the need for more "core" and less arts instructional time. For that reason, music administrators must be vigilant. We must be active in the community and serve as the liaison between the school system, parents, community groups, policy makers, and other stakeholders in order to speak to the importance of maintaining a strong music education program in the district regardless of the issues. Strong music programs can be lifelines for students in urban districts and can serve as the impetus for staying in school. How often do we hear of students who are so dedicated to the marching band that it becomes the surrogate family they might not have? Yes, urban music educators have quite a responsibility.

So then, with all of these challenges, how can the music administrator give the novice music teacher a firm foundation and prepare them for what they are about to encounter? Music administrators must examine this issue and develop a plan to provide comprehensive support. In Norfolk Public Schools in Norfolk, Virginia, teachers and administrators have taken the challenges of an urban setting seriously and turned them into positive opportunities. Rather than focusing on what some school systems see as negatives, in Norfolk the "Urban Advantage," as it is called, focuses on valuing cultural diversity, makes sure that all students have equal opportunities, and provides the high-quality support necessary for all teachers to succeed.

The new teacher support system developed for new music teachers in Norfolk involves a three-strand approach. First, a comprehensive new teacher orientation or induction program is provided so that new music teachers can connect with the districtwide music program. Second, a well-defined plan for in-depth music instructional support, that focuses on issues common to first-year teachers, helps teachers survive in the classroom. Finally, a music teacher mentor system assists teachers with making professional connections that are so critical to their growth and development.

NEW TEACHER ORIENTATION PROGRAMS

Providing the first-year urban music teacher with a comprehensive new teacher orientation program is vital. Most school districts have some sort of new teacher induction program that focuses on school system policies, health insurance information, and so forth. It is equally important that new teachers have the opportunity to meet in content-specific groups (i.e., music) with content administrators to get a feel for their area of instruction before they face a class. This meeting also gives the music administrator the opportunity to present curriculum guides, lesson plans, the annual events calendar, and instrument rental and repair policies, and introduce music mentors. A sample agenda for such a meeting is shown below. The meeting should include time for new teachers to talk, ask questions, and air their concerns openly in a nonthreatening atmosphere.

Sample New Teacher Orientation Agenda

Wednesday, August 25

9:30 a.m.–11:00 a.m.	Welcome and Introductions, Music Office Support, NPS Music Calendar and Handbook

Thursday, August 26

10:25 a.m.–11:25 a.m.	NPS Curriculum/ Support Documents
12:15 p.m.–2:25 p.m.	Content Groups (elem/band/chorus/orch) Meet the Mentors!!!
12:30 p.m.–4:30 p.m.	School Visits with Mentor

An extensive packet of informational materials is distributed at the new teacher orientation session to give new teachers an opportunity to review what is expected of them many times during the first few months of school. We have had success with a packet that includes the following:

1. Instructional documents: annual music handbook with calendar of events, curriculum guides, sample lesson plan formats, curriculum guide roadmaps, sample music CRT tests, best practices guide, sample interdisciplinary units
2. Mentor contacts: names and numbers of mentor teachers
3. Professional contacts: professional music organizations (the state Music Educators Association [MEA] as well as the National Association for Music Education [MENC] and any local affiliates)
4. District materials: policy statements and dates of district events such as festivals, regionals, and all-city events

New teachers will be comforted by having the tools to seek out the information they may need. That, in itself, can reduce the stress level tremendously. They will need time to absorb the information; they may be on "information overload" at the conclusion of the sessions, especially if this is their first teaching assignment. Administrators can give them the peace of mind they need to start the year by coupling this new teacher information packet with time for talking to music mentors and peers.

MUSIC INSTRUCTIONAL SUPPORT

Novice music teachers may not know that they are expected to align their music curriculum, lesson plan format, instructional strategies, and discipline plans with those sanctioned by the building or district in which they teach. A good music administrator will make certain that these expectations are clear and well defined so new teachers can formulate their lessons to meet the appropriate requirements. Using a variety of methods for content-based instructional support will help new teachers begin to build a foundation to start creating their own instructional tools. The administrator is also responsible for translating districtwide instructional programs into music instructional terms and developing strategies to help music teachers implement them into their teaching. Urban districts, in an effort to overcome expectations of low student achievement and high teacher frustration, often latch on to the latest "educational panacea." Music administrators must stay abreast of these programs and guide novice teachers through the "translation" of these programs into their music classes.

One invaluable tool for the new urban music teacher is a music procedural handbook. This handbook, created by the music administrator, should contain everything from a calendar of yearly events to financial forms to sample lesson plans. The handbook can serve as an immediate resource for "How do I?" questions. It should be sent to each new teacher in hard copy form and can also be placed on the school system website, providing multiple means for locating information. A sample of the handbook used in Norfolk is shown below.

Sample Procedural Manual, Norfolk Public Schools
Office of Music Education

Table of Contents

Another good way to provide support for the new urban music educator is to develop a best practices guide. A sample guide can be seen below. Such a guide can easily be created by collecting proven teaching strategies used by the teachers in the district as well as materials from conferences. The guide should be divided into special focus sections such as general music and music à la cart. It has a profound impact on new teachers when they see their colleagues' opinions about what really works with their students in their school system.

Sample Best Practice Guide: Elementary General Music

- Have class rules posted and review frequently.
- Be consistent with rules and consequences.

- Each lesson should include a variety of activities—singing, playing, moving, and listening.
- Use short activities with follow up the next week. Introduce a form activity:
  1st Week: Listen & steady beat
  2nd Week: Sing songs and move to form
  3rd Week: Play instruments to form
- Develop a behavior modification plan that works well for you: stars, stickers, stamps.
- Put staff on the board with a note backed with masking tape. Throughout the class move note up as class completes activities. Should behavior problems arise, begin to move note down. Class gets sticker only if note makes it to the top of the staff. Once this is in place, you will rarely have to address negative behavior.
- Reinforce the positive, not the negative.
- Always use entering music. It sets the tone. Have students wait at the door until music begins—have them echo your steady beat.
- Seat students in color-coded teams with labels on chairs.
- Number chairs and give students a music number. Use this number throughout the year for classroom management as well as grading. This also eliminates arguing over chairs.
- Use competition between teams to reinforce good participation and class rules.
- Have chairs in U shape if possible. This helps with monitoring student behavior as well as participation.

Sample Best Practice Guide: "Music à la Cart"

- Make the room become yours when you enter.
- Prepare a guide for your teachers at the beginning of school called "How to prepare for music" (chairs facing front, desks cleared, etc).
- Remember that each class is different. You may have to adjust certain routines based on class size and logistics.
- Focus on flexibility, adaptability, and creativity in solving problems such as movement space.
- Get students focused using warm-up activity.
- Capture students' attention upon entering each classroom. This may be achieved by playing music as you enter the room.
- Have a student lead a steady beat activity. This gives you time to set up charts, books, and instruments.
- If students are seated at tables—make them teams—drop a color or shape in the center of the table so teams can be called.

To expand this idea one step further, the music supervisor can capture these best practices in action by using a digital or video camera to document observations and create a digital warehouse of best practices. Videotaping model lessons taught by exemplary teachers from throughout the district provides a direct and effective way to share instructional strategies and classroom management techniques. These visual models are much more impressive than a lecture, even when given by a well-meaning teacher or administrator. When new teachers see successful teaching strategies being used by their colleagues, they can imagine them working with students just like theirs. This eliminates comments such as "You can't do that in my school." Concerts, general music programs, and superior festival performances presented by colleagues in other urban schools can also be videotaped to help new teachers identify performance standards. Combining a best practices guide with the digital warehouse provides hands-on support for new teachers as well as a visual representation of the concepts. This is particularly vital in the urban district where time for peer observation or collaborative planning is not an option due to overloaded teaching schedules.

Interaction with other music teachers is yet another critical need for new music teachers in an urban school district. While working with music mentors and the music administrator develops a foundation of support, interacting with music teachers from different schools provides multiple perspectives on the role of the music teacher in the school. Monthly staff meetings, in-service opportunities, and idea exchanges can provide valuable opportunities as well. While these meetings are generally held after school hours and cannot be mandated in many districts, most music teachers will jump at the chance to interact with their colleagues. It is critical that these meetings and in-services are organized such that there is plenty of time for informal discussions. The music administrator must take on the role of facilitator and guide the discussion with creative problem-solving techniques so this time does not become a "gripe session." The formal agenda should include current instructional topics and best practices, clinicians, and staff-directed presentations. These topics can serve as a springboard for small group discussions and sharing. Often, sharing ideas and materials in small group conversation is where the real learning takes place for new teachers. Often veteran teachers have already successfully dealt with issues that new teachers are just beginning to see and can serve as a resource for helpful solutions.

NEW TEACHER–MENTOR PROGRAMS

Most school systems provide building-level peer mentor programs when new teachers are assigned mentors in their schools. Peer mentors can share suggestions about school policies, record keeping, managing nonteaching tasks, and some elements of classroom management. This type of mentor program is especially important for traveling teachers, as procedures often vary drastically from school to school. Most often, however, these mentors are *not* music teachers. Thus, it is critical for the music administrator to initiate a mentor program for novice music teachers from day one.

While creating a content-based mentor support system can be a scheduling challenge, benefits for the new music teacher are numerous and worth the effort. Music mentors can offer a wide variety of support to new teachers, including assistance with program planning, guidance on selecting "tried and true" performance literature, lesson planning, and effective music classroom management strategies. Other hot topics include dealing with parents, addressing student attendance, or counteracting apathy for the music program among the school staff. Since there is usually only one music teacher per building, music teachers may feel isolated in their schools. Without content-specific support, school districts are likely to lose new teachers that have not yet learned to tap their full potential.

Serving as a music mentor also has many benefits for veteran teachers. It provides them with a renewed sense of vision, an opportunity to share their knowledge, and a chance to hear new ideas from their mentees. With the frequency of burnout associated with urban schools, this is a great way to revitalize a veteran teacher. One experienced music mentor from the Norfolk Public Schools says that the best part "is the collaborative aspect . . . you have this running dialogue of questions, suggestions, and ideas between the mentor and the new teacher. They generally lack confidence at first so you keep the conversation going and they begin to see the possibilities for delivering curriculum *and* having fun! I am so rewarded when they begin coming up with their own ideas and want to share with me!" Another Norfolk music mentor said that mentoring "keeps me looking at my teaching through fresh eyes. I love seeing new ways to look at the same things. I also love helping new teachers use the survival techniques that it took me years to figure out!"

The first step in creating a music mentor program is to identify veteran teachers who are not only master teachers but have also demonstrated exemplary communication skills. Often, mentors spend as much of their time listening to venting and frustration as they do offering instructional support. They have to learn to redirect a negative conversation while at the same time offering a sympathetic ear. It truly does take a special person. Good mentoring skills include:

- Patience—Knowing when to talk and when to listen
- Consistency—Having the ability to gently redirect and get back on task
- Optimism—Talking about the positive rather than the negative

- Acceptance—Taking people as they are and helping them move to where they need to go.

After the mentors have been chosen, the next step is to arrange time for them to meet with the novice teachers. To begin this process, set up a meeting with the mentor teacher's principal to share the exciting news of this teacher's appointment as a music mentor. Be sure to offer the principal special congratulations for supporting such an outstanding teacher who is willing to make a difference in the lives of new teachers. Generally, principals take pride in the fact that their music teacher has been selected for this honor. At that point, a discussion about scheduling availability for observation time can take place. The goal is to have at least one half-day each week designated for outside school visits to allow for mentors to see new teachers in action. That is why it is imperative to get the principal on board early. Once the schedule has been determined, the mentor teachers can be assigned. The responsibilities of the mentor include sharing strategies for curriculum implementation, lesson plans, classroom management, and support for district-level performance events. If it is not possible to encumber an additional pay stipend for the mentor teachers, as is the case in most urban districts, other means of remuneration may be discovered, such as providing funding to send mentor teachers to conferences. This not only serves as a "thank-you" but also provides the mentors with new ideas to share with their mentees. The music mentor will become a lifeline for the first-year urban music teacher.

New teachers generally face rigorous evaluation procedures with multiple observations by principals, assistant principals, and department chairs. While principals clearly have the capacity to evaluate general classroom instruction and management, they often need assistance with content issues and may ask the music administrator for help in that area. It is difficult for the music administrator to attempt to serve as both mentor and evaluator, but sometimes that happens. A better solution is to make music mentors part of the teacher improvement plan. An effective means of supporting the evaluation process begins with the music administrator observing the new teacher, assessing their instructional needs, and sharing these needs with the new teacher and the mentor. Allowing the music teacher and mentor to work together is a very effective procedure for evaluative support. It also provides the new teacher with a supportive confidant who is not involved in the evaluation process. The administrator and principal can then work together to complete the evaluation. If in fact, the goal of the evaluation process is to improve instruction, this method provides tremendous opportunities for doing just that. Clearly, a centrally organized music mentor program can have a tremendous impact on the first-year urban music teacher.

CONCLUSION

Getting off to a good start is vital for the first-year music teacher in an urban setting, and having a strong support system is key. Developing a three-strand support system that includes a comprehensive new teacher orientation program, in-depth music instructional support, and a music mentor program can provide the groundwork for a successful first-year teaching experience. In light of the negative impact that No Child Left Behind is having on school music programs in many urban school systems, it is incumbent upon the music administrator to provide as much support as possible to make certain that new teachers come into their positions with a level of comfort and strong foundation of support that will carry them through the first year. Surviving the first year of teaching music is in itself quite a challenge, but with the added issues that often come in an urban division it can seem like an impossible task. Having a strong support system can provide new teachers with the fortitude they need to meet those challenges head-on and make a difference in their schools, and in the lives of children.

3

The Power of Arts Teacher Leadership

Michelle Wiebe Zederayko

INTRODUCTION

This chapter describes a case study of the relationship between an arts program in an inner-city school and its turnaround through a major reform. Findings indicated that the arts program was an instrumental element in the school's reform, and that the arts program's success was a result of strong leadership behaviors exhibited by the arts teachers. Although it was clear that the leadership behaviors of the teachers had contributed to the development of an exemplary program, the teachers themselves did not see themselves as leaders. Examining their experiences helps us to understand the ways arts teachers can employ leadership to enhance their programs and improve their schools. This is particularly pertinent in the emerging discussion of the nature and importance of teacher leadership as a viable option to "the traditional school organization with the principal at the top" (Buckner and McDowelle, 2000, p. 35).

The School

The source of the data was a secondary school (grades eight through 12) in a large city in Canada. The site was identified as an exemplary school with a strong arts program by the National Report of the Exemplary Schools project conducted under the auspices of the Canadian Education Association (CEA) in 1994. The strong arts program was also identified as having had an impact on schoolwide reform.

The site was chosen in 1994 to be part of the Exemplary Schools project because it was a school that had reformed itself and become a model of a successful inner-city school. Before its reform, the school had a "reputation as undemanding, dangerous, and catering to non-university-bound students" (Gaskell, 1995, p. 33). At the time of the study, however, the school had improved retention rates, was seen as a safe place to be, and had many graduates who went on to postsecondary education.

The research site was in a working-class area of a large city and had a culturally diverse student population. This secondary school strove to meet the needs of its diverse student population by favoring a school-within-a-school approach. In the midst of multiple programs, however, a majority of the student population was involved in the arts program. Indeed, it was because the research site had managed to carry out a successful reform effort and build a strong arts program that it was a worthy site in which to study the impact of teacher and administrator leadership on school reform.

Research Method

To conduct the study the researcher spent time in the school at various times over two school years. School visits ranged from three days to a week in length and involved observations as well as interviews with all of the teachers in the Fine Arts Department. In addition, present and past principals were interviewed and school records were studied. Observations and interviews were guided by the following research questions:

1. What was the impact of teacher and administrator leadership in school reform and on the development of the arts program?
2. What were the outcomes associated with the arts program that contributed to the school's reform and its exemplary status, if any?

TEACHER LEADERSHIP

Very often the way a behavior is conceptualized changes both the way it is labeled and the way it is perceived. This is true with regards to teacher leadership. According to Caine and Caine,

> *Leadership* is a deceptive word because it can be equally evocative to people for whom it has diametrically different meanings. We used to define leadership as the action of someone out in front or at the top of a hierarchy telling those below them what to do. While there is still an element of truth in this, leadership is now being dramatically reframed. Indeed, many of the qualities that we look for in leaders are precisely the same qualities that make people very good teachers. (2000, p. 7)

Ash and Pearsall add that the "new" model of teacher leadership "embraces the view that the process of teaching itself is a quintessential leadership function and rejects the notion that only activities outside the classroom constitute leadership" (2000, p. 20).

All teachers exercise leadership behaviors on a regular basis, but since they do not think of themselves as leaders, they do not conceptualize what they do as leadership. Considering that "the instructional leader is concerned with the technical core of operations, namely, well-designed and managed classroom instruction" (Griffith, 1999, p. 285), it is only reasonable that teachers should be involved in leadership. As Linda Lambert (1998) says, "school leadership needs to be a broad concept that is separated from person, role, and a discrete set of individual behaviors. It needs to be embedded in the school community as a whole. Such a broadening of the concept of leadership suggests a shared responsibility for a shared purpose of community" (p. 5). Leadership then becomes a dual responsibility shared by administration and teachers.

Teachers must realize the distinction between *leadership* and *management* if they are to successfully shift their perceptions. "Most of the researchers involved in exploring the concept of teachers as leaders agree that it is distinctly different from administrative or managerial concepts of leadership" (Wynne, 2001, p. 2). In addition, "leadership never involves just one person; it always involves two or more persons. Second, those involved in leadership are not just a collection of isolated individuals; rather, they interact with one another" (Heslep, 1997, p. 73). Reframing our understanding of the role of leadership in a school therefore involves a consideration of the ways in which teachers can and do behave as leaders.

This research was conducted to review the role of teacher leadership in school reform and in the development of a strong arts program. However, such behavior clearly is identified as leadership by school reformers: "We believe teachers are leaders when they function in professional learning communities to affect student learning; contribute to school improvement; inspire excellence in practice; and empower stakeholders to participate in educational improvement" (Childs-Bowen, Moller, & Scrivner, 2000, p. 28). The unexpected discovery in this research was that while it was obvious that individual arts teachers had a significant impact on the strength of the arts programs, and therefore the school itself, they gave themselves little credit for what they had done.

It is worthwhile to consider the factors that contributed to the strength of the arts program. To a large extent, the program was a result of specific actions and behaviors on the part of the arts teachers. In their drive to create a strong program the arts teachers had multiple foci. Specifically, they focused on the development of program excellence, accessibility, authentic learning, and program visibility. They developed a shared vision and worked with tenacity to enact that vision. Beyond their work in their own programs, the arts teachers also provided administration with essential curricular knowledge. Because arts-specific curricular knowledge is something that administrators may lack, leadership on the part of arts teachers can provide instructional support in the arts area (Burnham, 1997; Seidel, 1994). In spite of all these leadership behaviors, the arts teachers did not view themselves as school leaders and were not inclined to give themselves credit for leadership.

Arts Teachers' Perceptions of Leadership

The arts teachers were quick to acknowledge their drive to provide an excellent program, but they did not feel that their actions to achieve that goal exemplified leadership on a schoolwide scale. They did, however, identify several consistent themes that they believed increased the success of their program: excellence, accessibility, being involved in scheduling, authentic arts learning, visibility, and working toward a shared vision.

Excellence

The goal of program excellence was highlighted by a comment made by one of the arts teachers on the importance of evaluation:

> I guess it's about keeping students accountable and balancing that with self-improvement. It's about meeting a standard I've set by myself. It has to do with the quality of the program. It's one thing to do things just "'cause it's fun" but there has to be more sense of pride. Your name should mean something; it shouldn't be garbage.

Teachers spoke of the importance of communicating to students that the arts were serious disciplines and strove to create program quality throughout the curriculum. Comments such as, "we never let things go at fine—we've gotta be brilliant" exemplified the approach. This was also evidenced in comments from other faculty in the school. One said, "I do feel that the fine arts program has an impact on the rest of the school because the kids are proud of their achievements and excited to be a part of the band."

Accessibility

Teachers in the fine arts program believed they had to take initiative in reaching students to keep their programs strong. There was an underlying conviction that since arts classes were good for students it was important to get them in the door. As one teacher observed:

> I make it really accessible. For example, I have lunch rehearsals and lots of performances in the community, at seniors' homes, at elementary schools. The ele-

mentary schools are really important for raising the profile of the program. Those performances really bring students in.

Another teacher elaborated on the idea of accessibility by explaining how he helped students learn "their" music:

> I get music from the students—I tell them, "If you give me the song I'll figure it out for you." Usually if I just spend an hour or two, I've got it. I don't think it is a copyright thing really—I'm not giving them the music and the words are easily available anyway. That way the kids'll like the songs.

Being Involved in Scheduling

The arts teachers devised creative scheduling approaches to make their programs as accessible as possible. The choir teacher came up with possible solutions to a schedule that restricted student choice and then developed a workable format to present to the school administration. By studying the school timetable he realized that allowing students from different grades into each period would increase his numbers and make the course available to students who otherwise might not take choir simply because they could not fit it into their schedules.

Another approach to accessibility was to offer split classes, which made more work for the teachers involved but accommodated students' schedules. The band instructors incorporated a team-teaching component, which allowed for a larger band and provided a greater opportunity for band students. In addition, all of the teachers made themselves available when students needed to see them.

Authentic Arts Learning

Accessibility was only one of the areas in which teachers demonstrated their leadership capacity. They also considered the subject of authentic learning to be important. Teachers commented on the ways in which they made their programs as real and as meaningful as they possibly could because authenticity increased student learning and because, as one teacher pointed out:

> It's always an issue of balancing it. Where, because it's an elective, the bottom line is that the kids have gotta like it. So that balance is a fine line because you have to have consistency and accountability and enjoyment.

Commenting that she liked to make her students' experience "as authentic as possible," another teacher talked about providing assignments for the students that were connected with activities happening in the city.

Visibility

The arts teachers were also aware of the importance of program visibility and made efforts to increase the visibility of their programs whenever possible. One school administrator commented on the efforts made by the arts teachers to increase visibility of the program:

> [A]ny opportunity to get out into the community strengthens program. So, the band going out to elementary schools or the choir going out into the community—all of that is important.

Both the band and the choir teachers also spoke of the value of performances outside of the school as a way to build positive perceptions in the community for both the school and the program.

Visibility was approached in another way as well. Teachers spoke of sending information home to keep parents informed and to let families know of student achievement in arts classes. When appropriate, this communication was in the form of achievement certificates. As one teacher pointed out, the arts were not always perceived as important by parents, but when parents understood that their children were achieving in the program, it worked to increase positive feelings and shift perceptions of the value of those classes.

Working toward a Shared Vision

The arts teachers had a strong belief in the value of their program and in the value that the arts could add to the school. They developed a vision for a viable program that would contribute to the whole school and worked to enact it in the belief that access to the arts would enrich the students' lives and thereby reinforce efforts aimed at lowering the dropout rate and increasing test scores. This in itself represented leadership behavior, because "leadership and productive change begin with the creation of a compelling organizational purpose" (Schwahn and Spady, 1998, p. 45).

Arts teachers were clear about their vision for the fine arts program and its importance in the whole school, and they were tenacious about adhering to their vision even in the face of pressure to the contrary from the school administration. As the choir teacher explained:

> Every now and then somebody "down there" will get an idea. They're coming through and they want to do something—make a name or something—and they'll come up with some idea. Like one fellow really wanted to move the choir room down to that big barn of a room down there [*pointed toward auditorium*]. Can you imagine trying to have a choir down there? All echo-ee. Well, he just persisted and persisted, and I resisted and resisted. Really, have you seen my storage room? And I have all the hanging mikes in here and the sound system,

and can you imagine moving? It would be ludicrous! So he finally gave up. Why would I want to move?

This teacher, whose tenure at the school had been lengthy, pointed out that it took years to build such a good facility for the choir and that "someone who had just come into the school didn't have a sense of the history and therefore was in no position to start changing things." The teacher had a strong sense of what was best for his program in addition to his belief in the importance of the program within the school, and he worked hard to communicate that to the administrator proposing a detrimental change.

Thus, observation revealed consistent proactive leadership behaviors on the part of all teachers in the fine arts department. The initial comment of one very involved teacher, however, encapsulated the general feeling among the fine arts teachers. When asked specifically about his views on instructional leadership the response was, "Oh I'm not really into that sort of thing—I just do what I do and I'm involved here [*pointing around the room*]. Well, yes, I do what I do to keep my program strong but . . ." This teacher exhibited strong leadership behaviors on a regular basis but did not view what he did as "leadership"; it was just "doing what I do." Another teacher highlighted the "doing what I do" position in a way that also clarified the attitudes of many of her colleagues. After some thought, she expressed this view:

Teachers are trained in the way that they're trained and they don't want to change. They get working and they don't see outside and they get good at doing what they're doing. *But* we have to be aware of what is happening in the rest of the world and try to get on the bandwagon.

Another arts teacher responded that he viewed leadership as being important but not part of his daily experience in the classroom:

Ooooohhhhh, one of those "educational" words. How do I answer this one? [*long pause*] Trying to provide number one, a physical environment that allows or enhances people to do their job. People need to know that there is support and guidance. I think it is also holding people accountable, which doesn't always happen in education. Leadership means that you will also rock the boat when it is needed.

In contrast with their perceptions that what they did on a daily basis did not necessarily involve leadership, these teachers readily gave examples of the importance of leadership when asked whether instructional leadership was significant in building a strong arts program. For instance, a band teacher commented, "From the band perspective leadership really is important. Who is directing affects the program. The program really is the director. Great coach pretty good team—lousy coach pretty bad team." Or as a choral teacher suggested, "Although resources and facilities have to be there, programs will run themselves if you have the right people. Get the right people and then let them do the job." When asked whether or not instructional leadership was important, the response was an emphatic "Oh, *Doh*! Through personal experience I can say definitely, absolutely, undoubtedly, etc." The arts teachers frequently exhibited leadership behaviors and also believed that leadership was important in building a strong program but did not view the kinds of leadership that went into building a strong arts program as the same kinds of skills that built a strong school. The distinction in teachers' minds between personal initiative and leadership became clear when teachers were asked what they did personally to strengthen their programs, at which point they were both willing and able to talk at length about initiatives they had undertaken.

Teachers tended to view leadership as something apart from their jobs and, when the subject of leadership came up, referred to their department head or to some "person" other than themselves. One teacher pointed out:

> An instructional leader would be an experienced teacher who informs younger teachers of the "ropes." It is someone open to questions about department and school policy. That person should be informed and make an effort to keep other individuals in the department informed of policy and administrative decisions which affect the department and the curriculum. They must demonstrate *good communication skills* and act as a liaison and a resource for others in the department.

When teachers were asked how problems in the fine arts program were dealt with, however, they mentioned leadership considerably more often. Several made comments like this; "I don't have too many problems. Basically our Department Head is the leader of the arts program . . . so if there is a problem . . . but really there aren't problems." Leadership in the context of problem solving in the department was discussed in a different manner. One teacher said, "The arts are unique in that we're all our own bosses. We're all leaders in our own areas." Others echoed the belief that the fine arts teachers ran their own shows and, in that respect, were involved in personal leadership. "Each one of us is our own leader. Leadership is really important in building a strong arts program. Every single arts teacher is a leader and good at communication. Then you can build something greater than yourself." While the speaker felt that each arts teacher was a "leader" the leadership was considered personal and not a behavior that impacted the whole school.

Another view in the department was that "if decisions come from above, we consult as a department. I think we do that a lot." This view was reiterated by another teacher, who indicated that "we communicate well within the department." The comment was made that within the department communication was possible because "we have a lot of trust" and that means "I don't feel isolated at all."

In this study it became clear that teachers and administrators conceptualized school leadership roles very differently. Although the fine arts teachers regularly engaged in proactive leadership behaviors, they did not view what they did on a daily basis as leadership. Their actions and opinions suggested that leadership was a role for someone else and that school leadership was separate from them. When teachers were questioned directly about specific behaviors that could easily be constructed as leadership, they demurred and said, "[O]h yes, well I do *that* but that's just part of my job."

Arts teachers, for the most part, viewed themselves as *teachers* and did not conceptualize their actions as containing elements of leadership. Administrators, on the other hand, often commented upon those same behaviors as contributing to the efficacy of both the arts program and the school. Administrators conceptualized the arts teachers' behaviors as *leadership*, whereas the arts teachers saw the same behaviors as "just doing what I do." These opposing views had the capacity to hinder communication since the vocabularies the two groups were employing was disparate.

This lack of understanding about how administrators constructed leadership meant that the arts teachers did not believe they had deterministic power over their programs. Principals and vice principals, on the other hand, viewed the arts teachers as having substantial power to determine both program strength and the degree of student engagement. Principals made comments such as "any program success rests entirely with the teacher," "if you have a good teacher you can have a good program in a tent—it's not about resources or the room, it's about the teacher," and "the key is to get good staff."

Teachers vacillated between recognizing their own power to determine program strength and deferring to the principal's control. One teacher indicated that "unless there is huge support from administration," it is hard to have a strong arts program. This statement appears to contrast with earlier comments by teachers suggesting that the "key is hiring" because "programs will run themselves if you have the right people. Get the right people and then let them do the job."

These differing modes of understanding reflect Schein's description of "individual reality" as "what a person has learned from her or his own experience and that therefore has a quality of absolute truth to that person. However, that truth may not be shared with anyone else" (1992, p. 100). According to Schein, it is necessary to "clearly articulate what our actual experience base is" so that we can "move forward" (p. 100).

THE ROLE OF ADMINISTRATION

The administration in the study school showed a willingness to view the pro-active behaviors of the arts teachers as leadership. Because a former principal had believed that "everyone in the school should be involved in leadership," the current operating model of the school was built on the expectation that everyone should be involved in leadership. One current administrator explained his view of teacher leadership by suggesting that

> For me it is teachers being professionals. I believe in transformational leadership. Transformational leadership should transfer into the class, but students should be fully engaged. This is especially true in the arts; it's true in all disciplines, but especially in the arts. The teacher has to be a role model not only through delivery but also through his or her own activities as an artist.

All three vice principals at the school also voiced clear expectations for teacher leadership. One explained:

> Teacher leadership is essential for a successful program but also essential in terms of providing direction for the school. For instance, input to administration in terms of decision making is vital. Strong teacher leadership demonstrates ownership of programs. So much energy and commitment goes into making a strong program. Strong teacher commitment builds a strong reputation and a strong program and that is going to attract students.

Administrative support, as an important aspect of encouraging teacher leadership, was expressed repeatedly. A vice principal expressed her views on teacher leadership when she observed:

> My sense of a strong school is that it should be a place where any teacher who has an idea they want to pursue should be supported in doing so. Teachers should be encouraged to do things and they should be supported with their ideas.

As the principal pointed out:

> I think that instructional leadership comes in a variety of ways. It comes about when colleagues are able to talk with one another. It means that someone, and I don't mean the principal (it can be anyone—an administrator, another teacher, etc.), but someone provides the energy to make learning possible and exciting and gets talking happening.

The way these administrators described what they believed to be effective teacher leadership was telling in two ways. On one hand, their comments could easily have been describing the behaviors of the arts teachers. On the other hand, however, their comments indicated a willingness to accept and support teacher leadership within the school as a viable means to increase program strength and to improve the school as a whole.

SUGGESTIONS FOR TEACHER LEADERS IN THE ARTS

The impact the arts teachers had on the daily operations of the urban school in this research suggests that the kinds of leadership behaviors seen by arts teachers as "just doing my job" may in fact have a powerful influence on the life of a school. The following suggestions for teacher leaders in the arts are based on the conclusions drawn from this research.

- Allow yourself to realize that program development and many elements of your daily work with students is leadership.
- Create and measure programmatic excellence and promote the arts as a serious and worthwhile venture for students.
- Actively promote and increase your program's visibility and importance in as many appropriate ways as possible. Take a leadership role in promoting the music programs in your school by thinking about the ways in which they can benefit the whole school. For example, a great concert makes the whole school look good. Send notes home to parents so they understand that the arts mean accomplishment.
- Work with your colleagues to promote the fine arts in your school. The arts teachers in the present study were able to promote their programs more successfully by working together.
- Get involved in the whole school and strive to see the big picture so that you can actively strive to make your program as accessible as possible.
- Interact with the administration in a manner that shares leadership. Make efforts to share curricular and program knowledge as a way of promoting your program and making your school a better place. If you can show that you have thought about your program and how it fits into the mission/vision of the whole school, you are more likely to get heard.
- Finally, be tenacious and do not give up. Worthwhile change and development takes time.

REFERENCES

Ash, R. C., & Persall, J. M. (2000). The principal as chief learning officer: Developing teacher leaders. *NASSP Bulletin*, May 2000, pp. 15–22.

Buckner, K. G., & McDowelle, J. O. (2000). Developing teacher leaders: Providing encouragement and support. *NASSP Bulletin*, May 2000, pp. 35–41.

Burnham, T. (1997). Public policy and arts education. Drumbeat 96: Proceedings, survey results and recommendations. A report from "Drumbeat 96," the Mississippi Conference on Arts Education. T. M. Brewer (Ed.) (SO 028 971). Hattiesburg: University of Southern Mississippi (ED 426 004).

Caine, G., & Caine, R. N. (2000). The learning community as a foundation for developing teacher leaders. *NASSP Bulletin*, May 2000, pp. 7–14.

Childs-Bowen, D., Moller, G., & Scrivner, J. (2000). Principals: Leaders of leaders. *NASSP Bulletin*, May 2000, pp. 27–34.

Gaskell, J. (1995). *Secondary schools in Canada: The national report of the exemplary schools project*. Toronto: Canadian Education Association.

Griffith, J. (1999). The school leadership/school climate relation: Identification of school configurations associated with change in principals. *Educational Administration Quarterly*, 35(2), 267–291.

Heslep, R. D. (1997). The practical value of philosophical thought for the ethical dimension of educational leadership. *Educational Administration Quarterly*, 33(1), 67–85.

Lambert, L. (1998). *Building leadership capacity in schools*. Alexandria, VA: Association for Supervision and Curriculum Development.

Schein, E. H. (1992). *Organizational culture and leadership*, 2nd ed. San Francisco: Jossey-Bass.

Schwahn, C., & Spady, W. (1998). Why change doesn't happen and how to make sure it does. *Educational Leadership*, 55(7), 45–47.

Seidel, K. (1994). Developing successful arts program evaluation. *NASSP Bulletin*, 78(561), 7–19.

Wynne, J. (2001). Teachers as leaders in education reform (ED462376).

4

Five Simple Steps to Becoming a Music Teacher Leader in an Urban School

Michele A. Flagg

There was a time when music education in the large cities of the United States was cutting-edge, innovative, and at the forefront of educational change. Then something happened. As suburbia grew and expanded, business owners moved their families out of the urban areas and into the comforts of large houses, quiet streets, and safer neighborhoods. What was left were the "have-nots," the factory workers, minimum-wage earners, and new immigrants from a variety of cultures and religious beliefs. The new urban mix, brimming with traditions and cultural differences, altered the face of the city. Boards of education underwent transformations as parental involvement and consideration changed. Affordable housing, sprawling apartment complexes, and abandoned buildings changed the face as well as the academic climate of the neighborhood. Adequate funding for the education of these multicultural communities became an issue, and in some cases, state governments stepped in to assist urban districts in raising student achievement.

As a result of these social changes, arts education suffered serious indignities in many urban areas. Although cities once served as models for exemplary programs, this was no longer the case. With the arrival of national performance standards and diminishing test scores in the urban districts, many misguided educational leaders, far removed from the classroom experience, had the astounding idea that urban students no longer needed a general music class to be an integral part of their public education. After all, many of these students couldn't read on grade level or multiply and divide. How could the district possibly justify keeping a music teacher instead of hiring another basic skills teacher? And so a new chapter in music education was written. The "haves" got more exposure to the arts, and the "have-nots" got less. Instead of subscribing to the intelligent philosophy of educating the *whole* child, many urban districts across the country decided to cut and paste, starting with the arts.

The day of an elementary school music teacher from an urban school often looks like a scene out of a bad sitcom. Teachers trudge down long hallways pushing carts that are loaded with outdated books, battered CD players, chipped rhythm sticks, and ever-changing class lists. Their patched-together schedules provide no continuity, and they are often met by grade-level teachers who see them only as much needed relief, "prep givers." In many cases this is the norm, not the exception. In a recent meeting of urban music educators from various districts across New Jersey, the common mantra "I have no place to hang my coat!" echoed through the hall. Elementary band instructors who are lucky enough to have a teaching space may work in an empty closet, a reserved spot under a stairwell, or in rare cases an actual classroom with a door! Music teachers work in varied settings as unique as our students. We may see our students on a rotating schedule, perhaps by the week or perhaps by semester. While district policies for math, language arts, science, and even physical education are clear districtwide, instruction in the arts is open to interpretation by school leaders. No one doubts the importance of music in the urban school systems, but urban music teachers are like the scavengers in the food chain. We must find the leftovers and feast on them!

You may ask: What does this have to do with leadership? What does being a music teacher leader in an urban district have to do with leadership? It has everything to do with it! Urban music teachers are natural leaders because we are survivors! Who we are and the way we perceive what we do is how we learn to lead. We develop a vision, value our relationships with our students, and work to instill our deep-seated beliefs in the necessity of arts education in public education. We influence relationships and remain highly accountable for our actions. We have learned that in order to be effective, we must often reframe our situations because traditional notions of leadership in our schools are not within our locus of control.

Music teachers don't often see themselves as leaders, yet they exhibit all the qualities and use them on a daily basis. They have focus, negotiating skills, and many, like me, are on a continuous mission to accomplish the impossible in the face of adversity. My time is precious, my materials are coveted, and the chances of making a difference in the lives of my very important students take strength, stamina, and determination. These are all characteristics of leadership. Unless your perspective changes to encompass one of school leadership, success and fulfillment will remain elusive whether you are a novice or a veteran general music teacher.

I have taught in urban schools for 15 years. Like many music educators across the country, I have had the unique learning experience of teaching in more than one district during my 27-year career. I've taught in suburban districts where my students came to school well fed, well clothed, highly engaged, and ready to learn. Those schools had generous budgets, strong supervisors, and energetic principals who actually took the time to walk the building, smiling and happy to engage in conversation. There was never a question as to whether chorus students would come to concerts dressed in crisp white shirts and ironed black trousers or skirts; this was a given. The music room was spacious, carpeted, and came with a key to a lock that actually worked. Concerts were held at night, and were a full family affair with fathers, mothers, grandmothers, and aunts and uncles in attendance.

The students' music education moved forward with consistency and intellectual rigor. Two 40-minute music periods each week gave students the time to thoroughly learn musical concepts and theory, recorder playing, and rhythmic movement. As a teacher, I often left the quiet building happy and humming, with a voice to sing along to my favorite songs on the radio during my ride home.

All this would change when life events led me to take a job just over the hill from my comfortable suburban home. As I hastily drove through the city for the first time, I began to wonder about what differences were evident between an urban music teacher's experience and my own. I started to drive slower, allowing the rhythm of the city to invade my pleasant thoughts. What would it be like to work in the city? Why did I sense vibrancy and life pulsating around me when I stopped for a light? How different could it be? Children are children wherever you teach. Whether it was curiosity or a personal challenge still remains a mystery to me. I had resigned my post in suburbia and accepted a position in Paterson, New Jersey. Armed with knowledge, experience, and a vast repertoire of teaching tools, I came to urban music teaching in the middle of my life with an intense desire to explore the new world and succeed. I had no idea what I was getting myself into. I stubbornly argued with my family, turned a deaf ear to the music supervisor, and began working in two very different schools at opposite ends of the city, entering midyear into a system of more than 3,000 educators.

Leadership exists in all music teachers to a certain degree. Those who have the spirit and dedication to teach successfully in an urban district are almost certainly music teacher leaders. Whether it is a lack of space, nonexistent supplies, disruptive students, large class sizes, or difficult administrators, the music teacher must access the leader within to continually provide our most needy children with quality arts education. Music on a cart, lessons in a closet, classroom on the stage, or travel between multiple schools takes determination and stamina. Yet when all is said and done, it is the children that matter most. As I reflected on the lessons I've learned during my time in

Paterson, I came up with some simple yet essential steps to explain how this music teacher leader emerged.

STEP ONE: LEARN TO CELEBRATE
THE BABY STEPS

The two low-performing schools to which I was assigned were part of a paradigm experiment. This meant that students struggled through reading and math with physical education as their only special subject. My arrival signaled that arts teachers had recently been hired and now the students would have music too! The two schools found dedicated music space (which I insisted on). Brand-new CD players were waiting for me along with a current series of music books. I decorated my rooms with vibrant bulletin boards and artifacts accumulated throughout my teaching career. The teaching staffs were welcoming and helpful and I was eager to get started. Then reality set in.

Taking attendance became my first challenge as I tried to correctly spell and pronounce names that were unfamiliar to me. I passed out the new music books only to find that the majority of my middle school students couldn't read the words. In spite of the new CD player, the recordings to give meaning to the brand-new textbooks had not been purchased by the district. Since the last music class they had was in kindergarten, eighth graders did not know what a staff or a treble clef was. To say that my eyes were opened to the unique problems of urban music teaching would be an understatement. I went home the first week disappointed, disoriented, and discouraged. My five-minute drive over the hill to suburbia was one of reflection, frustration, and defeat. What on earth was I thinking when I took this position? Was it ever going to be possible to make a difference?

I began to see my challenge as that of a mother raising a child. I didn't expect my children to go from crawling to walking—there was a crucial step in between the two when I held their hands and raised them up to a standing position. Then I guided them gently through baby steps, teaching them how to put one foot in front of the other and tentatively begin the process of standing on their own two feet unaided by me. Whether this vision was divine intervention or my own mind finally finding an answer, I do not know. When I came back to school on Monday, I thought "baby steps" and I held on to that vision for survival. Every time I began to feel frustrated I readdressed my vision and transferred it to my teaching.

One of the wisest decisions I made was to enter a new Masters of Professional Education program at a local university. Like many talented music teachers across the country I knew *what* to teach, but learning *how* to teach it was the key! By transferring terminology and procedures from regular subject areas, I began to create and modify rubrics and learned to develop a process-folios format to fit urban students' needs. "Chunks" of important knowledge were broken down into digestible "bites" for the students, which allowed them to move at a slow but steady pace toward deeper understanding. Listing two or three new terms on the board for each lesson enabled students to remain focused and kept the major objective of each new lesson in sight. Short assessments that followed lesson-centered activities (even if it was an open book "can you find the term and use it in a sentence" variety) enabled students to see their progress.

Eventually I created a process-folio for each of the 600 students I saw weekly. My lesson plans reflected echoing rhythms, drawing music symbols creatively, and listening to selections of a variety of music styles from my own CD collection. Students wrote about music during every class, and we read the music lessons from the textbooks together. Each lesson would include a two-sentence reflection on what was learned that day. I read everything they wrote, giving grades for effort as well as content, and praising their treble clefs and note writing. Comments were always positive and encouraging and As and Bs given generously. My students would succeed with baby steps and so would I.

The language used with my students in music class changed. *Rubric* replaced rules, *assessment* replaced test, and *engaged in learning* replaced pay attention! I sat at eye level with the students and involved them in conversations, looking for every opportunity to discuss the history of music and lives of composers. Child abuse became a segue for a discussion about Beethoven, large families for learning about Bach, and living in a foreign country for talk about Chopin's music. I made everything into a story and invited their questions, often using them to springboard a conversation centered on the performing arts. Slowly but surely two written sentences turned to three and eventually a paragraph. Listening to Vivaldi and Bach became the norm, and identifying major and minor tonality correctly brought about new self-assurance in marginal students whose aptitude for listening excelled over their writing ability.

Leaders are change agents. They know how to dream and how to turn a vision into a reality. They see challenges instead of obstacles and they know that it's the little things that matter most. There is a point when others begin to buy into a leader's vision. Once my students could see their progress and came to the realization that they were learning in a unique and creative way, they wanted to learn more. Tangible success was within their reach and new learning behaviors emerged. Above all, they grew to trust my judgment and happily embarked on an educational journey with me. Good leaders make a positive impression on their followers, prove that they will make a difference, and encourage others to change.

How does one become a teacher leader in urban music? By taking baby steps in student success, documenting student performance, and proving to your students that you are tougher than them and twice as stubborn.

STEP TWO: NEVER GIVE UP; NEVER GIVE IN

The very nature of teaching music is collaborative, and this encourages us to be leaders. Music teachers have an advantage over other teachers when it comes to leadership because so many of our tasks involve the democratic process of working harmoniously with a group of people. In a school this means a large number of grade-level teachers, administration, and other educational leaders; students of different ages and of diverse abilities; and even the maintenance staff. It is part of our training to inspire the members of our choruses, marching bands, and orchestras to do their best. We wear an assortment of hats during the school day as classroom teacher, choral director, band conductor, private instructor, and choral accompanist. Taking notes on a page and transforming them into a meaningful and precise presentation takes stamina, stubbornness, and insight. We make important decisions on a daily basis that effect student self-esteem. We select music, plan concerts, prepare significant and creative encapsulated lessons, and represent our district in the community. We assist our students in making real-world connections between practice, accountability, cooperation, commitment, and compassion. We are comfortable thinking both inside and outside of the box, fostering critical and creative thinking skills. We speak a language that transcends cultural and economic differences and we are practitioners of inclusion in everything we do. How are we not teacher leaders?

Authentic leaders never give up. They refuse to give in to apathy and defeatist attitudes. They are as tough and obstinate as the challenges that unfold around them. The urban setting is rampant with such tests of character. Many students in urban districts have been given up on. They are mired in the false belief that their test scores are indicative of low achievement, low moral character, and poor self-esteem. Administrators scurry around us because as urban schools struggle through Category One status due to No Child Left Behind and budget constraints, music is the first subject placed on the chopping block as incidental versus absolute necessity. But there is hope.

The music teacher leader will stand tall and prove that music makes a child a better student and raises moral character and self-esteem. We document our success with every new performance. The music teacher leader gets involved with action research to provide evidence that our students outperform others on achievement tests. We demonstrate that activities in our subject area contribute to creating good citizens who become productive members of our democratic society.

The music teacher leader refines and retools the unpolished gems in his or her classes. Some of the most creative and expressive individuals that I have taught have lived in urban settings. These talented children don't give up and give in to the many dangers they face living in the heart of a city. So why would I ever give up on them and give in to pressured administrators that have been brainwashed into believing that 40 more minutes of reading or math is going to turn them into suburban scholars? Isn't it amazing how that same span of teaching time can transform an urban child into a dreamer of dreams, a happy eight-year-old singing an African song, or a confident fourth grader who can play the low C on the recorder?

The music teacher leader practices and refines leadership skills every day. It is within our capability to demonstrate that we will not give up on our mission to promote musical growth and understanding and we will never give in to misinformed central office administrators who try to marginalize our discipline.

STEP THREE: BECOME A LIFELONG LEARNER AND YOUR STUDENTS WILL MODEL YOU

Neither of my parents went beyond the seventh grade, but every morning as far back as I can remember they read and studied the entire daily newspaper. Many mornings I would pick up one of the few books that I owned and sit with them, mimicking their intense faces. This taught me that learning is a lifelong process, and that my thirst to know why and how was something I had to pursue on my own. Because of my gregarious and outgoing nature I loved to share my new bits of wisdom with anyone who would listen. It eventually led me to the classroom where I have a captivated audience of over seven hundred students a week. It is often said that music teaching is not a profession but a vocation. The ability to be a teacher leader may come naturally to some and may be a learned skill to others. Either way, the teacher leader models lifelong learning for students and peers. Collaboration, professional dialogue, and discussion and a desire to see others succeed drive us to be the best music teacher we know how to be. Sharing unconventional teaching tips, making ourselves available to novice and preservice music teachers, and inviting administrators to participate in our lessons should be the norm.

The music teacher leader raises the bar for peers and students. One way of doing this is through weaving the core curriculum through our subjects in every lesson. Math, social studies, language arts, geography, art, physical education, and science are all connected to the music lesson. A music teacher leader should be on a constant quest to infuse core content into every lesson. Experimentation, valid and short assessments, and informal student surveys continue to spark student interest. Reading and researching about brain-based learning and backward designed curriculum will put your classes back on the cutting edge of music education. When your students are aware of your desire to learn and to know more, they model you.

I have learned to Google with the best of them! There is so much information at our fingertips today. Just typing a word into that little box on the computer opens a whole new world of learning. Reading articles; sharing them with my principal or supervisor; questioning and reflecting on different teaching techniques, methods, and general music lessons available at no cost on the web have broadened my educational horizon.

We are never too old to learn or to try a new approach in our classrooms. The music teacher leader embraces change, continues to grow, and models lifelong learning for his or her students. Urban students require role models. They have to have individuals who practice what they preach. Urban education calls for dedicated teachers who are not afraid to say "I don't know but I'll find out for you." Students want the security of seeing you day after day, committed to their need to know and ready to guide them on a journey though our very interesting and exciting subject. They learn discipline and commitment by practicing it in the classes taught by music teacher leaders. Preservice and novice teachers necessitate the supervision and support of seasoned music teacher leaders because soon they will be in our shoes. Take your learning to the next stage and transport others with you into the world of learning as a way of life. Change the climate of your school one child at a time. Secure your position as a vital and essential staff member in your building by being the best you can be and continue to learn.

Fostering leadership proficiencies through classes in educational administration and supervision should be encouraged as important components to professional development. Taking the progressive step into an educational leadership program led me to better understand the role of music in public education. My students are constantly interested in my assignments and take delight in the fact that they often become my homework! We are in the same place—learning and growing while trying to make sense of it all, challenging ourselves to know more, and developing the strength of character to continue our journey.

STEP FOUR: RELEASE THE MUSIC TEACHER
LEADER IN YOU AND PASS IT ON

Whether or not you have seen yourself as a leader is inconsequential: if you are a successful music teacher in an urban school, you already are. You are not "only the music teacher." You are a vital connection to other subjects, other teachers, and a powerful link to your administrators. You see the entire school population every week, network with every teacher of every grade level, and have practiced core content integration with students since their first contact with you in kindergarten. Community members and family members attend your concerts—possibly the only cheerful and constructive interaction that inner-city parents have with your school. Whether you have a chorus, a marching band, or a recorder class, every student learns the ability to work collaboratively and creatively from you.

The urban setting provides us with a larger view of the world and our place within it. The music teacher as leader builds bridges across cultures, subjects, grade levels, and personalities. These bridges continue beyond the classroom door. Urban students who participate in meaningful collaborations learn tolerance and acceptance. Their worldviews expand as their unique future places in society become more apparent.

"A rock pile ceases to be a rock pile the moment a single man contemplates it, bearing within him the image of a cathedral" (Antoine de Saint-Exupery). When I stand back and visualize my position as music teacher leader, I can begin to see the bigger picture. When I step out of my isolated classroom-on-a-stage and see myself within my building and this rich community, I begin to broaden my view and gain a perspective of myself as a music teacher who has learned how to lead. It helps to refocus my thinking to encompass the vision of myself as a leader within the school.

Instead of comparing yourself to other grade-level teachers, compare your abilities to those of the administrators in the building. Like them, some of us network with 10 or more staff members every day. Special subject teachers of art, music, and physical education are often more engaged in student growth and development than the grade-level teacher because we move beyond specific age groups and see the school as a whole. Multiple grade level interaction exists in our activities. It is often in our classes, our choruses, our bands and orchestras where moral character is developed and long-lasting connections are made to numerous forms of knowledge and understanding. This is not a teacher's view. It is a leader's vision.

STEP FIVE: MAKE TIME TO REFLECT ON HOW FAR THOSE BABY STEPS HAVE TAKEN YOU ON YOUR PERSONAL JOURNEY TO BECOMING A MUSIC TEACHER LEADER

Successful music teacher leaders take the time to glance backward as they progress forward. They reflect on where they have been, where they are, and where they are going. After eight years in the same school I can see how far I have come, and it is humbling. Those baby steps have turned into confident strides. I never would have believed the incredible things my students are accomplishing on their educational journeys.

Our school now has a chorus of more than 100 students and our concerts include songs in many different languages. The students read vocal scores because they now understand notation and expressive markings. We have a variety of black-and-white outfits on hand that have been donated to our school to ensure that on the day of the concert every student is able to participate with pride and dignity. Our concerts have become an important part of our school culture.

General music class students write major and minor scales and are able to identify the differences visually and aurally. Seventh graders bring their recorders to class and proudly play along with the songs in the music books. Students are fascinated with video clips on opera, Irish dancing, or short orchestral vignettes, often writing three-paragraph essays on what they see and what they have learned. They use Kodály hand signals and recognize intervals. First graders make connections between *ta* and the quarter note and second graders are able to identify ABA form in haiku poems as well as simple vocal scores in their books. My students retain an amazing amount of information from week to week. Watching them take ownership of their knowledge is a source of never-ending joy for me, and it makes me want to do more to help them learn.

The supportive administration of my school has allowed me to take my students on a wonderful musical expedition. My principal knows that I represent our school with integrity and honor. There is mutual respect between us. If I present a problem to her I have two solutions ready to suggest, at all times keeping the students' best interests in mind.

This is what being a music teacher leader is about—working together with other educators toward a common goal. As Michael Fullan (2003) states, "school leadership is a collective enterprise. . . . it is the combined forces of shared leadership that makes a difference." Educational leaders who are successful in urban settings build a collegial and trusting atmosphere. They engage all stakeholders in education. They are reflective and creative thinkers. They lead by their actions and their reactions to unusual and often complicated situations. Their efforts affect school climate and school culture. They are important and necessary components to an urban school's traditions and values. As teachers of the arts, we are in a pivotal position to fulfill the role of teacher leader in urban schools. It is through the experience of teaching the meaningful subject of music that the leadership ability in all of us is encouraged, fostered, and nurtured.

REFERENCES

Fullan, M. (2003). *The moral imperative of school leadership*. Thousand Oaks, CA: Corwin Press.

II

TEACHER EDUCATION

5

I Plant My Feet on Higher Ground: Music Teacher Education for Urban Schools

Marsha Kindall-Smith

In a voice similar to her famous late father, Rev. Martin Luther King, Jr., Rev. Bernice King captivated the audience with her eloquent delivery:

> A father and his son went fishing one day. While they were out on the lake, the little boy started giggling. The father asked, "What is so funny, Jimmy?" . . . Little Jimmy pointed his finger under his Dad's feet and said, *"Dad, you're going to drown. You have a hole in your side of the boat."* Little Jimmy did not realize that he was in the same boat, and that if Dad was going to drown, then so was he. *Brothers and sisters, we may have come here on different ships, but we are all in the same boat now.* Black and white, rich and poor, north side and southside, learned and unlearned, we will either make it in together or ultimately drown in the sea of indifference. (King, 1996, p. 26)

While urban schools have a multitude of challenges, they can provide hope for millions of poor people. Amidst these challenges music teachers often serve as beacons of hope. Presently, however, too many urban music teachers are inadequately prepared. We need changes in public policy to keep us from drowning, but changes in music teacher education are also necessary. When teacher education programs fail to prepare teachers to engage the many diverse needs of urban children, our society suffers. The intent of this chapter can best be summarized in words from a well-known contemplative hymn sung in denominations of African American churches:

I have no desire to stay
Where doubts arise and fears dismay
Though some may dwell where these abound,
New heights I'm gaining every day
I plant my feet on higher ground
I'm pressing on the upward way. (Oatman, 1898)

This chapter describes methodology in teacher education that is specifically geared toward strengthening music teaching placements in urban schools. After describing major problems in urban schools, I will explain the disparities and present proactive strategies. Although public policies that exacerbate inequalities in jobs, health, and other areas that impact education must be consistently addressed, this chapter is limited to what music teacher educators should know and be able to do about diversity and social change in their settings.

As an insider, an African American musician-teacher and teacher-musician who is grounded in music education, my immersion in the research for this chapter created a change in my thinking, a change to include social justice in multicultural instruction, a change toward culturally relevant pedagogy. Perhaps Cochran-Smith best expresses these concerns:

> How can we open up the unsettling discourse of race without making people afraid to speak for fear of being naïve, offensive, or using the wrong language? Without making people of color do all the work. . . . Without eliminating conflict to the point of flatness. . . . How do we help children develop their own racial and cultural identities and establish meaningful relationships with children of other races and cultures when we ourselves are uncomfortable with that? When, in fact, we have failed for most of our adult lives to talk directly and constructively with others about issues of race and culture? (1996, pp. 374 & 388)

I HAVE NO DESIRE TO STAY: PROBLEMS, PREDISPOSITIONS, ATTITUDES

A demographic factor characteristic of urban schools is the racial, ethnic, and cultural mismatch between the students and the teachers. The 100 largest public school systems enroll 23% of all public school students and 69% of those are students of color. But the 1999–2000 census indicated that 84% of teachers and 61% of students are Caucasian; 8% of teachers and 17% of students are African American, 6% of teachers and 16% of students are Latinos, and 38% of schools do not have one teacher of color (Kindall-Smith, 2003, p. 7). (Notice that *students of color* is the politically preferred term because it emphasizes differences; the term *minorities* emphasizes deficiencies.) Diverse students are not, however, confined to large cities. Forty-two percent of all public school students are students of color according to the 2003 U.S. Census and Department of Education (Peterson, 2005). Furthermore, seven out of 10 students of color attend high-poverty schools with more inexperienced, out-of-field teachers and fewer resources than the public schools most White children attend (Cashin, 2004). Thus, urban schools also have a higher than average pupil-to-teacher ratio and fewer experienced teachers to handle these challenges.

Details about how intergroup educators confronted problems with immigrants, people of color, and divisions between groups after World War II shed light on current events. Cherry Banks articulates that it takes several generations to close the gap between social conflicts and American creed values of freedom, justice, and equality (2005). From 1928 through the 1960s civil rights struggle, scholars created transformative knowledge, inspired change in textbooks and curricula, and discovered that subject matter teachers did not know how to deal with race and culture. My childhood participation in annual brotherhood assemblies involved materials to promote cultural understanding and peace, and the Council on Human Relations was my favorite extracurricular activity in high school.

Another problem in urban education is many teachers' attitudes about their students' abilities. An overview of research on preservice teachers' predispositions and attitudes indicates consistency with national trends because the majority of preservice teachers are White, female, and middle class. They are also from small towns or suburbs, with limited diversity experiences and negative attitudes and beliefs about people who differ from themselves (Hollins & Guzman, 2005). I participated in Jeff Howard's Efficacy Institute, with teachers and parents in Massachusetts, which highlighted how stereotypes, assumptions, and labels limit students' academic achievement. Previously the major explanations for low achievement involved blaming the students themselves and their families (Cuban, 1989). Haberman (1995a) notes that blaming the victim is the most powerful predictor of teacher failure. Preservice teachers must learn to avoid rationalizing student failure by blaming the students, parents, or society because these beliefs influence teachers' expectations of students and students' achievement. Delpit goes so far as to say that if all African American children were taught how to dance in school, "by the time they had finished the first five workbooks on the topic, we would have a generation of remedial dancers!" (1995a, p. 83).

WHERE DOUBTS ARISE AND FEARS DISMAY:
THE ACHIEVEMENT GAP

The most pervasive challenge in urban schools is the persistent academic achievement gap between students of color and Whites. In July 2005 the president of the National Education Association declared that closing the achievement gap is the union's top priority (Keller, 2005). For 50 years failure has been documented for African Americans, Latinos, Native Americans, poor Whites, and recently Asian and Pacific American immigrants (Nieto, 2002). This achievement gap results from many problems, and teacher educators should avoid superficial explanations by understanding their fundamental assumptions.

Jeff Howard points out some disappointing assumptions that appear in *A Nation at Risk* (National Commission on Excellence in Teaching, 1983). He suggests that the authors' emphasis on balancing "the twin goals of equity and high-quality schooling" so that all students have a "chance to learn and live according to their aspirations and abilities" (p. 13) actually contributes to the pervasive culture of disbelief in the learning capacity of many students by promoting a sliding scale of expectations. In other words:

> Attributing poor skills to low ability leads naturally to the low expectations for future performance . . . and to the tenacity with which they are held. (Howard, 1983, p. 83)

The commission's suggestion to resolve this dilemma involves assisting "all students to work to the limits of their capabilities" (National Commission on Excellence in Teaching, 1983, p. 13). Again, Howard explains that this promotes relative standards because it could be mistaken for "an enlightened, liberal flexibility—a standard for each child based upon his or her own characteristics and potential" (p. 86). If teachers believe that urban students cannot achieve high standards, then the teachers resist procedures to define clear standards and do not see themselves accountable for low student achievement. Music teacher educators can join general and special teacher educators who are currently finding new ways of teaching all learners by preventing "misidentification, misassessment, miscategorization, misplacement, and misinstruction" (Obiakor, 2004, p. 51).

Pedro Noguera, a keynote speaker at the Closing the Achievement Gap Summer Institute at University of Wisconsin-Milwaukee (UWM) in June 2005 described four challenges that contribute to the wide achievement gap: preparation, opportunity-to-learn, relationships between adults and students, and the parent–school gap (Noguera, 2003).

The Preparation Gap

Early childhood music teacher educators can address the preparation gap by forming partnerships with urban childcare centers. In spring semester 2005, I gave music majors a choice in an early childhood course: either take the traditional final exam or plan and deliver an "interactive conference presentation with handouts" for 30 caregivers at UWM Children's Center. The students decided on the latter and collaborated in developing and teaching unfamiliar songs, dances, and one short listening lesson that would be appropriate for children ages three to five. Workshops for early childhood caregivers are available at the new Wisconsin Center for Music Education.

The Opportunity-to-Learn Gap and the Relationship Gap

Consider the opportunity-to-learn gap and the relationship gap between teachers and students. As a result of complex issues previously described, poor urban children have fewer books, read less at home, and learn fewer words. Yet students with weak work habits often produce results for caring teachers while refusing to work for others. Researchers believe that children who exhibit expertise in real-life settings often have difficulty decontextualizing knowledge for written assessments, and performance assessments are beneficial.

James Comer, a child psychiatrist, believes that the relationship between the teacher and child is most critical, and relationships among staff, parents, and students also improve the social psychological climate of the school. During the last 35 years Comer's School Development Plan, a structural intervention model with collaborative decisions by a school governance team, a mental health team, and parental participation, has enabled students at 600 low-performing schools to raise their achievement levels (Comer, 2004). Hollins and Guzman (2005) reported a study of 59 first-year teachers who had three different student teaching approaches. Two approaches were in urban schools, one approach with the Comer reform model, one approach without the model, and one approach was in rural and suburban schools. Results indicated that teachers who student taught in urban schools were better prepared to interact with parents from diverse backgrounds compared to those in rural and suburban schools regardless of the Comer model. Neither details about the conceptualization nor the implementation of the model were described, but the study suggests promising new practices for preservice teacher education.

Parent Communication Gap

Closing the communication gap between parents and schools is another challenge. In St. Louis during the fall of 2004 teachers visited 300 students' homes more than 500 times simply to meet the parents (Howard, 2005). The home visits were deemed successful because students who had been visited completed more homework and exhibited better school behavior, and teachers gained insight about students' concerns, interests, and needs. I suggest that music teachers contact parents to provide positive feedback about their children, plan or attend a community activity with several students and their parents, arrange for school music ensembles to perform at community events, and find ways to use parents as cultural resources even if they cannot leave work to come to school.

THOUGH SOME MAY DWELL WHERE THESE ABOUND: MUSIC EDUCATION

Some music educators in all areas and levels exclaim *Edict A*: "I teach music, quality music is paramount, and music is color-blind." Some music teachers espouse *Edict B*: "I don't teach music, I teach students." But such attempts at neutrality may actually "mask a 'dysconscious racism'" (Ladson-Billings, 1994, p. 31). Research has indicated that many well-meaning teachers who have difficulty accepting differences may be assuming that "normal" students are "White, middle class, heterosexual, and at least outwardly well adjusted to school—the presumed majority" (Darling-Hammond, French, & Garcia-Lopez, 2002, p. 9). If Edict A and Edict B music teacher educators believe in equality, then their beliefs should be incorporated in their instruction.

As I write, I remember challenges that music teachers had in relating to students in urban schools in the past, and MENC's response—the publication of a *Music Educators Journal* focus issue in 1970. In that issue I noted that "appropriate music literature in the inner city is a two-way street. One—the teacher must understand the music of the inner city. Two—traditional music literature can be made relevant for the inner-city child" (Kindall-Smith, 1970, p. 62). During the same period of time, James Standifer described how the desegregation of schools

> [R]equired that the teacher training program reevaluate itself because teachers were going to schools, and couldn't cope with, or couldn't focus on, the kind of music that the black students were doing. (Volk, 1998, p. 94)

Although the music of African Americans and other cultures of color has been studied, understood, and taught, proactive music educators must change music in the schools to avoid losing the participation of some of the best young musicians in the country. As Carter lamented, "Please, no more hyperbole or philosophical papers; rather, we need Herculean deeds and actions to change the situation" (1993, p. 228).

Socioeconomic challenges in schools threaten the very existence of music instruction. Not only are arts teachers among the first to lose their jobs during fiscal crises, but several music teachers have told me that many principals now ask classroom teachers, "Would you prefer to have a music teacher or an art teacher?" Urban principals often cut weak music teachers by reducing or eliminating the programs. On the other hand, urban principals have been known to increase music programs because music teachers provide excellent instruction for underserved students.

Libby Larsen, the famous composer, challenged attendees at the 2005 Mountain Lake Symposium to think beyond traditional music instruction. In Larsen's words:

> For our students to be responsible and responsive, we must teach music elements so that they can apply it to music they access. . . . Cultures evolve the music they need. . . . Our students care deeply about music; they share their lives through sharing their music with each other.

Larsen's references to culture and students' active music making are similar to Elliott's beliefs about teachers engaging students in active, cultural, artistic problem finding and solving. Elliott declares:

> If MUSIC consists in a diversity of music cultures, then MUSIC is inherently multicultural. And if MUSIC is inherently multicultural, then music education ought to be multicultural in essence. (1995, p. 209)

Furthermore, Elliott's beliefs and Larsen's suggestions would especially appeal to urban students who prefer their music to the teacher's music. How interesting to realize that a concert takes place anytime, anyplace there is a sound system, such as a microphone, computer, sequencer, recording, or iPod. Larsen tells students, "You're a composer until you're not." That is another way of saying, "I believe in you; try it; discover what happens"—a message delivered by successful urban teachers to their students.

Music teacher educators should understand that the intent of the No Child Left Behind law (NCLB) signed by President George W. Bush on January 8, 2002, is to close the achievement gap with standardized testing and consequences (*No Subject Left Behind*, 2004). At the February 2005 conference of the National Association for the Study and Performance of African American Music (NASPAAM), I facilitated a discussion about the impact of the ambitious law on urban schools. After my presentation, angry responses from urban music teachers indicated feelings of helplessness and unfairness. Their concerns were based on the results of its implementation, for example, the omission of students who need extra tutoring and the elimination of music, recess, and field trips for a narrow focus on preparation for testing. Afterward, a White music teacher educator thanked me and confessed that she was astounded by the consequences for urban students. This caused me to wonder. Do music teacher educators discuss the positive and negative impact of NCLB? Do preservice music teachers know that the law promised to eradicate the achievement gap and improve teacher quality? Do they know that the arts are included as a core academic subject in the 1,000-page law? During conference presentations I play a CD that continues the tradition of protest songs with references to "students working hard" "focused on testing" and "now the music is gone" (Drake, 2005).

NEW HEIGHTS I'M GAINING EVERY DAY: PREJUDICE REDUCTION THROUGH MULTICULTURALISM

Music teacher education programs must have a common basis for multicultural education before establishing programs. Several definitions of multiculturalism are needed to grasp the nuances in this chapter. James Banks, whose Multicultural Education Series sets the standard in general education, developed the definition, dimensions, and conceptual framework for multiculturalism in each book in the series and in the *Handbook of Research on Multicultural Education*. According to Banks and Banks:

> We may define multicultural education as a field of study designed to increase educational equity for all students that incorporates, for this purpose content, concepts, principles, theories, and paradigms from history, the social and behavioral sciences, and particularly from ethnic studies and women's studies. (Banks, J. & Banks, C. M., 2004, p. xii, emphasis in original)

In the foreword for each book in Banks' multicultural education series, Banks states that the five dimensions of the "metadiscipline" of multicultural education must be attended to for its successful implementation: *content integration, the knowledge construction process, prejudice reduction, an equity pedagogy*, and *an empowering school structure and social structure*. He explains that teachers should:

> [U]se content from diverse groups when teaching concepts and skills, help students to understand how knowledge in the various disciplines is constructed, help students to develop positive intergroup attitudes and behaviors, and modify their teaching strategies so that students from different racial, cultural, language, and social-class groups will experience equal educational opportunities, . . [and assist in transforming] . . . the total environment and culture of the school . . . so that students from diverse groups will experience equal status in the culture and life of the school. (Banks, C., 2005, p. xii)

In separate research reviews 10 years apart, both Jordan (1992) and Lundquist (2002) assert that multicultural music education for preservice and inservice teachers is inadequate and fragmented. Definitions of multicultural music education have paralleled changing definitions in general education.

Volk presents the following guiding principles of multicultural music education from divergent ways of thinking that have been supported by ethnomusicologists and music education researchers for almost three decades:

- There are many different and equally valid music systems in the world.
- All music exists within its cultural context.
- Music education should reflect the inherently multicultural nature of music.
- Given that the American population is made up of many diverse cultures, music education should also reflect the diverse music of the American population.
- Authenticity is determined by the people within the music culture. (1998, p. 15)

With reference to Banks's definition, these principles emphasize multiculturalism in music as content integration and knowledge construction with small doses of an equity pedagogy.

Some crucial human relations concepts appear in the approach that Anderson and Campbell developed:

> A multicultural approach to learning centers around organizing educational experiences for students that encourage and develop understanding and sensitivity to peoples from a broad spectrum of ethnic backgrounds. If students are to learn from a multicultural perspective, teachers need to develop an educational philosophy that recognizes the inherent worth of endeavors by different cultural groups. Multicultural education develops the understanding that there are many different but equally valid forms of musical and artistic expression and encourages students to develop a broad perspective based on understanding, tolerance, and respect for a variety of opinions and approaches. (1989, p. 2)

Inclusiveness and balance is the first step, but multiculturalism does not automatically take care of racism; it should be antiracist and antidiscriminatory by including prejudice reduction (Nieto, 1996; Stephens, 2002). Prejudice reduction includes activities and lessons designed by teachers to help students develop positive attitudes about diversity. Consistent, sequential multiethnic teaching materials with positive images of racial and ethnic groups help students develop more positive intergroup attitudes (Banks, 2004). Currently, choral teacher educators are confronting some resistance to certain multicultural choral works attributed to political and ethnic concerns (Gratto, 2005). Mary Goetze (Goetze & Fern, 1999) and other choral and instrumental teacher educators who study authentic world repertoire in the field must persevere and teach music through cultural traditions and prejudice reduction.

Definitions of multiculturalism depend on the development of personal, collective, and institutional ideas. Nieto's definition is: "Multicultural education is an anti-racist education that is firmly related to student learning and permeates all areas of schooling" (2002/2003, p. 7). Teacher educators should confront the topic either by infusion in courses or separate courses in addition to extracurricular activities. She presents the following often unasked questions for teacher educators:

- How many of us as teacher educators have grappled with our own biases?
- How do we prepare future teachers to confront racism in their classrooms?
- What knowledge do future teachers need to possess in order to develop affirming, inclusive, and rigorous curricula?
- What types of experiences do future teachers need to help them understand culturally responsive education?
- What skills must we give students so that they can develop viable alternatives to tracking?
- What skills do future teachers need to develop so that they learn to assess all students in an equitable manner?
- What experiences do we provide future teachers so that they understand the important role of parents in educational decision making and help them confront their fear, anxiety, or superiority concerning parents? (2002, pp. 187–198)

As Nieto declares, it is easier to plan an assembly program of ethnic music than to provide quality music instruction for all students (1996). Culturally responsive pedagogy, according to Nieto, is an outgrowth of multicultural education based on the idea that students' backgrounds are assets, not deficits, and all teachers should learn how to skillfully, effectively teach diverse students.

If teacher educators teach multicultural music without helping preservice teachers understand conditions contributing to prejudice, then it is like a half-baked cake, an inedible pudding. They get credit for trying, but teacher educators who have never taught multicultural music, those who have not even tried to bake the cake, need a reality check.

Koza (2001) is a music educator with a chapter in a multicultural text for general educators; her ideas have the potential to influence educators who are not familiar with our discipline. She argues that pragmatism contributes to meager allotments of time and resources for elementary music education and summarizes:

> The struggle is a commentary on the values of those who decide what constitutes worthwhile knowledge, and thus the marginalization of music is, in a broad sense, a multicultural issue. (p. 246)

Koza advocates adopting Grant and Sleeter's multicultural and social reconstructionist concepts; I prefer the following language in their lesson-based companion.

- To promote an understanding and appreciation of cultural diversity in the United States.
- To promote alternative choices for people, with full affirmation of their race, gender, disability, language, sexual orientation, social class background.
- To help all children achieve academic success.
- To promote awareness of social issues involving the unequal distribution of power and privilege that limits the opportunity of those not in the dominant group. (Grant & Sleeter, 2003, pp. 200–201)

Koza and other authors warn music teachers to avoid using decades-old books with biased content that might still be in classrooms and libraries.

In contrast, an experience described by Campbell is a model for our profession. She escorted 14 University of Washington students from their White middle-class framework for a one-week "Cultural Immersion Project" living with families and teaching children on the Yakama reservation. Preparation involved having students write their personal music profiles, reading/ discussing Delpit's *Other People's Children* (1995), and six weeks researching the musical culture (locating songs, dances, and stories; transcribing the music; and preparing to teach songs in the ethnic languages with authentic instruments from China, Ecuador, Zimbabwe, Vietnam, and Ghana). Many reflections by university students are applicable to teaching music in urban schools, including Molly's:

> My view is that the Yakama children adapt well, moving in and out of white mainstream culture, from home to school to home again, with the greatest of ease. At the outer edge, perhaps there are issues of the lesser motivation to meet school expectations, to respond to teachers and the experiences they design for the children. But in this (preliminary) expedition, I see as much (or more) that is alike than different about these children when compared to those I know better in suburban schools. (Campbell, 2001)

Social justice educators have concerns about short-term immersion experiences that can exploit the indigenous students for the benefit of education students, but this experience developed from intensive student teaching preparation that benefited the Yakama children. Elliott believes that the immersion of students in unfamiliar musical practices links the most important values of music education to the broader goals of humanistic education. In this way students have "the opportunity to know one's self (musical and otherwise) and the relationship of one's self to others" (1995, p. 209). This immersion experience and these ideas create a bridge to culturally relevant pedagogy.

I'M PRESSING ON THE UPWARD WAY: CULTURALLY RELEVANT PEDAGOGY

Gloria Ladson-Billings's theoretical notion of culturally relevant pedagogy is based on academic achievement, cultural competence, and sociopolitical consciousness. Ladson-Billings, the keynote speaker at the Closing the Achievement Gap Conference, used a banking metaphor to describe outmoded assimilationist pedagogy where there are slots for everyone, culture is an impediment, and skills are an end. In contrast, the metaphor for culturally relevant pedagogy is mining, which requires excavation to make it better, culture is a resource, and skills are a means to an end. She stressed that teachers "cannot look down at the kids and up at the curriculum and say that they [the students] can't reach it."

Her ideas were developed from a three-year study of eight elementary classroom teachers, including five African Americans and three Whites as described in *The Dreamkeepers* (1994). She warned, "Don't get caught up in skin color because teachers' beliefs are far more important." She described an incident that typifies the transformative thinking of successful urban teachers. Throughout one school many teachers described a student as "an accident just waiting to happen," but the successful teacher in the study described him as "a piece of crystal." In *Crossing Over to Canaan* (2001) Ladson-Billings describes the implementation of culturally relevant pedagogy in urban schools by eight novice teachers. The teachers were enrolled in "Teach for Diversity," a masters-level teacher education program developed by Ladson-Billings and her colleagues at the University of Wisconsin. Zeichner, codirector of the program, explained that the focus should be more broad than "transforming White, monolingual teachers to teach students of color"; the focus should be on "preparing all teachers to teach all students" (Zeichner, 2003, p. 513). Indicators of culturally relevant pedagogy (Ladson-Billings, 2001) are academic achievement, or the current terminology, *promoting student learning*, when the teacher:

- presumes that all students are capable of being educated.
- clearly delineates what achievement means in . . . his or her classroom.
- knows the content, the learner, and how to teach content to the learner.
- supports a critical consciousness toward the curriculum.
- encourages academic achievement as a complex conception not amenable to a single, static measurement.

Ladson-Billings's propositions of cultural competence are that the teacher:

- understands culture and its role in education.
- takes responsibility for learning about students' culture and community.
- uses student culture as a basis for learning.
- promotes a flexible use of students' local and global culture.

Finally, sociopolitical consciousness occurs in classrooms when the teacher:

- knows the . . . sociopolitical context of the school-community-nation-world.
- has an investment in the public good.
- plans and implements academic experiences that connect students to the larger social context.
- believes that students' success has consequences for his or her own quality of life. (Ladson-Billings, 2001, pp. 74–121)

I PLANT MY FEET ON HIGHER GROUND:
MUSIC TEACHER EDUCATION

The question that prompted me to write this chapter was this: Since I teach similar multicultural music and resources in both methods courses, why are most students from the UWM School of Education extremely enthusiastic about these materials in their methods course and some music education students from the UWM Music Department indifferent about these materials in their methods course? The following reflection is a typical response from a School of Education preservice teacher:

> The Native American flute has a distant lonely echo sound, an empty hollow sound. I jumped back and forth on the CD to hear and compare the difference between the piccolo, the Indian flute, the pipa. . . . I want to play the Native American flute! Is there any professor on campus who can demonstrate his love of this instrument to me? I'm hooked. . . . I had never heard "Lift Every Voice and Sing." Eighth notes as triplets move the song, but the power in this tune is the force of the dotted quarter notes. The words and the music complement each other. . . . Listening to you sing motivated us. We must teach music from diverse cultures. Our students should have an opportunity to get "hooked" on this music. (Kindall-Smith, 2002, p. 115)

In contrast, a typical reflection from a music education major is: "I like brainstorming about how to introduce the listening. Thank you, I will keep all these resources."

Klinger's analysis of the differences between the two groups of preservice teachers concurs with my observation: it is discouraging but true that young preservice music teachers are uncomfortable with world music and classroom diversity (2002). Perhaps the scenario will change when college-level "music departments begin to integrate world music into all curricular offerings with the same enthusiasm as many elementary schools" (p. 212). Robinson agrees that teacher education is the key and outlines a 21st-century undergraduate music education curriculum with multicultural teaching and learning in all courses throughout the music department or school (2002). The reality of too many music education programs is that the missions are traditional with a focus on excellence and individual student growth and a benign neglect of social justice. Social justice should be modeled and taught.

Culturally relevant pedagogy is emphasized throughout the entire curriculum at the UWM School of Education. Perhaps that is the reason for the different responses between the general education and music education students at my university. Similar programs exist at other universities, including the University of California at Berkeley and Stanford, and colleges, including Alverno, Bank Street, Evergreen State, and Wheelock. These institutions have transformed multicultural programs and multicultural faculty to "attempt to confront and alter undemocratic, and biased teaching behaviors of future teachers" (Vavrus, 2002, p. 99). At UWM education students must complete the introductory course with 50 field-based observation hours in Milwaukee Public Schools (MPS) before applying to the School of Education. Readings include either *Lies My Teacher Told Me* (Loewen, 1995) or *The Dreamkeepers* (Ladson-Billings, 1994) and two favorite books, *White Teacher* (Paley, 2000) and *Growing Minds: On Becoming a Teacher* (Kohl, 1984), plus a coursepack with 19 social justice articles by various authors. This course helps students understand culturally responsive/relevant education for urban teaching. (The program coordinator and professors credit Felicia Saffold, organizer of the course, for its success.)

The unique aspect of UWM's Middle Childhood-Early Adolescent Program is programmatic coherence from: "(1) standards that actively support our urban mission, (2) a collaborative faculty model, (3) linking seminar, and (4) faculty development as a function of performance assessment" (Pugach, Longwell-Grice, & Ford, p. 87, 2006). Student cohorts take a four-semester sequence of program block courses concurrent with clinical experience in Milwaukee Public Schools and a linking seminar, which connects courses and experience. All program faculty, including university professors, current or retired MPS teachers, and six urban teachers-in-residence, lead students in open discussions about multicultural concerns. Each semester review indicates that students develop stronger urban education identities.

Curriculum specialist Beverly Cross frames graduate courses at UWM around big ideas in the struggle for freedom, justice, and equality, that is,

Where is the question that will guide you and your students in thinking about how this learning experience relates to their ability to understand the world and how people experience it differently? (1998, p. 50)

Teachers in her courses admit that answering this moral question presents a struggle because their perspectives about teaching had been limited to academic terms and general ideas about respect instead of the social reality of groups of people. This confession is similar to my concerns about certain music educators' multicultural methodology.

What are characteristics of successful urban teachers? Haberman's interviews of more than 1,000 teachers revealed 14 functions of the 5 to 8% of "star teachers" in each school district, teachers identified as outstanding by other people. For example, star teachers convince students that "I need you here"; they use "gentle strategies in a violent society"; and

they act as if they can teach anything they care about—and they care about a great deal. Perhaps the most accurate term for describing this quality is neither stamina nor enthusiasm, but irrepressibility. They are not worn down by children. (1995b, p. 73)

Four of Irvine's characteristics of successful urban teachers include being members of caring communities, culturally responsive pedagogues, antiracist educators, and pedagogical-content specialists (2003). I used the same characteristics to describe how teachers of various ethnicities impacted my musical success as an urban student; this is found in "On My Journey" (Kindall-Smith, 2004).

Haberman's (1995a) memorable metaphor is that traditional teacher education programs prepare students to swim the English Channel by swimming in the university pool. He calculates that selection for urban teachers counts approximately 80% more than training. He and his colleagues developed The Haberman Urban Teacher Interview (1995a). If the structured interview is used in combination with observations of the candidates teaching children the summer before employment, there is less than a 5% error rate. Without observations the error rate is 8 to 10%.

We must reevaluate music education programs in light of social justice instruction. A reason why schools of general education have been more successful in recruiting students of color than music schools or departments is that they do not require an understanding of educational theory prior to admission. This issue was brought to my mind at a recent board meeting of Wisconsin music educators. A teacher educator from another university expressed concerns about the number of students who are rejected, despite a commitment to teaching and excellent music backgrounds, because of failing music theory placement exams. Considering this *sacred cow*, this problem is even more prevalent with freshmen students of color who do not have access to quality music instruction in their urban high schools.

"Teachers Teaching Teachers: Revitalization in an Urban Setting" describes my successful recruitment, retention, and revitalization strategies (Kindall-Smith, 2004). The mentoring course I established in 2000 for beginning Milwaukee Public Schools music teachers continues to be successful. A sampling of last semester's comments from teachers who were not my former students are:

> I survived the first few days [of urban teaching] standing on both feet, but just barely. . . . Kindall-Smith has been wonderful in helping us "get through," reminding us that our challenge is great . . . but also encouraging us to keep on and use our strengths to find success, even in small doses.

Music teacher educators should consider these other findings about diversity from Hollins and Guzman (2005). Although many preservice teachers feel inadequately prepared to teach in urban schools, many of them are willing to try. Many studies about prejudice reduction have mixed results. Most of the studies reviewed had generally positive short-term impacts, but little evidence is known about long-term effects. Program evaluations suggest that universities are at various stages of development about multicultural education. There are many issues in research about candidates' program experiences. Teacher candidates of color often feel alienated at White majority institutions because their cultural and experiential knowledge is not valued. Researchers agree that studies are needed about the relationship about teacher preparation for diversity and pupils' learning and other outcomes. Also needed are longitudinal studies from the initial preparation of preservice teachers to their career experiences. According to Hollins and Guzman (2005) Sleeter suggests starting with questions about good teaching and working backwards to questions about teacher preparation.

I requested suggestions for teacher educators from conference participants at the 2005 NASPAAM conference. The overriding response from numerous music educators of color was to *require* appropriate courses so that preservice teachers can get grounded with the desired *values* for social justice. How do you begin? The entire learning community should be involved. Begin with *Transforming the Multicultural Education of Teachers* (Vavrus, 2002). Individually, start with a commitment to change, discard ideas in Edict A and Edict B, keep an open mind, read, reflect, contact experts, form a group for continuous discussions, admit mistakes, correct errors, and try again. I commend music teacher educators who are in various stages of this process.

Rev. Bernice King remarked about getting the message beyond a listening audience:

Rosa Parks was just one lady, but because she sat down, a whole race of people could stand up to confront racism and inequality. The good news is that when one individual does something good, it can create a domino effect. . . . Everybody has the power to do something to help those who have become victims of our society. . . . the Samaritan gave of himself. . . . He didn't even pick up his cellular phone to call 911. . . . I don't know of any program or organization that ever made real progress without people who were willing to give personal time and attention. . . . The songwriter was right who said,

> "If I can help somebody as I pass along,
> If I can cheer somebody with a word or song,
> If I can show somebody he's traveling wrong,
> Then my living shall not be in vain." (1996, p. 175)

I plant my feet on higher ground: There will be music in urban schools—public, private, charter, and voucher schools—but will music educators be part of it? I plant my feet on higher ground: We must change music teacher education to keep administrators in urban schools from tapping the delete key on their computers and eliminating the discipline of music education as we cherish it. I plant my feet on higher ground: We will not drown by indifference if we embrace multicultural education that provides for content integration, knowledge construction, prejudice reduction, equitable pedagogy, and an empowering school and social structure. I plant my feet on higher ground: Music teacher educators must enable preservice music teachers to promote student learning, to teach for cultural competence, and to develop personal sociopolitical consciousness.

I plant my feet on higher ground: Music teachers will strive for irrepressibility and make a difference even if they activate social justice only with their students and their students' caregivers. I plant my feet on higher ground: Music teacher educators will make a greater difference as they prepare all preservice music teachers for social justice in all urban, suburban, and rural schools across the country. I plant my feet on higher ground: Music teachers of the 21st century will learn how to teach music classes with less talking because the students are engaged in sharing their lives through quality music. I plant my feet on higher ground: Individually and collectively we will ensure that certified, qualified music teachers provide a balanced, comprehensive, sequential program of music instruction in all schools. I plant my feet on higher ground: These are the ways that music educators can enable millions of students to experience the joy of music in urban schools.

REFERENCES

Anderson, W. M., & Campbell, P. S. (1989). *Teaching music from a multicultural perspective*. Reston, VA: Music Educators National Conference.

Banks, C. M. (2005). *Improving multicultural education: Lessons from the intergroup education movement*. New York: Teachers College Press.

Banks, J. & Banks, C. M. (2004). (Eds.), *Handbook of research on multicultural education* (2nd ed.). San Francisco: Jossey-Bass.

Campbell, P. S. (2001, Spring). Lessons from the Yakama. *The Mountain Lake Reader*, pp. 46–51.

Carter, W. L. (1993). Minority participation in music programs. In M. Mark (Ed.), *Music education: Source readings from ancient Greece to today* (pp. 227–228). New York: Routledge.

Cashin, S. (2004). *The failures of integration: How race and class are undermining the American dream*. New York: Public Affairs.

Cochran-Smith, M. (1996). Uncertain allies: Understanding the boundaries of race and teaching. In T. Beauboeuf-Lafontant & D. Smith-Augustine (Eds.), *Facing racism in education* (pp. 369–401). Cambridge, MA: Harvard Educational Review.

Comer, J. P. (2004). *Leave no child behind: Preparing today's youth for tomorrow's world*. New Haven, CT: Yale University Press.

Cross, B. (1998). Mediating curriculum: Problems of non-engagement and practices of engagement. In R. Chavez & J. O'Donnell (Eds.), *Speaking the unpleasant: The politics of (non) engagement in the multicultural education terrain* (pp. 32–55). Albany: State University of New York Press.

Cuban, L. (1989). The "at-risk" label and the problem of urban school reform. *Phi Delta Kappan*, pp. 780–784, 799–801.

Darling-Hammond, L., French, J., & Garcia-Lopez, S. (2002). *Learning to teach for social justice*. New York: Teachers College Press.

Delpit, L. (1995). *Other people's children: Cultural conflict in the classroom*. New York: The New Press.

Drake, D. HB. 2005. *No Child Left Behind CD for Teachers* [CD-ROM]. Available from Organic Arts LTD., PO Box 1642, Milwaukee, WI 53201-1642.

Elliott, D. J. (1995). *Music matters: A new philosophy of music education*. New York: Oxford University Press.

Goetze, M., & Fern, J. (1999). *Global Voices in Song* [Interactive CD-ROM]. New Palestine, IN: MJ Publishers.

Grant, C., & Sleeter, C. E. (2003). *Turning on learning: Five approaches for multicultural teaching plans for race, class, gender, and disability*. New York: Wiley.

Gratto, S. (2005). Ethnic and multicultural perspectives. *Choral Journal*, 45(8), 51–54.

Haberman, M. (1995a). Selecting "star" teachers for children and youth in urban poverty. *Phi Delta Kappan*, pp. 777–781.

———. (1995b). *Star teachers of children of poverty*. West Lafayette, IN: Kappa Delta Pi.

Hollins, E. R., & Guzman, M. T. (2005). Research on preparing teachers for diverse populations. In M. Cochran-Smith & K. Zeichner (Eds.), *Studying teacher education: The report of the AERA panel on research and teacher education* (pp. 477–548). Washington, DC: American Educational Research Association.

Howard, J. (2003). Still at risk: The causes and costs of failure to educate poor and minority children for the twenty-first century. In D. Gordon (Ed.), *A nation reformed? American education 20 years after a nation at risk* (pp. 81–98). Cambridge, MA: Harvard Education Press.

Howard, T. L. (2005, January 3). Home visits by teachers pay off in the classroom. *St. Louis Post-Dispatch*, www.stltoday.com.

Irvine, J. J. (2003). *Educating teachers for diversity: Seeing with a cultural eye*. New York: Teachers College Press.

Jordan, J. (1992). Multicultural music education in a pluralistic society. In R. Colwell (Ed.), *Handbook of research on music teaching and learning* (pp. 735–748). New York: Schirmer.

Keller, B. (2005, July 6). NEA president says achievement gap to go at top of union's priority list. *Education Week*, http://www.edweek.org/ew/articles/2005/07/05/42neagap_web.

Kindall-Smith, M. (1970). Godliness is next to nothing [Special report on urban education]. In C. Fowler (Ed.), *Music Educators Journal*, 56(5), 90.

———. (2002). Comparison of arts PROPEL and teacher-directed approaches to teaching music education to pre-service teachers (Unpublished doctoral dissertation, Boston University).

———. (2003). "Music Education and Minorities." Letter to the Editor. *Teaching Music*, 11(3), 7–8.

———. (2004, Spring). On my journey: Minority teachers and teaching beyond the curriculum. *Mountain Lake Reader*, 14–20.

———. (2004). Teachers teaching teachers: Revitalization in an urban setting. *Music Educators Journal*, 91(2), 41–46.

King, B. A. (1996). *Hard questions, heart answers*. New York: Broadway Books.

Klinger, R. (2002). A materials girl in search of the genuine article. In B. Reimer (Ed.), *World musics and music education: Facing the issues* (pp. 205–218). Reston, VA: Music Educators National Conference.

Kohl, H. (1984). *Growing minds: On becoming a teacher*. New York: Harper & Row.

Koza, J. (2001 [1996]). Multicultural approaches to music education. In M. Gomez & C. Grant (Eds.), *Campus and classroom: Making schooling multicultural* (pp. 239–258). Upper Saddle River, NJ: Prentice Hall.

Ladson-Billings, G. (1994). *The dreamkeepers: Successful teachers of African American children*. San Francisco: Jossey-Bass.

———. (2001). *Crossing over to Canaan: The journey of new teachers in diverse classrooms*. San Francisco: Jossey-Bass.

Larsen, L. (2005, May). Navigating the universe of possibilities. Paper presented at the Mountain Lake Colloquium for Teachers of General Music Methods, Mountain Lake, VA.

Loewen, J. W. (1995). *Lies my teacher told me*. New York: The New Press.

Lundquist, B. (2002). Music, culture, curriculum and instruction. In R. Colwell & C. Richardson (Eds.), *The new handbook of research on music teaching and learning* (pp. 626–647). Oxford: Oxford University Press.

National Commission on Excellence in Teaching. (1983). *A nation at risk: The imperative for educational reform*. Washington, DC: U.S. Department of Education.

Nieto, S. M. (1996 [1992]). *Affirming diversity: The sociopolitical context of multicultural education*. White Plains, NY: Longman.

———. (2002). *Language, culture, and teaching*. Mahwah, NJ: Lawrence Erlbaum Associates.

————. (2002, December/2003, January). Profoundly multicultural questions. *Educational Leadership*, 60(4), 6–10.

No Subject Left Behind: A Guide to Arts Education Opportunities in the 2001 NCLB Act (2004). Washington, DC: Arts Education Partnership, et al.

Noguera, P. (2003). *City schools and the American dream: Reclaiming the promise of public education*. New York: Teachers College Press.

Oatman, J. (1998). I'm pressing on the upward way: Higher ground. *African Methodist Episcopal Church Hymnal*. Nashville, TN: The African Methodist Episcopal Church, 347.

Obiakor, F. E. (2004). Impact of changing demographics on public education for culturally diverse learners with behavior problems; implications for teacher preparation. In L. Bullock & R. Gable (Eds.), *Quality personnel preparation in emotional/behavioral disorders* (pp. 51–63). Denton: University of North Texas.

Paley, V. G. (2000). *White teacher*. Cambridge, MA: Harvard University Press. (Original work published 1979.)

Peterson, K. (2005, March 30). Need school info? New site probably has it. www.stateline.org.

Pugach, M. C., Longwell-Grice, H., & Ford, A. (2006). UWM's collaborative teacher education program for urban communities and the pursuit of program coherence. In K. Howey & L. M. Post (Eds.), *Recruiting, preparing, and retaining teachers for urban schools* (pp. 83–100). Washington, DC: American Association of Colleges for Teacher Education.

Robinson, K. (2002). Teacher education for a new world of musics. In B. Reimer (Ed.), *World musics and music education: Facing the issues* (pp. 219–238). Reston, VA: Music Educators National Conference.

Stephens, R. W. (2002). Memory, multiculturism, and music: An African American perspective. In B. Reimer (Ed.), *World musics and music education: Facing the issues* (pp. 91–102). Reston, VA: Music Educators National Conference.

Vavrus, M. (2002). *Transforming the multicultural education of teachers: Theory, research, and practice*. New York: Teachers College Press.

Volk, T. (1998). *Music, education, and multiculturalism: Foundations and principles*. New York: Oxford University Press.

Zeichner, K. M. (2003). The inadequacies of three current strategies to recruit, prepare, and retain the best teachers for all students. *Teachers College Record*, 105(3), 513.

6

New Millennium Music Education: Alternative Certification and the Urban Setting

Corinne Mills

The growing need for music teachers who will be prepared to work and thrive in an urban district is of significant concern to the public education system. One of the most pressing issues for urban school districts is hiring teachers that are qualified to meet the certification requirements of No Child Left Behind (NCLB). By the 2005–2006 school year, all teachers in core academic areas (which include the arts) in Connecticut public schools must meet the "highly qualified" criteria described in NCLB.

As a result of the high need for music teachers, some urban districts are turning to alternative certification programs to find teaching candidates. These programs offer training to preservice teachers who have training in a content field with at least a bachelor's degree, but lack teaching credentials. These candidates are often professionals from diverse backgrounds who wish to change careers and become teachers. With the rising cost of college tuition and the large number of credits that are necessary to complete an education degree, acceptance into the Alternate Route program provides a far less expensive way for college graduates to get into the teaching field. The cost of the Connecticut Alternate Route to Certification Program is about $3,600, including tuition, fees, and books. This is far less expensive than pursuing the necessary credits to complete an additional degree. As Mutari and Lakew (2004) state: "Even the most narrow-minded economists agree that improving access to education generates benefits for society as a whole—it produces what economists call *positive externalities*. Better access to education creates higher levels of skill and knowledge in the workforce, for instance" (p. 356).

The Connecticut Alternate Route to Certification (ARC) Program was not designed to be a full-scale teacher preparation program; rather it is a certification program that assumes that accepted candidates have the necessary content skills. Connecticut Alternate Route candidates are professionals from a vast array of professions (including the arts) who are seeking a career change. The program offers certification preparation in 15 fields. There are two major sessions, a full-time summer program known as ARC I, and a part-time program during the academic year known as ARC II (p. 3). Music candidates must present a minimum of 30 semester hours of credit in music studies prior to entering the program (p. 6). Upon completing the program, candidates receive a Record of Completion. This credential qualifies candidates for certification in any Connecticut public school pending the successful completion of the Praxis II or ACTFL exam(s) and upon the recommendation of the employing superintendent (p. 12).

The three major components of the Connecticut Alternate Route to Certification as explained in the Core Curriculum Framework are: core or foundation presentation, methods instructions, and clinical experiences (p. 1). Teacher candidate schedules are packed with either a full day of classes or a combination of classes and clinical experiences. Homework assignments are required in all three component areas. The goals specific to urban education include:

- Exhibiting an understanding of the societal and classroom issues of urban education, race, and gender and
- Applying the theories of multicultural education to lesson and unit design.

These goals are accomplished through the successful completion of clinical experiences and the development of lessons that incorporate multicultural approaches to learning.

The Connecticut State Department of Education does not accept any other alternative programs for certification purposes. The program was specifically designed to train teachers in shortage areas such as music with the secondary goal of alleviating the teacher shortages in urban districts. Only about 20% of applicants are accepted into the program. Admission is based on academic strength and breadth of knowledge with consideration of professional and teaching-related experiences. Other qualities that are considered are the applicant's communication skills and overall character disposition, which is determined through their application essay. About 75% of annual graduates are hired within six months of completing the training. Since 1988 the Connecticut ARC program has produced over 2,700 graduates in numerous content areas with music ranking fifth in sought-after certification areas (Connecticut Department of Education, 2004).

According to LeRoy E. Hay, director of the Connecticut Alternate Route to Certification program, 54% of ARC placements are in priority and transitional districts. The Hartford Public Schools has been identified as a priority district, and currently 20% of the music staff are ARC graduates. In his lecture *Recruiting Quality Candidates: Alternate Routes Are Not Alternate Standards,* Dr. Hay (2003) identified the factors that contribute most to success in the classroom and prioritized them as follows:

- Classroom management and discipline (32%)
- Personal qualities (30%)
- Ability to build rapport (15%)
- Organizational skills and preparation (12%)
- Family and school support (6%)
- Subject area knowledge (6%).

As Dr. Hay's statistics indicate that classroom management is the biggest concern of ARC graduates. Thus, ARC candidates need authentic urban clinical experiences during their training. While a well-developed lesson plan and solid pedagogical background are essential for creating a successful classroom environment, these things must be coupled with an effective discipline plan that emphasizes prevention rather than reaction. The MENC position statement on this matter concludes, "alternative certification programs must prepare prospective teachers to meet the same rigorous standards established for college and university trained music educators" (2003, p. 2). Part of these standards must include frequent opportunities to observe quality teaching in an urban setting.

Connecticut requires a music teacher to either obtain either a master's degree or 30 graduate credit hours in order to obtain a professional-level teaching certificate. Some school districts in Connecticut require a master's degree rather than the bachelor + 30 in order to be compensated at the master's level. Connecticut ARC music graduates who have not obtained an undergraduate degree in music education may have difficulty being accepted to a Connecticut university for a master of music education unless they complete additional music education courses prior to applying to the program. This requirement creates a dilemma for the ARC music graduate who is working full-time. Unless the required courses are offered in the evening hours, ARC graduates may not be able to fulfill this requirement. At least one Connecticut university has designed a schedule to accommodate this need. More universities need to broaden their course offerings in this area.

With 37 as the median age of an ARC graduate, these candidates are frequently more mature because they have real-life experiences. Consequently, they often prove to be well suited in coping with the multitiered needs of high-risk students. They articulate an awareness of and willingness to carry the mantle of mentorship for high-risk students and, in some cases, have supplanted the traditional music-education graduate applicant who may not have the emotional maturity to handle the challenge of a classroom. Haberman (2004) states: "while traditional teacher preparation programs seek to attract more young people into the teaching profession, past experiences suggest that many of these graduates will not seek employment in large urban school districts where most of the new hires will be needed" (p. 14). Often ARC candidates have their own children and adeptly transfer, revise, and reapply the parental involvement strategies their children's school districts are using to form parent/guardian partnerships with their students' families. These same skills are often useful for developing a discipline framework that will promote student learning. These candidates come to the interview wanting to make a significant contribution and willing to accept the challenges that, once overcome, will create a positive musical experience for urban children to build upon.

The music teacher can be a powerful force in an urban school. Hamann and Walker (1993) found that the music teacher was often the most significant "teacher" role for African American high school students. Some ARC music candidates come to teaching with this vision. They are crossover professional musicians who seek to combine their performance experience with a teaching career. Many candidates have had rewarding teaching careers in private studios or other educational institutions that do not require state certification. Based on these experiences, they passionately believe that the arts can contribute to student success and hope to transfer the joy they get from performing into a joy of teaching disenfranchised students.

Music is classified as a "high need" teaching area in Connecticut for several reasons. Numerous factors are contributing to the growing number of vacancies in school districts (primarily urban districts), including a large portion of the current workforce nearing and entering retirement, a troubling teacher retention rate, and a limited supply of new music graduates. Recent statistics provided by the program show that 68% of graduates are applying to the suburbs and only 52% are applying to urban districts. Teacher retention statistics reported during *The First Northeast Regional Conference on Alternate Routes to Teacher Certification*, held in October of 2003, show that one third of all teachers leave the profession after three years and almost half (46%) of all trained teachers leave the profession after their fifth year. This dramatic decline, in conjunction with retirements, teachers transferring out of district, teachers returning to higher education, teachers returning to other/changing careers leaves one third of the teaching force in any school in transition. The lack of sufficient preparation in child psychology is the main reason cited for teachers leaving the profession. The regional conference also concluded that providing teachers with an extensive support system early in the induction period keeps them in the field. The solution suggested by the conference planners is to provide a strong mentoring program coupled with professional development. Though this solution is costly, the benefits outweigh the educational consequences of teachers leaving the field in such large numbers. Table 6.1 shows the retention rate of ARC candidates in relation to that of traditionally trained teachers.

Table 6.1. ARC Persistence as CT Public School Teachers (Retention Rates)

First to Second Year	ARC 85%	Traditional 93%
After 3 years	ARC 85.7%	Traditional 84.4%
After 5 years	ARC 79.9%	Traditional 78.7%

Part of the discussion at the conference centered on recruitment procedures. Since the challenge of urban teaching is not for everyone, it would be a great asset to identify the right people to be teachers. Simply put, we need to get the wrong people "off of the bus." The conference also concluded that higher education has largely escaped the focus of No Child Left Behind and has been minimally affected by Title I. Because of this, teachers in general are not equipped to deal with the poorest or least prepared students.

The Connecticut Beginning Educator Support and Training Program (BEST) is a two-year mentorship and certification program that is required for beginning teachers from all subject areas regardless of their path to certification. This program includes live and online seminars to help novice teachers develop pedagogical skills. In their second year of teaching participants are required to develop a portfolio of four to six lessons that are centered on student learning. These novice music teacher portfolios are scored by master music teachers and administrators from throughout the state that have been accepted into the scoring program based on their professional reputation and qualifications. To be considered qualified as a BEST program assessor, scorers are required to attend 55 hours of initial training, update training annually, and pass a proficiency-scoring exam. Portfolios are rated on a scoring rubric of one (failure) through four (exemplar). Statistically over half of the ARC graduates throughout the disciplines receive either a three or four on their portfolio submissions.

At the 2005 MENC Eastern Division Conference in Baltimore, Maryland, a group of colleagues gathered to discuss the attributes of a successful urban music teacher. Participants described the successful urban music teacher as a person with mettle who is resourceful, innovative, able to push the envelope, and is supported by both their colleagues and administration. Haberman (2004) describes successful urban teachers as: "predominantly women, they are over 30 years of age, attended urban schools themselves, completed a bachelor's degree in college but not necessarily in education, worked at other full-time jobs and are parents themselves. This successful pool also contains a substantially higher number of individuals who are African American, Latino and male" (p. 13). It is important for both preparatory programs and employing districts to seek teachers who meet these descriptions and to provide training opportunities that help teachers develop and utilize these skills.

In response to the need for improved teacher induction the Connecticut program has launched an outreach effort to provide classroom-based coaching and mentoring for ARC graduates. Recent program graduates are offered the chance to be observed at least twice during the first 90 days of teaching. This coaching supplements the Connecticut State Department of Education's BEST mentoring program. ARC's "coaches" are professionals who hold administration certificates. Most are BEST-trained for observations and assessments. They are retired professionals from public schools, and bring a wealth of knowledge and wisdom to new teachers. ARC graduates are placed on a 90-day Temporary Certificate before moving onto an Initial Certificate. Once on the Initial Certificate, they go through the same licensure procedures as any other beginning teacher (Connecticut Department of Education, 2004a).

In my role as the district music coach for the Hartford Public Schools, I have seen firsthand the challenges that face music teachers in urban schools. These include cultural differences between students and teachers and the communities where they work; concerns about developing a curriculum that will produce engaging, interesting, and relevant lessons; and disciplinary policies that are agreeable to and understood by the students, their parents/guardians, and the school administration.

INFORMAL ALTERNATE ROUTE SURVEY

For the purposes of this chapter I surveyed numerous Connecticut ARC I graduates who are currently working or have worked in the Hartford Public Schools over the past 10 years. This was not a formal survey; participants were not chosen at random and the questions were designed to be brief and accessible to encourage the teachers to respond. The survey addressed six topics: program preparation, student home life, mentorship, administrative support, job search, and ways to improve future candidates. Teachers were surveyed independently and were not aware of any of the other teachers who had been contacted or had responded. They were assured that they would not be quoted, but rather their responses would be a collective summation. The answers were analyzed separately and then collectively for similarities and differences.

How did the alternate route to certification address the issues of urban education?

The ARC graduates who had completed the course over the span of the past decade were unanimous in their response that the music education methods classes offered through the ARC program did not address issues pertinent to urban education. The music education methods classes adhered solely to music pedagogy, while classroom management strategies were taught in the general education classes by a separate consultant. While cooperating teachers did provide good experiences, they were in affluent suburbs or "transitional" communities that did not prepare the candidates to work in an urban district. They indicated that this is a serious shortfall of the Alternate Route program. If strategies and curriculum relevant to urban teaching are not taught in the methods classes, it can be very discouraging to someone who gets a job in an urban district. Without adequate preparation some teachers will quit immediately, thus perpetuating the myth that these districts are not teacher friendly and that the children are not teachable.

It is important for the ARC program to charge interested, qualified teachers to go and make a difference for the future of urban districts and their students. A few of the Hartford music teachers said that they were actively discouraged from applying to an urban district and were frightened by the horror stories that were circulating. One African American teacher told of how a colleague had set up an interview for her in an affluent suburb to discourage her from entering an urban setting. More recent ARC graduates (within the past two to three years) report that things have changed somewhat. The ARC program has begun to show sensitivity to urban issues by offering two core workshops (three hours each) to help teachers communicate with urban students, and multiple workshops and lectures are offered about multicultural classroom instruction. Recent graduates also report that the new music methods instructors have begun offering tips for classroom management.

What resources did the ARC program provide for preparing the student teacher to deal with the learning issues associated with single parenthood, high poverty levels, and transience?

The answers from respondents were unanimous: "Absolutely none." The respondents stated that the music curricula they had learned would not fly in an urban setting. Few of the general music resources they had used would appeal and relate to upper elementary and middle school urban kids. Further, the candidates were not provoked into asking questions or even thinking about multicultural issues during their training. Resources often pale compared to the impact of actually teaching a pregnant teenager or looking into the eyes of a high school sophomore who has given you an essay to edit about being raped by her father when she was five.

Several years ago, the book *Small Victories* by Samuel G. Freedman was a required text for high school teachers, and candidates were required to write a paper on the book prior to the start of classes. Unfortunately, the book and the issues presented were never analyzed or discussed during the eight-week summer training.

Did the ARC program work with students to provide them with realistic expectations as they entered the classroom?

Respondents answered "yes" to this question in a general sense but "no" relative to urban issues. They indicated that the student teaching preparation coupled with classroom lectures was based on an idealistic teaching situation. As one respondent said: "They are teaching you how to operate in a prime situation and this may discourage teachers later." It is difficult to get a real sense of the dynamics, culture, and community responsibility of a school with only three weeks of summer student teaching. It is also challenging to anticipate the interaction that is necessary between a music teacher and the rest of school personnel.

What follow-up mentorship and guidance is being offered by the ARC program once the graduate starts teaching in an urban district?

ARC graduates indicated that ongoing workshops are offered by ARC at many sites. These mentoring programs are optional. The respondents expressed disappointment in the mentoring that was offered as a follow-up by ARC during their first year. The mentors have been experienced classroom teachers and/or administrators, but because they were never music teachers they could only offer limited help with content.

What support should urban districts be providing to ARC graduates?

The responses were emphatic on this question: Any brand-new teacher, no matter what district he or she is placed in, needs support in classroom management. Regular meetings with experienced music teachers are invaluable and integral for developing teacher understanding and setting expectations for both the beginning teacher and their students. Due to their limited student teaching experience, ARC graduates felt that they needed a more extensive evaluation process than was offered. This should be a constructive, fair process that will lead to positive evaluations, thus encouraging and retaining beginning teachers, particularly in classrooms where management is difficult.

Why did you apply to an urban district?

Answers ranged from job availability, positive interview experiences, wanting to make a difference for city kids, and (disturbingly) not being considered "qualified" by suburban districts. Unfortunately, those who are shunned by the suburbs are funneled into urban districts, whether or not they are suited for their rigor.

A few noncertified teachers had started working in Hartford through specially funded programs. The positive experience that they had working with city kids lead them to apply to ARC for certification. They have remained fully committed to these children despite changes and/or eradications of the original program that enticed them to the district. One teacher firmly believes that the educational system must provide city kids with the same advantages offered to those in the affluent suburbs. This wonderful teacher is building a first-rate program and never wants to teach anywhere else. Urban districts need can-do, self-starter, highly motivated, and organized teachers with solid lesson and discipline plans. These teachers also must be flexible to the needs of the students they are seeking to serve, and many ARC graduates feel that they can fit this description. The challenge is real and very great, and many that are applying feel ready for this challenge.

Why have you stayed in urban teaching?

Without hesitation the answers indicated that special connections and bonds with the students kept these teachers in the urban schools. Positive experiences and support from other music teachers and department heads were also important factors in teachers' decisions to return for a second year and beyond. ARC graduates also enjoy having the opportunity to bring unique and important musical programming to their school sites. They see results in the hard work that they are putting in and are enjoying the trust, growth, and love that the students return. They have learned that you can never assume that a child has had breakfast or dinner, experienced love or companionship, peace or harmony, or any support from home. They all have had a student whose father is in prison or encountered a child whose home was burned out or may be passed from one relative to another during the night so that the parent/guardian can go to work.

A recent ARC graduate music teacher had a very difficult year due to the behavior of several sixth-grade boys. They came into his classroom on the last day to shake his hand and say that they had never learned so much from any other music teacher. This left him with a sense that his unfailing resolve and dedication throughout the year did pay off.

What will improve the quality of the ARC music candidate?

The respondents agreed that an interview process is necessary to determine whether a candidate is a good match for teaching music in an urban public school. "Looking good on paper" does not mean that an individual has the demeanor to work with children effectively. Ironically, Connecticut is among the states with the highest standards, based on the Praxis and the Beginning Educator Support and Training program.

The field of music education encompasses general, choral, instrumental, jazz, theory, history, and technology. It continues to broaden as the need for multicultural ensembles such as world drumming, steelband, strolling strings, and mariachi becomes apparent. Connecticut certifies music teachers to teach prekindergarten through grade 12. Very few disciplines are certified this broadly. Without careful screening by certified music specialists for candidates with a solid musical base for success, the program is merely filling enrollment quotas without viable and lasting results. The failure to carefully screen a music applicant's musical credentials ultimately saddles districts with candidates who are not wholly suited to teach music to children. It also perpetuates the poor music teacher retention rate.

Recently the Connecticut ARC program has been working to increase its focus on teaching in an urban setting. Dr. Gloria Holmes from Quinnipiac College designed a new CORE workshop entitled "Teaching in an Urban School." Six teachers from urban districts, all with less than four years of experience, were invited to be part of the presentation. ARC students are asked to read *A White Teacher Talks about Race* by Julie Landsman in preparation for the workshop. In addition the State Department of Education has facilitated a workshop on multicultural education during the summer ARC program. Additional funding entitled "Urban Fellows" was earmarked for two urban districts in Connecticut to provide special support, including topical seminars and coaching for ARC students holding either a Connecticut 90-day temporary certificate or those still teaching under a DSAP (Durational Shortage Permit). Connecticut will not issue an Initial Teaching Certificate to an ARC graduate until the teacher has completed 90 days of service authenticated by the district's superintendent. Teachers who are under a DSAP must show progress toward obtaining certification through completion of the Praxis I and Praxis II and/or be enrolled in a certification program. While this is a step in the right direction, there are several Connecticut urban districts (hence ARC teachers) that are not covered by the "Urban Fellows" funding. Further, the ARC "coaches" available to any requesting graduate may not have experience in urban areas or in music classrooms. This reality is a stark contrast to the kind of mentoring suggested by the National Association for Music Education: "MENC believes that for the mentoring experience to be meaningful and of value, the mentor must be an experienced music teacher with proven successes in the same music specialty area, i.e., band, choir, general music, or orchestra, as the teacher being mentored."

The conclusion of the distinguished panelists at the 2003 Northeast Regional Conference, which was made up of national experts in teacher preparation, was that there is an immediate and continued need for strong mentoring and in-service programs for its graduates. The cost of this support is expensive both for ARC programs and hiring districts. The educational price for urban communities hiring these candidates and not providing mentoring and classroom support is far greater than just dollar figures. The future of public education in urban areas depends on the successful induction and retention of alternatively certified teachers to provide quality education in hard to fill areas in needy schools. Criticizing the ARC music program and its graduates is easy; it is finding solutions that is difficult. It is a challenge that can only be met through the cooperation and collaboration of federal, state and community resources.

The Connecticut Alternate Route to Certification Music Class of Summer 2004 may well be the last such graduating class. Although the summer Connecticut ARC program will be continuing, music certification has been dropped from the list of course offerings. It will still be included in the 24-week ARC II program. As part of my work over the last four years as the district music coach for the Hartford Public Schools, I have been fully committed to providing mentorship and resources to teachers in the Connecticut BEST program, many of whom are Alternate Route to Certification graduates. Several things have led to an increase in fully certified teacher retention, including creating a network of mentors, recruiting teachers and portfolio scorers from long-time music staff, encouraging professional development to increase teachers' pedagogical base, streamlining procedures, and being available to communicate with new teachers through several means. The awarding of federal funding for professional development to our district has promoted music education and provided numerous resources that would have been unattainable given our limited music budget. The 2004 ARC graduates in our district have completed their first year, discovering that they need to dig deep within themselves to find the wisdom and fortitude to make music a workable vehicle for student learning in a high-stakes testing district. They have discovered that urban music education requires exploring resources and developing innovative programming. It is absolutely necessary to think outside the box to reach urban kids and important to be flexible under the crushing demands of failing schools. The 2004 graduates will be back next year, along with all the other ARC graduates who have remained committed to making music with some of the nation's poorest children. The mentoring system that is in place is not flawless, or seamless, but it is there, a work in progress, and accessible for the taking to these very dedicated teachers. Qualified professionals wishing to pursue a career in public education should be keenly aware before embarking on this program that is it only the first step in an educational career. Districts facing shortages should be vigilant in their screening of alternative candidates for their qualifications, training, talent, and potential for being successful in suitable classrooms. Districts must provide the necessary and ongoing teacher induction essential for developing successful teachers. Universities and alternative certification programs must work together for the benefit of students and beginning teachers. High-quality teacher preparation programs, whether traditional or accelerated, should be able to show a pattern of evidence of success among their graduates and ultimately the students they seek to serve.

REFERENCES

Connecticut Department of Education. (2004a). *Alternate route to certification fact sheet*. Hartford, CT: Author.

———. (2004b). *The alternate route to certification program information and application 2004*. Hartford, CT: Author.

Connecticut Department of Higher Education. (2003.) *Alternate route to certification core curriculum framework 2003*. Hartford, CT: Author.

Haberman, M. (2004). *Urban education: The state of urban schooling at the start of the 21st century*. Retrieved August 11, 2005, from www.EducationNews.org.

Hay, L. (2003). Recruiting quality candidates: Alternate routes are not alternate standards [speech]. *The first northeast regional conference on alternate routes to teacher certification*. Farmington, CT, October 29–31, 2003.

Ladson-Billings, G. (1994). *The dreamkeepers*. San Francisco: Jossey-Bass.

MENC: The National Association for Music Education. (2003). *Alternate certification position statement*. Retrieved on June 5, 2003, from www.menc.org.

Mutari, E., & Lakew, M. (2004). Class conflict: The rising costs of college. In J. Skolnick & E. Currie (Eds.), *Crisis in American institutions* (p. 356). New York: Pearson.

Nierman, G., Zeichner, K., & Hobbel, N. (2002). Changing concepts of teacher education. In R. Colwell & C. Richardson (Eds.), *The new handbook of research on music teaching and learning* (pp. 818–839). New York: Oxford.

7

Real-World Methods: Preparing Future Music Teachers in Today's Classrooms

Patrick M. Jones and Fred P. Eyrich Jr.

INTRODUCTION AND PURPOSES

Music education in the urban centers of the United States faces many challenges. Issues such as underfunding, lack of administrative and community support, scheduling, and cultural conflicts are daily realities. While all of these are serious issues that need to be resolved, the greatest threat to music education in urban schools is perhaps the difficulty in attracting and retaining music teachers. Without qualified and dedicated music teachers, urban districts are left with three choices: have grade-level teachers teach music, which could result in music education as solely "appreciation" and social studies; outsource music education to the music industry through outreach programs geared toward building audiences rather than developing children's musicianship; or eliminate music instruction altogether. Intellectual honesty requires us to admit that one of the major reasons many university graduates don't consider teaching in urban districts is because they are afraid to do so. Therefore, what is needed is an approach to music teacher education that both prepares students for teaching and also eliminates their fear of teaching in urban schools. This chapter is an overview of a program that is just such an approach.

The model used for this program is the professional development school (PDS) model that was suggested by the Holmes Group (now known as the Holmes Partnership) and outlined in three reports (Holmes Group, 1986, 1990, 1995). The essence of the PDS is that it is a collaborative effort between universities and schools that serves simultaneously as "a school for the development of novice professionals, for continuing development of experienced professionals, and for the research and development of the profession" (Holmes Group, 1990, p. 1). Susan Wharton Conkling and Warren Henry pioneered this approach for music teacher education and provided the theoretical framework for applying the PDS approach in music teacher education in previously published articles to which we refer you (Conkling & Henry, 1999, 2002; Henry, 2001). Using the groundbreaking work of Conkling and Henry as our inspiration and model, we developed a site-based pedagogy program between the University of the Arts (UArts) and Abraham Lincoln High School (ALHS) in spring 2004. We focus here on one portion of the PDS model: developing novice professionals, as a collaboration between the university professor, a special area teacher, and preservice teachers. In this model the professor and teacher share responsibility for instruction, and the preservice teachers are empowered to contribute their own expertise and strengths and give liberal amounts of input. Responsibility for teacher education is then shared between the university and high school, breaking down barriers between theory and practice.

Professional development schools develop organically within the context and cultures of the communities, institutions, and personnel involved (Holmes Group, 1995, p. 81). Therefore, no two look exactly alike. With that in mind we do not propose that this chapter offers a prescribed solution to be superimposed onto other situations. Instead we offer a practical description of our program, steps we are taking to improve it, and tips for implementing similar programs in other schools. Our goals are to bring the PDS model to the attention of those who are part of the urban education conversation—particularly those interested in music education. The PDS model enables urban music teachers to infuse energy and bring resources they otherwise could not afford into their program, and enables university professors to provide practical, real-world experiences to their classes. It provides a way for urban schools to take an active part in educating and recruiting teachers who might otherwise never consider teaching in those settings, and helps urban school administrators who face a dearth of music teacher candidates applying for jobs in their schools. Policy makers at the state and national level should support mutually beneficial models such as this kind of partnership between higher education and K–12 schools.

PROGRAM OVERVIEW

School District of Philadelphia

The School District of Philadelphia is the nation's seventh largest by enrollment and serves a racially and ethnically diverse student population that includes approximately 200,000 students (K–12) enrolled in 264 schools and an additional 7,500 children enrolled in early childhood programs. The overwhelming majority of the students in Philadelphia public schools come from low-income and historically underserved racial minority backgrounds. In the 2002–2003 school year 71.1% (or a total of 139,756 students) were identified as low-income (i.e., eligible for free or reduced price lunch under federal guidelines). Student population racial demographics for that year were as follows: 65.3% African American; 16.4% White; 13.1% Latino; and 4.9% Asian. Over 23,000 students have been diagnosed with physical and/or learning disabilities severe enough to require special educational services. Nearly 13,000 have limited English proficiency, coming from homes where over 60 different primary languages are spoken (Grants Office, 2004).

The School District of Philadelphia has trouble recruiting music teachers. Many schools simply do not have one. Of those that do, many are uncertified and unqualified. Thus, the music education of students is spotty at best (Grants Office, 2004).

Abraham Lincoln High School

Abraham Lincoln High School is a large comprehensive high school. It is not a first choice school, since the top students tend to go to the various magnet or academically oriented schools in the district. ALHS had 2,402 students in grades 9–12 in the 2003–2004 school year with 46.8% identified as low-income. During that same year 343 received special education services and 58 were in the English for speakers of other languages (ESOL) program. The student population racial demographics for 2004–2005 were as follows: 43.0% African American; 40.2% White; 13.1% Latino; and 3.7% Asian (School District of Philadelphia, 2005).

The music program at Lincoln offers many students their first opportunity for formalized musical study. The high school program offers concert, jazz, and marching bands; concert choir and madrigal singers; and classes in music appreciation, music theory, and music technology. There is no feeder program, so most instrumental students are beginners in high school. There are two full-time music teachers at the high school and several itinerant music teachers who teach group lessons on band and orchestra instruments once a week.

The University of the Arts

The music education program at the University of the Arts is a master of Arts in Teaching (MAT) degree, which is a graduate-level teacher certification program. All students have a bachelor's degree in music in an area other than music education. This is in keeping with the Holmes Group's vision that teachers should receive bachelor degrees in their content areas and education degrees at the master's level (Holmes Group, 1986, pp. 93–95). Within the MAT there are currently professional development partnerships for two courses: MUED 520 Music Pedagogy III: PreK–4 and MUED 531 Conducting & Rehearsing Techniques: High School & Community Ensembles. Both of these courses occur during the first seven weeks of each semester. The university students, referred to from here on as interns, spend six hours each week at the school (two days a week for three hours each day) as a full class with the professor present. During the second half of each semester they move on to traditional student teaching placements. The fall semester is devoted to elementary pedagogy and student teaching, and the spring semester is dedicated to secondary pedagogy and student teaching. This schedule provides a direct connection between pedagogy and student teaching at the two levels required for K–12 music certification in Pennsylvania. This chapter describes the partnership for MUED 531 Conducting & Rehearsing Techniques: High School & Community Ensembles.

Daily Schedule

The daily schedule for MUED 531, which is held at ALHS, follows the two full-time ALHS music teachers' schedules. The interns are at the school for five periods a day, two days a week, and one after-school rehearsal. They are thus immersed in a plethora of responsibilities such as teaching lessons, music theory, music technology, music appreciation; organizing and rehearsing small ensembles and sectionals; working with students on solo literature; and conducting concert band, jazz band, and choir. In addition, the professor, instrumental teacher, and interns have a "class meeting" one hour each week during which assignments, lectures, and demonstrations occur just as they would in a campus-based course. Both the university professor and instrumental teacher provide instruction and input during the meeting. This session, however, is more of a strategic planning session than a lecture hour. The agenda consists of both predetermined content and emergent issues identified by the interns, professor, or teacher. Questions are answered, issues are discussed, and group planning takes place.

Course Content

The major emphasis of the course is on developing pedagogy rather than covering a list of topics related to methods of instruction. The critical focus is on developing the interns' habits of mind relative to the teaching cycle of preparation, delivery, feedback, reflection, and adjustment. A necessary component for achieving this is working with actual high school students. Therefore, the course goals cannot be accomplished on a college campus.

Assignments for the course are similar to those used in campus-based methods classes. They include score study, unit plans, lesson plans, repertoire selection, and reflections on videotaped conducting experiences as well as noncurricular responsibilities such as budgeting and parent booster organizations. The course includes two major real-world scenarios for which the interns are responsible. One is a recital in which the high school students perform chamber works and solos that the interns organize, select, and coach. The other is a *Music in Our Schools Month* concert. Everything having to do with the performances are prepared and generated by the interns. They rehearse the pieces, create the programs, send the invitations, stage-manage the events, conduct the concert, and so forth.

How It Works

- Each intern receives a piece or a movement of a larger work to rehearse with either the band or chorus (depending on the intern's area of specialization) for the duration of the course. These pieces are new ones for the ensembles, so the interns prepare them from scratch.
- Each intern conducts at least once a week for a 10–15 minute block of time with either the full ensemble or a sectional.
- Rehearsals are videotaped and the university professor and the high school teachers provide comments verbally and/or in writing.
- The interns review their tapes at home and perform a self-critique using an instructor-designed assessment scale. They complete a one-page reflection that includes goals and strategies for improvement, which they bring to the next class for discussion.
- The professor meets with interns once a week in small groups during their free times (while others are teaching lessons) at ALHS to review their tapes and self-critiques. Conducting exercises and advice on lesson planning and rehearsal strategies/techniques are provided during these small group sessions. All interns in the small group provide input and advice in these sessions as well. Thus, everyone learns from the issues raised by each intern.

While the majority of course content includes assignments determined by the professor and high school teachers, the instruction actually grows from the needs and concerns of the interns, making it organic to their experience, relevant to their context, and immediately applicable to their next class or rehearsal.

Benefits

To borrow an oft-worn phrase, this program is a textbook example of a "win-win" situation. All members of the partnership learn from each other.

The university professor and high school teachers learn from each other as well as from the interns and students, and are challenged to reconsider their values and theories regarding pedagogy, educational theory, course content, and instructional methods. The end result has been more innovation and improved learning for all participants. Two examples demonstrate how the interns have transferred their musical expertise from their real-world performing lives to the classroom. These illustrate the value of allowing student input rather than predetermining and prescribing all of the course content.

Music We Don't Normally Get to Hear

Most interns perform a variety of genres in cover and original bands throughout the Greater Philadelphia region. When developing the schedule for the music appreciation class they decided that live performances would make the music in these classes more interesting and accessible to the students. To do this they formed bands from among themselves, brought other performers with whom they work into the classes, and got the students performing as well. This resulted in a variety of genres such as jazz, blues, bluegrass, reggae, and Middle Eastern musics, and instruments such as the didgeridoo and the doumbek being presented with integrity and authenticity. Without the input of the interns, many of these genres and instruments would not have been included in the curriculum. This approach generated much more interest from the students than looking at pictures of instruments and listening to recordings. One of the ALHS students commented on an attitude survey that "having the interns play music in class made it real," and another commented that "the interns brought all kinds of music to class we don't normally get to hear" (Eyrich, 2005b).

Head Tunes

Some of the interns decided the students in the high school band should learn to play "head tunes" by ear like members of professional cover bands do. They thought that learning how to play songs they hear on the radio or CDs would make music instruction more applicable to students' daily lives and provide motivation to continue playing their instruments outside of school and after graduation. They asked for volunteers to stay after school on Wednesdays. About a dozen students participated. As a group the students and interns listened to several tunes. They selected "Chameleon." The interns led the students through the process of learning the tune by ear and crafting an arrangement by ear. So many drummers wanted to participate that they used marching percussion instead of a drum set. This gave them mobility so they developed staging, which included the drum line entering from the front of the auditorium and the horns entering from the rear and better rehearsal participants after sitting side by side with the interns, improved more quickly in their individual performance techniques, and learned more about relating music to their daily lives.

The teachers also learned about their own students and their own teaching from watching and critiquing the interns. They identified learning styles and strengths in their students that they might not have noticed from in front of the class. They saw similar traits in the interns and were able to help them be successful. They provided guidance and assistance to preservice teachers and gave real-world insights and tips for handling the day-to-day responsibilities of being a music teacher. Thus, they became "Career Professional Teachers," which the Holmes Group claims are crucial in the preparation of beginning teachers (1986, pp. 12–13; 40–41). This kind of interaction—having to explain what they do and reevaluate its impact when executed by an intern—helps teachers refine their own understanding of theory and practice. Working with a university music education colleague also gives the teacher insights and professional development at a different level than normally experienced in the school setting.

Professors

University music education professors are extremely busy. The pressure to either be on campus or home writing leaves little time to be in the schools interacting with K–12 colleagues and students. The PDS approach facilitates such interaction. For the university professor, the PDS approach also means giving up control. Whereas in traditional campus-based classes one has complete control of the schedule, calendar, lectures, and choices of repertoire, in this scenario that is not the case. The school dictates the daily schedule, the repertoire is chosen by the high school teacher, and the course calendar remains fluid based on real-world scenarios such as snow holidays and fire drills, input from the interns as they grow, and a final concert only seven weeks in the making. As a result, this professor learned to include less content and to rethink and prioritize what is really important to prepare university students for student teaching. This project, in fact, operationalized a previously raised concern about making band and conducting classes relevant to the future needs of music education majors (Jones, 2005b). In addition, pedagogy and educational theories were not only discussed, but put to action when the interns worked with actual students in a real high school. The interns contributed to the evaluation of course techniques, pedagogy, and content through healthy professional dialogue. And as the interns responsibility for their own learning the professor's role shifted to a consultant rather than a lecturer. The end result was a dynamic learning environment for all concerned. The professor was rewarded with seeing in action, being able to test and refine his ideas and approaches, and

walking through the audience while playing. Needless to say this piece was the hit of the *Music in Our Schools Month* concert.

These ideas came from the interns' real-world experiences as working musicians. They were supported by our theoretical work in foundations courses where the interns were challenged to go beyond the experiences they had in school music to develop useful and relevant musical experiences that would connect students to their out-of-school musical lives. Giving the interns a voice in the course content allowed them to draw on their own expertise, bring ideas to the class the instructors would never have imagined, and provide motivating and meaningful musical experiences for the high school students. As one intern noted, "In my experience at Lincoln I realized the more a teacher is able to relate the school/educational experience to the lived experiences of the students, the more the students relate to the education they receive and the more responsibility they take for it. I also realized that music may be the most effective way to bridge this gap between life in school from the life outside it because adolescents in particular tend to define themselves in large part by the music they listen to" (Decker, 2005). This is an important point for us as a profession to bear in mind as we struggle to redefine music education in general and in urban settings particularly. Our traditional approach to music education has been a one-size-fits-all model of general music and large ensembles, usually band, choir, and orchestra. If we intend to reach a wider segment of the population, particularly those in urban settings who come to school with a rich diversity of musical backgrounds, we should customize our offerings to the communities in which schools are located (Jones, 2004). Such an approach is in line with the Holmes Group's belief that "What is important is that teachers be engaged, that they observe their students, follow them closely, find out what excites them, and then help them to do that" (Holmes Group, 1990, p. 16). Nowhere is that approach perhaps more relevant in terms of curricular content than in music class.

HIGH SCHOOL STUDENTS

Working with the interns helped me improve my playing because they are experts on their instruments and can show me things my regular teacher can't. [Anonymous ALHS student]

(Eyrich, 2005a)

Because of this partnership, the ALHS students receive a level of attention and expertise that would not otherwise be available. As a result of this reinforcement, musical concepts and strategies are often absorbed by the students more easily than when presented by the teacher alone. Students receive much more personalized instruction on their instruments and they learn a variety of genres such as jazz, funk, rock, and world musics and receive instruction in improvisation, composition, arranging, and transcribing. The interns are young, motivated, and close enough in age to the high school students that they are musically in touch with the students' interests. Their age also allows them to serve as realistic role models. ALHS students admire the musicianship of the interns and try to absorb as much from them as they can.

The Lincoln students know the interns are accomplished musicians but that they are novice teachers. They see the interns take risks that sometimes don't work out as planned. They are supportive of the interns and want to see them do well. Thus, while the students learn music from the interns, they simultaneously provide an encouraging laboratory environment in which it is safe for the interns to take chances, grow, and learn from the students. This leads to a positive sense of empowerment among the students. Many have commented that they want to pursue music studies at the university level and a few of the graduates have auditioned at several universities.

UNIVERSITY INTERNS

> It's very easy to get quick feedback from both your peers and the students you're working with. The short amount of time in front of the class at different tasks, getting feedback from your peers, getting immediate feedback from your teachers, and also getting to work with students privately or in groups with things you feel most comfortable with was ideal.
>
> (Martin Brown, UArts MAT Class of 2005)

The interns receive direct feedback in an authentic school setting. They learn from each other, the students, in-service teachers, and the professor. They quickly realize that the students are depending on them and they are having a positive impact on the students. This sense of efficacy helps them develop the reflective practice mind-set necessary for success as a teacher much more quickly than in standard scenarios where methods are held on campus with limited field experience until student teaching. Their cooperating teachers comment that they are much more prepared for student teaching after this site-based course than students from previous campus-based methods classes were. By the time the interns begin student teaching they have already made the mental transition from student to teacher, having developed a teacher identity during the site-based course. They have experience in planning, delivering, assessing, and refining lessons; are much more comfortable on the podium; and have a more advanced rehearsal technique.

They have realistic expectations of what the job of a music teacher actually entails, and as a result they know how to set teaching goals, are comfortable multitasking in the music classroom setting, and understand how schools function. After teaching in this urban setting, they have very few problems with classroom management when they student teach, which is a major difference cooperating teachers have noticed since the start of this program.

Of great importance is the positive attitude change on the part of the interns regarding urban education and teaching in urban settings. Not only do they comment on this personally and in their journals, but some have made life choices to live and teach in the city. Whereas not a single alumnus of UArts was employed as a music teacher in the School District of Philadelphia prior to this program, 33% of the class of 2004 are now teaching in the district or in district-related charter schools, and two students from the class of 2005 have accepted employment in city charter schools as of July 2005. While this may not be a huge number, dedicated and better-prepared teachers who otherwise probably would not have even considered teaching in the city are now teaching in urban classrooms. Their experiences at Lincoln opened them to an option they might not otherwise have considered.

THOUGHTS FOR INSTRUCTORS

The initial fear of both the university and high school faculty is that this approach requires them to forfeit control, and this is true. However gains far outweigh any losses. The PDS model is better for students, teachers, professors, and administrators than the traditional approach K–12 schools and universities operate in isolation from each other Group, 1990, pp. 45–54).

Teachers

High school music teachers often feel pressure to be in con minute because of impending performances. The model mos in the university was that of the professional large ensemble v as conductor/maestro/decision maker. This approach has strung our profession and keeps us from adopting the inn approaches we need to meet a diverse and changing socie 2005a). Developing a PDS partnership means growing p approach and giving up instructional time in both class ensembles in order to let the interns teach. What teacher however, is made up with the individualized attention from the interns. The benefits in our program were app ning. The students were more excited about taking les

having a class that was motivated by richer and deeper experiences than could be created on campus.

STEPS FOR IMPROVEMENT

The experiences of the past two years have helped us refine our expectations, identify weaknesses, and make adjustments to the program as necessary. We will be making two major changes for the third year that we hope will improve the program even further.

Course Expectations

The interns were so successful in the second year of the program that ALHS students would come to the band room for assistance during every period on the days they were there. This made the scheduled "MAT class meeting" difficult to maintain as part of the daily schedule. The result was fragmented instruction and frustration among the interns regarding course assignments and expectations. To resolve this we will take an hour from an existing seminar and devote it to the class meeting. During that time we will introduce new assignments, review previous happenings at the high school, plan next steps in the course, and make sure everyone is clear on assignments and expectations.

Reflective Practice

According to the Holmes Group, "The improvement of teacher education depends on the continuing development of systematic knowledge and reflective practice" (Holmes Group, 1986, p. 66). Sharing reflections in the class provides opportunities for group input and unique and multiple perspectives on resolving issues, and creates a team approach to solving problems. Therefore, we began online weekly journals during student teaching last spring. This approach, which is essentially an electronic bulletin board, extended the group meetings held during MUED 531 into the student teaching portion of the semester. We plan to continue the use of online journals.

TIPS FOR IMPLEMENTING A SIMILAR PROGRAM AT OTHER INSTITUTIONS

Developing a partnership requires support from all concerned: administrators, teachers, interns, and students. The first step is to find the right partner teacher. In our case, this relationship was fostered through Philadelphia

Academies Incorporated, a nonprofit organization committed to improving the Philadelphia Public Schools (www.academiesinc.org). Both of us are active in this organization, and this is how we met. After a brief discussion of the model, we developed the basic outline for the site-based course. We then drafted a proposal and presented it to the school principal. With his approval we moved forward and continue to refine the program. The following are some tips from our experience:

1. Prepare a written proposal that outlines the program elements to include who, what, when, where, why, and how.
2. Impress upon the school administration that hosting such a program does not require any additional resources from the administration, school staff, school budget, etc.
3. Have interns get background checks, clearances, and any other paperwork required by the state and school. They should also be provided with school IDs and copies of the school handbook.
4. University professors: Determine what content you want to cover and reduce it by 10% right from the beginning. Be flexible and prepared to eliminate more once the course begins. Do some hard thinking about what is truly important in preparing teachers. It is impossible to prepare students for every potential scenario and to teach them every technique. We decided to focus on developing reflective practice and pedagogy as the emphasis of this course.
5. School teachers: Realize from the beginning that you are a valued and equal member of the team and do not shy from giving input. The interns will look up to you and want your guidance. The music curriculum must be in place and adhered to in order for the program to be successful. Give a copy to the interns at the beginning. They need to see that you have a curriculum and where they can fit into it during the brief time they are there. This helps keep your program moving in the direction you desire, as you are ultimately the one responsible for concerts, performances, assessment, etc.

CONCLUSION

My expectations changed during the course. Essentially, kids are kids, no matter where you go. This holds true at Lincoln. They may be slightly more urbanized (i.e., street smart, etc.) but they have the same tendencies as a suburban school. I even think that the urban factor could be a positive thing. Wealthy suburban school students tend to get bogged down in "keeping up" and having the latest gadgets. In this school, that is less of a concern, and you can get down to the nitty gritty of teaching music.

(Ryan Stroud, UArts MAT class of 2005)

Site-based courses are exciting and enriching experiences for everyone involved. Our course could almost be described as group student teaching, a preparatory phase where interns go twice a week with their classmates, professor, and a teacher who together serve as guides and a safety net. Moving on to student teaching simply continues the process with the professor and other class members no longer present.

Not only has this program alleviated the fear of teaching in urban schools, we believe it has made the interns better prepared for student teaching than the traditional campus-based course, regardless of the setting. Cooperating teachers and student teaching supervisors alike have noted the difference in the interns' preparation for student teaching. Both groups have commented on how the interns have been much more prepared for student teaching than in the years prior to this program. Particularly noted is their easy assumption of the teacher role, comfort level in front of the class, and their abilities to reflect on their teaching and to improve it. After having dealt with real-life scenarios before student teaching they were able to concentrate on teaching and learning, which is the goal of all teacher education programs.

REFERENCES

Brown, M. (2005). MUED 531 Journal: The University of the Arts.

Conkling, S. W., & Henry, W. (1999). Professional development partnerships: A new model for music teacher preparation. *Arts Education Policy Review*, 100(4), 19–23.

———. (2002). The impact of professional development partnerships: Our part of the story. *Journal of Music Teacher Education*, 11(2), n.p.

Decker, T. (2005). MUED 531 Journal: The University of the Arts.

Eyrich, F. (2005a). Student attitude survey—instrumental students: Abraham Lincoln High School, Philadelphia, PA.

———. (2005b). Student attitude survey—music appreciation class. Abraham Lincoln High School: Philadelphia, PA.

Grants Office. (2004). Demographic data. Philadelphia, PA: School District of Philadelphia.

Henry, W. (2001). Music teacher education and the professional development school. *Journal of Music Teacher Education*, 10(2), 23–28.

Holmes Group. (1986). *Tomorrow's teachers*. East Lansing, MI: Holmes Group.

———. (1990). *Tomorrow's schools*. East Lansing, MI: Holmes Group.

———. (1995). *Tomorrow's schools of education*. East Lansing, MI: Holmes Group.

Jones, P. M. (2004). Returning music education to the mainstream: Reconnecting with the community. In *Proceedings of the International Society for Music Education*. Tenerife, Canary Islands, Spain: ISME.

———. (2005a). Music education and the knowledge economy: Developing creativity, strengthening communities. *Arts Education Policy Review*, 106(4), 5–12.

————. (2005b). A review of dissertations about concert band repertoire with applications for school and collegiate bands. *Journal of Band Research*, 40(2), 60–83.
School District of Philadelphia. (2005). Abraham Lincoln High School. Retrieved August 10, 2005, from www.phila.k12.pa.us.
Stroud, R. (2005). MUED 531 Journal: The University of the Arts.

8

Building Bridges: A Collaboration between Elementary Music Students and Music Education Undergraduates

Donna T. Emmanuel

EDUCATION UNDERGRADUATES

Collegiate music education programs and public school music programs have long been partners in implicit and explicit ways. In urban settings where unique challenges exist, however, traditional partnerships are often ineffective. Creative, nontraditional methods are often more useful to meet these challenges and span the gap between higher education and urban public school systems. The purpose of this chapter is to discuss one such relationship that evolved from the professional development school model. This collaborative partnership involves an urban elementary music teacher, her third-grade class, a university music education methods class, and the faculty instructor.

As an assistant professor in the Division of Music Education in the College of Music at the University of North Texas, I have a passion for urban education. I also have a strong interest in working with Latino student populations because of past experiences working in a Hispanic area in urban Detroit and traveling in Mexico. Because of my interest in urban education and my desire to work particularly with Latino students, I sought to partner with an elementary school in Dallas with a predominantly Hispanic student population. Another concern was to find a school in which a collaborative partnership could provide the impetus for a continued building of resources (rather than a school with many resources already in place). The Elementary and Choral Music supervisor in Dallas first directed me to a school that met some of my criteria, but was identified as a "Showcase School" in that it had received additional funding, materials, programs, and facilities. I continued to search for a more appropriate setting, and was referred to a school by a professor from the College of Education at the university.

An Example of a Collaborative Partnership

The partnership was eventually formed between an elementary music program in urban Dallas and the undergraduate music education program at the University of North Texas. It began in the fall of 2004 and is still evolving. In this school of approximately 1,200 students, there is only one music teacher. Because of the large enrollment, the school administrator had to design a creative schedule. So that every student in the school has music at some time during the year, music classes are scheduled in six-week units of 45 minutes each. At the end of every six-week period, a new group of classes begins. This means that most students in the school, with a few exceptions, have music for only six weeks out of the year.

The music teacher is certified, with a degree from the University of North Texas, and has many years of experience in teaching music in the public schools. She is an accomplished musician, both pianist and vocalist, and is African American. She says that her biggest challenge in this setting is the schedule.

I initially met with the Dallas music teacher to discuss the possibility of some type of collaborative partnership. With her experience and musical expertise, she seemed like a wonderful role model for my students to observe, a successful teacher in a challenging setting. Our discussion centered on ways that my students and I might assist her in her teaching. She indicated that while she is an accomplished pianist and can improvise at the keyboard, she did not know how to teach improvisation. We agreed that an improvisation project would be beneficial for all the participants; that that her students would benefit from being engaged in this type of creative activity, and that the undergraduate students would begin to understand how to teach improvisation themselves.

Preliminary meetings involved the teacher and me. During these meetings, we shared ideas and knowledge and tried to establish some common goals and objectives. Early on it appeared that she was more comfortable in letting me guide how the collaboration might work. In order to gain her input, I had to ask direct questions. It was important to me that she did not view me as an intruder in her classroom, implementing my ideas and values, but as an equal partner in a project. Trust building was an important issue from the onset. I attempted to gain her trust by asking for her input, ideas, and suggestions. Later, as we developed lesson plans, I made sure she received copies with any revisions that had been made. I also made sure that we were covering the content and skills that she felt were important for her students.

As our discussions progressed, we agreed to limit our focus to rhythmic improvisation because of the short amount of time we had to work with the students. We also agreed to focus on note reading. We were fortunate that one third-grade class met during a time when I could travel to Dallas. This class served as our collaborative project. My university students would develop the lesson plans, but they would not actually teach directly. Instead, they would observe videotapes of the classes to determine how effective their plan was and what changes needed to made. Because this teacher was not yet comfortable teaching rhythmic improvisation, I would teach the classes at first and she would take part in the teaching process during segments in which she felt comfortable.

This partnership was specifically designed to include the undergraduate music education students from my elementary methods class. This course, which is required for all music education majors, is typically the first methods course for these students, and most of the students have not had any type of classroom teaching experience prior to taking this course. For this reason, their direct interaction with the elementary students is limited. Later in the semester, they would have the opportunity for hands-on teaching experiences with actual students.

I introduced the music education students to this project on the first day of the university semester. Their role in the project was explained: they would create lesson plans that the music teacher and I would use with the elementary students. Members of the class were excited about being able to watch an experienced teacher in the teaching process and were curious about the students in this urban Dallas school. About six weeks into the university semester, after the university students had learned about the elements and concepts that are included in elementary general music, we started to discuss ways to move third graders toward improvisation. The university students worked on sequencing activities into an effective lesson plan that would be appropriate for the particular group with which we would be working. The lesson plans were shared with the elementary music teacher, who gave feedback so the plans could be refined.

Eventually the plans were complete enough to put them into practice. I then traveled to the elementary school and taught the first lessons under the watchful eye of the elementary music teacher. These lessons were videotaped. University students whose schedule permitted them to go with me could accompany me, but they were instructed to only observe or operate the camera. Several times one or two students volunteered to go along.

Since this third-grade class had music three times a week, the music teacher taught their Monday class and I visited on Wednesdays and Fridays.

The class was forty-five minutes long, and the number of visits varied depending on where the elementary schedule was at the time. Typically, I visited the class twice a week for four to six weeks during both the fall and spring semesters.

One of the goals of this experience was for the elementary music teacher to become comfortable enough to eventually teach the lessons herself and build an improvisation component for the curriculum. Because of her unfamiliarity with teaching improvisation, she requested to observe during the first lessons, and gradually move into team-teaching as her comfort level increased. A unique aspect of this type of collaboration, which is loosely built on the professional development school model, is that rather than having the experienced teacher instruct the university students, the students were actually helping the music teacher learn more about a concept that she was unfamiliar with. The students certainly benefited from watching this teacher interact with her students and lead teaching segments, but unlike the PDS model, the primary roles were reversed.

After teaching each lesson I took the tape back to the university where my students could see their plan in action. They were able to tell what worked well and what did not, and then to create the next plan based on what they saw on the tape. This process challenged a number of their assumptions about elementary students and urban students in particular. Many of them were surprised at how advanced the elementary students were in certain musical skills. Rhythmically, the elementary students were quite strong. They were skilled at ensemble participation. They also were comfortable engaging in activities in which they had never before participated, such as creating rhythmic conversations. The university students were also surprised about how well behaved the elementary students were and how much was accomplished in each lesson.

Pedagogical learning occurred as well. It quickly became clear how important sequencing is in developing a lesson plan. Another discovery was the level of detail that was needed for a good lesson plan, and the number of activities required to fill a 45-minute class. As the semester progressed, the music teacher and I continued to collaborate on the progress made by the elementary students and how to refine and enhance the process of developing appropriate lesson plans. The university students responded with lesson plans that were more sophisticated and detailed based on the experience of observing the elementary students.

The project ended with a culminating event that was an adaptation of what we envisioned. Ideally, the elementary students and their music teacher would travel to the university to participate in a jam session with the music education undergraduate students. The undergraduate students would bring in their instruments and play a standard 12-bar blues pattern while the elementary students would create a rhythm ensemble behind them. Typically, this would result in an enthusiastic and energetic group performance during which some of the elementary students could be spotlighted on percussion solos. This jam session could be videotaped so that the elementary students could view their performance at a later date. Then the elementary students would take a tour of the campus, sit in on rehearsals, eat lunch in a dormitory dining room, and visit the football stadium. All these activities would help the students begin to develop knowledge of the university and therefore consider a college education. Afterward, the elementary students along with some of the undergraduate students would perform for their local community, either at the school facilities or in a community gathering place. This step was seen as vitally important so that the parents and other community members see tangible benefits of such a partnership.

What actually happened was a modified version. Because of liability issues traveling from one district to another, the time to gain permission took longer than we anticipated, such that all buses were already booked. So several of the undergraduate students took their instruments to Dallas and the jam session took place there. The elementary students also performed a rap that they created under the guidance of their teacher. A question and answer session followed. Because the permission process has already been worked through, the elementary students will be making their trip to the university in the fall of 2005.

Collaborative Partnerships Defined

What specific characteristics make this partnership collaborative? Traditional partnerships between music education programs and public school systems typically involve either student teacher placements or faculty members conducting research. A partnership, however, with a stated purpose to build a better link between music education programs and urban schools must meet several specific criteria. These ideas are not novel, but emerge from the three reports of the Holmes Group: *Tomorrow's Teachers* (1986), *Tomorrow's Schools* (1990), and *Tomorrow's Schools of Education* (1995). As outlined first in *Tomorrow's Teachers*, these criteria include reciprocity, experimentation, systematic inquiry, and student diversity.

Reciprocity

All partners must benefit from collaborative partnerships. For a partnership like ours, the public school students, the public school music teacher, the university faculty member, and the university students should all receive explicit benefits. These benefits should be explored by both the elementary music teacher and the university faculty person, and should be clearly stated and defined before engaging in any project.

All parties must also share a common goal. This goal must be clearly defined and based on shared visions and expectations. Discovering common beliefs and values helps the participants move toward their goal. In our case, the cooperating teacher, the music education professor, and the university students all agreed that learning to teach improvisation was a worthy goal.

There must also be a feeling of equity among all participants. As Pacheco notes, "quite a few professors are out of touch with what is going on in schools and, in addition, often take an elitist stance toward their colleagues in the public schools, assuming the guise of the expert over a profession in which they have many stories but little current practice" (2000, p. 9). The university faculty member must be aware of these perceptions and ensure the music teacher is treated as an equal expert in this realm and his or her ideas and input valued. Roles must be clearly defined and each participant must feel free to contribute to the process and to make positive criticisms.

A sense of trust among all the participants is important. Curricular decisions must be made in such a way that the university faculty member and the music teacher trust each other to consider what is best for all. If the music teacher suggests changes, the university faculty member must be confident in his or her expertise and knowledge of the students and the setting.

A defined structure for decision making must also exist. If working toward a specific project, each participant must be allowed to contribute to the process. Consideration must be given to the music teacher's specific goals and how those goals might be incorporated in the project. If the project includes undergraduate music education students, their input must be allowed and encouraged under the guidance of the music teacher and the faculty member.

The reciprocity that collaborative partnerships develop can contribute to the music teacher's sense of worth. Having someone from an institution of higher education express an interest in working with a public school music teacher gives that teacher a sense of belonging to a larger musical and educative community and also a sense of respect by having their teaching knowledge and ability recognized and valued. The public school teacher gains access to information and concepts perhaps not previously explored, giving him or her new ideas to use and draw from. As a result of this initial partnership, the music teacher and I had the opportunity to share our experience at a regional conference that focused on teaching music in urban schools. She stood among her peers, administrators, and other educators, able to answer their questions and convey her ideas to them. I am sure this not only boosted her own self-image as an expert music educator, but also affirmed her value in the eyes of her school administrators.

Experimentation

Another criterion for a collaborative partnership is that all parties must be willing to explore new ideas to design a creative project that is beneficial to

dents had an opportunity to participate in activities they might not have experienced before.

Finally, in order to attract more music educators to pursue careers in urban areas, their objections to teaching in this setting must be overcome. Collaborative projects can be powerful experiences for future music educators who are not familiar with urban areas and hold preconceived ideas about the schools and students there. Because many of the undergraduate music education students are from mainstream suburban settings, they have developed beliefs and attitudes about what is "typical" in urban educational settings (McDiarmid & Price, 1990; Zeichner & Gore, 1990). These preconceptions may include that students in these settings have lower aptitudes than students in suburban settings and might require different standards and objectives, or that violent behavior and emotional instability is the norm. The only way to overcome these preconceptions is to give undergraduate students opportunities to see what teaching in these areas is like, and show them that while there are challenges that are specific to these schools, their beliefs about students and those students' abilities are often inaccurate. They begin to recognize the rich environment and the diverse musical backgrounds and skills students in urban areas possess. Rather than view teaching in an urban area as an almost insurmountable challenge, these students begin to see the rewards of working with urban students who have strong musical abilities and who are wonderfully creative and imaginative. This was evidenced by my own students who initially doubted the musical skills of the urban students.

CONCLUSION

After two exploratory semesters, the music teacher and I have agreed to continue this project, working with new students each semester. The benefits have been tremendous. My students, both semesters, have said that the Dallas experience was one of the most valuable they have ever had. They expressed that they felt they learned much more by watching experienced teachers at work, and by seeing their plans implemented with real students, than they would have in a traditional methods class. Several have expressed interest in continuing a relationship with Dallas schools. Most of them have begun to challenge their preconceptions concerning teaching music in an urban setting. I anticipate that some of them will request a student teacher placement in the Dallas school district.

Of the four principles mentioned earlier, reciprocity, experimentation, systematic inquiry, and student diversity, I feel the most vital component is reciprocity. Collaborative partnerships depend on mutual exchange and trust, sharing of experiences and expertise, and concrete benefits for all participants. The idea of reciprocity should also extend to school administrators and policy makers, who should be considered (and should consider themselves) equal allies and cocreators of viable links between music education programs and urban schools.

It is crucially important to build ongoing, vibrant, reciprocal relationships between students, teachers, and administrators in urban schools and institutions of higher learning. These types of collaborative projects will build bridges that will begin to fill some of the gaps that exist between university music education programs and music programs in our public schools, providing music teachers that are better prepared and looking toward achieving long-term goals of equity in our diverse world.

REFERENCES

Banks, J. (2001). Citizenship education and diversity. *Journal of Teacher Education*, 1, 5–16.

Groulx, J. (2001). Changing pre-service teacher perceptions of minority schools. *Urban Education*, 36(1), 60–92.

Ladson-Billings, G. (2000). Fighting for our lives: Preparing teachers to teach African American students. *Journal of Teacher Education*, 51(3), 206–214.

McDiarmid, G., and Price, J. (1990). *Prospective teachers' views of diverse learners: A study of the participants in the ABCD project*. East Lansing, MI: Michigan State University, National Center for Research on Teacher Education.

Pacheco, A. (2000). Meeting the challenge of high-quality teacher education: Why higher education must change. 40th Charles R. Hunt Memorial Lecture. Paper presented at the annual meeting of the American Association of Colleges for Teacher Education. Chicago, IL, Feb. 26–29 (ERIC Document Reproduction Service No. ED 468 988).

Zeichner, K., and Gore, J. (1990). Teacher socialization. In *Handbook of research on teacher education* (pp. 329–348). New York: Macmillan.

9

Music Education Students Teach At-Risk Children Private Instrumental Lessons

Cindy L. Bell and Nathalie G. Robinson

Music educators concerned with improving urban school music programs have been calling for preservice training in urban areas since the Tanglewood Conference of 1967 (Choate, 1968). This is a challenge for college music education programs. Such an experience may encourage these young professionals to student teach in these settings or seek jobs with disadvantaged children. But adequate exposure of prospective music teachers to school communities with cultural or socioeconomic backgrounds different from their own is lacking in most teacher education programs (Emmanuel, 2005; Nierman, Zeichner, & Hobbel, 2002).

Hofstra University's Department of Music (Hempstead, NY) and the Freeport Union Free School District (Freeport, NY) collaborated to address this issue in a unique partnership that combined music education majors with at-risk public school students for individual and small-group music instruction. This school district is identified by New York State as having "high student needs in relation to district resource capacity" (Freeport Public Schools, 2005). Other statistics reported by the Freeport district (2005) and the U.S. Census Bureau (2000) indicate that a high percentage of the pupil population meets the classic definition of at-risk students: students confronted with inequitable socioeconomic factors affecting family life, health/nutrition, community conditions, social status, and school performance (National Institute on the Education of At-Risk Students, 2002). This chapter will detail how this school/university partnership utilized funding from the No Child Left Behind Act to create a successful community of musical learners and teachers, and thereby probe preservice teachers' presumptions about urban school settings and at-risk youth.

For clarification in reading the chapter, the term *student teacher* refers to the undergraduate music education major who taught instrumental lessons, even though this experience was prior to their official student teaching experience. *Music teacher* refers to the licensed teacher employed by the public school district: in this case, a band or orchestra director. *Child* or *children* refers to the public school student (ages 10–15) who received the individualized instruction.

FEDERAL FUNDING FOR
AFTER-SCHOOL PROGRAMS

Federal funding for education programs has often focused on low-income or low-achieving schools (Arts Education Partnership, 2004, p. 3). Programs such as the 21st Century Community Learning Centers, created by the U.S. Department of Education in 1998, fund before- and after-school, weekend, and summer activities that enhance academic performance and provide enrichment, recreational, and social services (U.S. Department of Education, 2004). Additionally, the U.S. Department of Education (2002/2003) recognizes that at-risk children and youth are generally less likely to have access to and participate in arts education programs, which are often inadequately funded in urban areas (p. 2). Research indicates that schools that stay open after hours and offer local youth supplementary learning opportunities in safe environments are providing activities crucial to successful intervention for at-risk and disadvantaged students (Taylor, Barry, & Walls, 1997).

The No Child Left Behind Act of 2001 identified the arts as a "core academic subject," positioning music and arts on equal footing with reading, math, sciences, and other disciplines (Arts Education Partnership, 2004). Arts education advocates cheered the language of this government bill that allowed for a significant shift in funding to community-based arts education programs. Community leaders and school district administrators were urged to obtain funding for neighborhood projects (Arts Education Partnership, 2004), particularly as improved arts education is equated with improvement in overall student performance (p. 3).

Research has demonstrated other rewards of successful participation in music and arts activities, benefits that contribute to self-esteem and a greater sense of belonging within the school environment (Taylor et al., 1997). Ebie (1998) identified five points where music education affected the lives of at-risk children, including feelings of accomplishment through participation in ensembles. Taylor et al. (1997) affirmed that music and arts teachers are in a unique position to help at-risk students because of the satisfaction that many students find in participation in arts activities (p. 5). It stands to reason, then, that school districts applying for federal funding since the 2001 No Child Left Behind Act should consider a component of arts enrichment for at-risk children.

FREEPORT SCHOOLS, NEW YORK

Freeport is located 30 miles east of New York City on Long Island. It is an economically diverse town of 44,000 residents, wedged between the more affluent neighborhoods typical of Nassau County. The southern edge of the town borders the Great South Bay, where the evidence of several centuries of the maritime industry lingers in boatyards and marinas. In the 1960s, Freeport began to see a growing ethnic population that continues to transform the community (Bleyer, 2005). Recent census statistics (U.S. Census Bureau, 2000) place the racial makeup of the community at 43% White, 33% Black. In terms of cultural heritage, 34% identify themselves as Hispanic or Latino (U.S. Census Bureau, 2000). Note that the census reporting makes a distinction between race and cultural heritage. Those who identify themselves as Hispanic may classify their race as Black or White. Freeport Public Schools (2005) report racial/ethnic origin of the enrolled student body as 41% Black (not Hispanic) and 47% Hispanic, with 11% White (not Hispanic).

The school district, founded in 1890, is committed to quality education for its student body, and in 1962 was one of the first school systems in New York State to voluntarily desegregate its schools (Freeport Public Schools, 2005). The current school district buildings and grounds occupy over 100 acres and include a pre-K and kindergarten school, four elementary schools (grades one through four), separate schools for grades five and six and grades seven and eight, and a four-year high school. The district enrolls approximately 7,500 students and a professional staff of nearly 500. Freeport Public Schools (2005) distinguish themselves in the development and implementation of many innovative programs that have become models for other districts, such as magnet schools for elementary students. The vision of the Freeport Public Schools (2005) is to "empower students to embrace challenges and opportunities of the future."

No Child Left Behind Act

The Freeport Public Schools responded to No Child Left Behind (NCLB) by applying for federal funding to sponsor a 21st Century Community Learning Center in their school buildings. They channeled their grant funds from NCLB to create the after-school program for at-risk children titled

Families and Communities Together (FACT), which offered a variety of educational and social services. Capitalizing on the recent inclusion of the arts as a core curricula subject in NCLB, the district supervisor of music suggested that the FACT program extend to provide after-school lessons on musical instruments.

The criteria for implementing such a project required four divisions of personnel: (1) the school district supervisor of music to arrange all logistical issues at the school and district level (i.e., teaching space, scheduling, communications, appropriate permissions, musical instruments, teacher participation); (2) certified music teacher(s) to be present after school, and organize lessons and children; (3) a college music faculty member to handle logistical issues at the university level (i.e., scheduling, transportation, debriefing with students); and (4) preservice music education majors willing to share their talents and apply their classroom training with at-risk youth.

The Freeport district music supervisor approached Hofstra University to construct a plan for delivering instrumental instruction through the FACT program. Hofstra, a private liberal arts college with 200 music students out of 8,000 full-time undergraduates, had a history of educational collaboration with the Freeport Public Schools, as its close proximity to their campus makes it an ideal placement for participant observation and student teacher experiences in numerous subject areas. Hofstra's music education faculty recruited the student teachers, and the band and orchestra teachers from Freeport coordinated and oversaw the instrumental lessons for the after-school FACT program.

AFTER-SCHOOL MUSIC LESSONS

Parameters of the private instruction program were determined prior to the beginning of the lessons. Private lessons were offered at no cost to any interested Freeport child in elementary or middle school, and taught by a Hofstra undergraduate music education major. If a child did not own an instrument, he or she was provided with one by the Freeport music department. Lessons were offered one afternoon per week at each of the participating FACT schools (depending on the year, two or three schools participated). The music teachers announced the lesson opportunity during their large ensembles and group lessons. Interested children, with the assistance of their ensemble director, selected a regular half hour time slot for instruction. None of the participating children had private lessons outside of the school day, but all were participating in weekly group lessons typical of an instrumental instruction program in a public school.

It is critical to note that the Freeport Public Schools already maintain a well-developed and equipped music program, including high-quality instruments. Under the direction of an energetic and enterprising music supervisor, the district had hired and retained accomplished music educators. The district regularly sent children to participate in all-county and all-state ensembles. The high school select chorale recently performed at the ACDA (American Choral Directors Association) Eastern Division convention. Given the racial, cultural, and socioeconomic mix of the diverse community, the music department produced an outstanding performing arts program. However, very few, if any, beginning instrumental students had the financial means for access to private instrumental lessons.

The Hofstra student teachers coaching the private music lessons (either sophomore- or junior-level students with limited teaching experience) were paid by the lesson through grant funds and compensated for travel, parking, and general expenses. Participation was strictly voluntary, and was solicited in the undergraduate music education classes. The participating student teachers were at a midway point in their teacher training, having completed various foundational courses in music and educational theory and practice, and some instrumental methods classes. For many, this was to be their first experience teaching a music lesson one-on-one.

An upperclassman from Hofstra served as the on-site project administrator, managing children and student teachers and enforcing guidelines. First, it was agreed that any child arriving for a lesson should receive instruction, even if their assigned student teacher was unable to be present. Second, the student teachers were "on their own" in their approach to the lesson instruction. A licensed, certified music teacher (the band or orchestra director) from the district was always present and helped to organize space, but was usually working in the music office. The music teacher was available for problem solving, but would not interfere in the lessons, as the student teachers were to "figure it out" if faced with unexpected teaching issues. They had each other to confer with, but no specific adult intervention occurred during the lesson hour. After each lesson, the student teacher could consult with the music teacher on specific issues of teaching, and generate new ideas for the next lesson.

IMMEDIATE CONCERNS AND ISSUES

Two immediate issues surfaced as the experimental program began. First, there were far more children interested in taking lessons than the university had student teachers to supply. Therefore, several junior-level student teachers agreed to teach on secondary instruments to help cover as many lessons as possible. Some lessons expanded to two or three children with one student teacher. Second, the shortage of string teachers was evident, and one string bass player was engaged to teach violin.

Initially, the lesson program had a slow start, due to differences between the public school's and the college's academic calendars. Lessons were offered late in the afternoon, at the close of the school day, and Hofstra students arranged work schedules, class schedules, and transportation around lesson time schedules. But shortly, a routine of regular lessons was underway.

OBSERVATIONS AND REACTIONS

A post-program discussion was attended by the student teachers, the college supervisor, and school district music personnel at the conclusion of the first year. This dialogue permitted all involved to share their experiences and perceptions of the lesson program. Informal evaluation by the student teachers was in progress during the project, as they kept journals in their music methods class, and participated in weekly in-class discussions with the college supervisor. The discussion session was guided by questions directed at the music education students: how did your participation in this project influence your thoughts about teaching; and how would you describe the benefits to the public school child. Several common themes emerged in this exchange.

First of all, the student teachers describe the development of strong bonds with the younger students and, thus, an increased enthusiasm for teaching. Stated one student teacher, "I had a great experience with the one boy. We developed such a great rapport. We made each other laugh. He was like a sponge. I found myself (working) with him being so exciting. I could tell he genuinely enjoyed it, and it made it so rewarding for me." A second student teacher discovered her enjoyment for this particular age group (middle school), and was considering focusing her music career at that age level. Another student teacher offered, "It was a great experience; [it] firmed up that I really want to be a teacher, [and] I learned a lot about myself as a teacher."

Furthermore, the music student teachers revealed vast improvement in their instrumental techniques and development of teaching skills for lesson instruction. As one student teacher pointed out, college music education programs do not provide undergraduates with instruction on how to conduct private lessons. Another student teacher expressed her anxieties about the particulars of teaching a secondary instrument: "The first day I went I taught a trombone lesson. I was so scared, because I don't know anything about trombone, but it was [fine], because I had my fingering book with me." A third student teacher, a clarinet player, had to teach a flute lesson, and was greatly encouraged to realize that she could successfully teach a child on any instrument. Another student teacher told of his success with a somewhat disinterested string player who had placed rosin all over the fingerboard, and her subsequent improvement in the school's orchestra:

> One half hour with me, and she started to realize what this was all about. She likes [playing the violin] the right way, and got a mentorship with a teacher that she couldn't have in a [large ensemble] setting. Once we pounded in the fundamentals, when I watched her in the large group setting, she was up and playing.

Several student teachers described adapting their individual teaching styles based on their own previous lesson experience and educational training. For instance, one student teacher detailed how she transferred her own learning of the horn embouchure to help "Danny": "I had exercises that my teacher worked on with me, and I worked on the same exercises with him . . . In 45 minutes there was such a change [in his sound]." Another student teacher (saxophone player) made an important connection between his required observational hours and his own teaching: "Seeing the [middle school] teacher teach the trumpet really helped me when I had to teach [it myself]." He suggested coupling observations of group instruction with the after-school lesson.

One student teacher examined his own teaching style, and revised the way he taught. He stated, "I found out it's easier to know how to do something than it is to explain it. You have to find a number of ways to explain things." Another student teacher recognized the importance of having the children engage in self-learning and monitoring their practice time:

> One [clarinet student] showed up every week; she was very talented . . . she kept a practice log, not so much [the] time, but what organized her practice time. Little things like the placement of the reed. We did a lot of things, like expression. She came out with a firmer grasp of musicality and expression, the nuances of playing.

Several comments by student teachers suggested that their experience had forced them to consider educational issues, such as the establishment of unified teaching goals. For instance, while some taught with an emphasis on solo preparation for the upcoming all-county contest, others focused on developing fundamental playing techniques. "We have to weigh things equally," suggested a student teacher.

Even though children were initially grouped in lessons by ability level, the student teachers discovered the challenges of teaching as performance abilities branched. In describing a specific trombone slurring technique she was teaching to two children, one student teacher said, "One student was a little overwhelmed with [the] exercise. The other kid banged it out with no problem." The children, she noted, would "take off in different directions and have different problems" with playing their instruments.

Another student teacher, working with an advanced child who was also taking piano lessons at home, recognized the paradox of at-risk children participating in such after-school programs:

> It was great having an advanced student who was working so hard, but she was already doing that. . . . I would like to have worked with more kids . . . the ones in the back of the [clarinet] section.

SUGGESTIONS FOR FUTURE PROGRAMS

The student teachers encountered problems that are typical of a music teacher's day in a school. The oft-cited dilemma of adequate teaching space was noted by several student teachers. One was squeezed into a small practice room with two clarinet players, and another used the instrument closet to teach lessons. Often, two separate lessons were occurring simultaneously in one large space, such as the opposite sides of a rehearsal room. It was suggested that more classroom space be available for lessons.

Irregular attendance was another issue that troubled the student teachers, as some children were busy with sports practice or other activities, causing them to miss lessons. The district music supervisor suggested creating a lesson contract to be signed by the child and parent, to help bring more legitimacy to the commitment and an obligation of attendance.

One suggestion offered by the district music supervisor and the Freeport music teaching staff was the creation of a syllabus for teaching that clarified lesson content. In this way, the ensemble director could establish what specific issues were priorities for the different children taking lessons, and the student teacher would work "more in tandem" with the music teacher. Also, regular meetings following lessons would help the music teachers to notate progress by students, and ascertain performance goals for future lessons.

The student teachers proposed having a "sharing" at the end of the year, not specifically identified as a recital, but an informal evening of performance for friends and parents. Since some student teachers had practiced duets with the children, and others had incorporated improvisation and compositional activities into the lessons, there was ample material to be performed. Finally, the general consensus by the student teachers was a shift in emphasis from competition preparation to the enjoyment of playing, performing, and creating music.

CONCLUSION

The FACT Freeport Schools–Hofstra University collaboration depicts a model of cooperation and teamwork. Preservice music educators gain invaluable experience teaching instrumental lessons, often on secondary instruments, and exposure to culturally and economically diverse teaching situations. At-risk and disadvantaged children acquire private instrumental instruction, something to which they did not have access. It is a program rich in benefits for all involved. The collaboration project continues, and discussion is under way for expansion into other avenues of music education, such as piano and voice lessons.

Particularly for the Hofstra students, the mystique of teaching vanished: the experience either affirmed that they had made the appropriate career choice, or led them to the realization that a teaching career wasn't for them. Furthermore, they made connections to their music education classes, and understood the value of their undergraduate education. Faces and personalities replaced their perceptions of educational and sociological terms such as *at-risk* and *disadvantaged*. Ultimately, they discovered and understood what it was like to teach, and to teach within a supportive community.

POST-SCRIPTS

Several of the Hofstra students involved in this program in its first two years have since graduated. Five of 10 participants choose to obtain employment in high-needs areas. One student is attending graduate school at a major university with a graduate program committed to equality in urban (and music) education. One student returned to the Freeport district for a teaching position, and another chose to student teach in New York City, and is now teaching in Queens. One outcome is that one student decided not to become a teacher.

The authors wish to acknowledge Mr. Charles A. Puricelli, coordinator of the Arts for the Freeport Public Schools, for his initiative and vision of this collaborative program.

REFERENCES

Arts Education Partnership. (2004). *No subject left behind: A guide to arts education opportunities in the 2001 NCLB act.* Retrieved October 1, 2004, from www.aep .arts.org.

Bleyer, B. (2005). *Freeport: Action on the nautical mile.* Retrieved June 1, 2005, from www.newsday.com/extras/lihistory/spectown/hist001k.htm.

Choate, R., ed. (1968). *Documentary report of the Tanglewood Symposium.* Reston, VA: Music Educators National Conference.

Ebie, B. D. (1998). Can music help? A qualitative investigation of two music educators' views on the role of music in the lives of at-risk students. *Contributions to Music Education,* 25(2), 63–78.

Emmanuel, D. T. (2005). The effects of a music education immersion internship in a culturally diverse setting on the beliefs and attitudes of pre-service music teachers. *International Journal of Music Education*, 23(1), 49–62.

Freeport Public Schools. (2005). *Freeport Public Schools vision statement*. Freeport, NY: Author. Retrieved June 1, 2005, from freeportschools.org/admin/vision_state ment.htm.

National Institute on the Education of At-Risk Students. (2002). *National institute on the education of at-risk students*. Washington, DC: U.S. Department of Education. Retrieved September 1, 2005, from www.ed.gov/offices/OERI/At-Risk/.

Neill, S. (2004). Preservice music teaching field experiences utilizing an urban minority after school program. *Action, Criticism, and Theory for Music Education*, 3(3). Retrieved June 1, 2004, from mas.siue.edu/ACT/v3/Neill04.pdf.

Nierman, G. E., Zeichner, K., & Hobbel, N. (2002). Changing concepts of teacher education. In R. Colwell and C. Richardson (Eds.), *New handbook of research and music teaching and learning* (pp. 818–839). New York: Oxford University Press.

Taylor, J., Barry, N., & Walls, K. (1997). *Music and students at risk: Creative solutions for a national dilemma*. Reston, VA: Music Educators National Conference.

U.S. Census Bureau, Census 2000. (2000). Retrieved June 1, 2005, from www.co. nassau.ny.us/YouthBoard/GDCP2000/1603627485.pdf.

U.S. Department of Education. (2002/2003). *Cultural partnerships for at-risk children and youth program*. Retrieved August 1, 2005, from www.ed.gov/legislation/ FedRegister/announcements/2002-2/060602b.html.

U.S. Department of Education. (2004). *Twenty-first century community learning centers* (2004). Washington, DC: Author. Retrieved October 1, 2004, from www.ed .gov/programs/21stcclc.

10

Learning to Teach in the City: Privileged Music Education Majors Reach Underprivileged Children in an After-School Music Partnership

Patrice Madura Ward-Steinman

Urban university music education departments have much to offer their neighborhood elementary schools, and a successful partnership between the two can provide invaluable experiences for both at-risk children and pre-service teachers. However, with the time constraints felt by all, it is often difficult to bring an outreach program to fruition unless spearheaded by some outside force. The purpose of this chapter is to present the development of such an outreach partnership, as well as the children's and the pre-service teachers' reflections on the experience.

DEVELOPMENT OF THE PARTNERSHIP

During the spring of 2002, an urban university's music department was invited to partner with a small, independent music outreach program that had been active in bringing music lessons to inner-city youth from a nearby elementary school for eight years. Having grown up in the neighborhood, the outreach program's director knew firsthand the extreme importance of musical role models and educational resources in helping at-risk children develop their talents, self-esteem, leadership skills, and aspirations for life.

The outreach program's stated goal was "to give youth positive alternatives to gang activities and peer pressure through the performing arts," and its motto was "Giving back to the community."

The demographics of the elementary school were as follows: 45% of the students were African American and 55% were Latino; approximately 75% qualified for free meal tickets, while the remaining students received reduced-price school meals; and 43% were designated as English-language learners. This population's economic status differed enormously from that of the privileged students of the private university just a few blocks away.

This type of university–community partnership was strongly supported by the university and was eligible for a grant designed to enhance the quality of life in the neighborhood. Specifically, the grant was awarded to assist in bringing music classes to a local elementary school during the after-school hours in a safe and supervised environment. Although the school did have a regular music teacher who traveled to several schools in the city each week, and thus taught a minimal music curriculum, the outreach program provided additional music instruction and was open to all the children in the school.

The partners were awarded $13,000 for the 2002–2003 school year. The grant was to fund a graduate student coordinator for three hours per week at $15 per hour, music education majors to work as teachers for $13 per hour, and material needs (flyers, concert programs, brochures, concert tickets, musical instruments, and nutritious snacks). Volunteer positions included the outreach program founder, the university music education professor, and a public-school staff member to act as facilitator.

The elementary-school facilitator aided in the posting of flyers at the school and distributing parent permission slips (in both English and Spanish) to all students in grades one through five. Permission slips asked that parents commit to having their child attend all music classes. Within a few weeks of the announcement, 125 first through fifth graders had signed up for free music classes taught by university music education majors. One hundred twenty-five parents submitted permission slips for their children to participate; approximately 97 children came to the first class. Twelve of these were first graders, 18 were second graders, 22 were third graders, 26 were fourth graders, and 19 were fifth graders. Since the grant proposal specified that each music class would be limited to 20 children, separate classes were divided into one first grade, one second grade, two third grades, two fourth grades, and one fifth grade.

The elementary-school facilitator also arranged school rooms, including pianos, CD players, and storage for university-owned musical instruments, and helped coordinate the schedule. Classes for the fall semester were scheduled for nine consecutive Wednesdays from 2:35 to 3:30 p.m., starting a short 10 minutes after the school day ended to eliminate distractions that might lead to leaving the school premises.

The university music education professor who served as project director oversaw two main aspects of the program: its goals and implementation, and the music curriculum and teaching. A review of the research literature regarding effective after-school education programs for at-risk children identified both organizational and teaching characteristics, which became goals of this program. Effective organizational characteristics included: low teacher–child ratios; requirement of regular attendance; attention to safety, health, and nutrition; family involvement; quality staffing; goal setting, strong management, and sustainability; and evaluation of the program's progress (Otterbourg, 2000). These were all addressed in the planning stages of the after-school project.

Effective teaching characteristics included positive and flexible teacher attitudes; interesting, challenging, and extraordinary musical activities (Pierce & Vandell, 1999); and allowance for children to blow off steam, have snacks, play with friends, and build relationships with caring and competent adults (O'Connor & McGuire, 1998). These teaching characteristics were emphasized as goals for all the participating teachers. Additionally, lessons in the creative activities of improvising and composing, and involving basic skills such as singing, playing instruments, listening, performing, moving, and reading music were encouraged (Roman, 1998).

Ten undergraduate music education majors who were concurrently enrolled in an elementary methods course taught by the project director were asked to serve as teachers, and five other music education students were recruited to serve as additional teachers and as coordinator. The 14 university student teachers were given a packet of resources, which included a list of musical and teaching goals. Other resources included classroom management tips, lesson plan formats, student and self-assessment rubrics, the National Standards for Arts Education, and practical matters such as professional attitude and dress, teaching schedule, directions to the school, and emergency contact information.

The teachers worked in teams to develop the nine-week curriculum. Most classes were general music classes, with the exception of one recorder class and one chorus.

CHILDREN'S MUSICAL PREFERENCES

The nine-week program began with an exploration of the students' musical tastes in order to familiarize the university students with the musical "mindset" of the children. When asked questions about their favorite music, 80 children responded as follows: Nelly (14), Britney Spears (8), B2K (5), Bow Wow (5), Eminem (4), Shakira (4), Christina Aguilera (3), Rock (3), Jennifer Lopez (3), Ashanti (2), Ludacris (2), Sisco (2), and Barney (2). All the rest were individual responses. The university students, not known for prudishness, expressed shock at the questionable lyrics of some of these "favorites."

When asked the same question at the end of the nine weeks, 12 of the fifth graders responded that their favorite song was a choral piece that they performed in the final outreach concert—seven enjoyed "Changamano" best and five liked "Oye la Musica" best; seven second graders liked their performed "Shark Song" the best; nine children liked the live performance of a Scottish instrumental ensemble best; three third graders liked their performed recorder pieces best ("Hot Cross Buns" and "Jingle Bells"); two liked "Kumbaya" best; nine liked individual songs sung during classes; and only 12 continued to prefer rap and pop songs (Madura Ward-Steinman, 2006). While this result doesn't suggest that the after-school program permanently changed the children's musical preferences, it is encouraging that they enjoyed the experience so much that the music performed had become a "favorite," even if temporarily.

An exit questionnaire asked the children to identify their favorite part of the after-school music program. "Singing" was the overwhelming favorite, followed by "performing," "juice and treats," "the teachers," "playing recorders," "the band," and "instruments." One student's favorite part of the program was "learning something different from rap."

The nine-week program concluded with two weeks of live performances. One concert was a Scottish performing ensemble that regularly donated its time for outreach purposes, and the last was a concert by the children who participated in the after-school program. This final concert ended with the music teachers who were also members of the university marching band providing a rousing performance and leading everyone out of the auditorium in a large parade. All participating children received a Music Achievement Award and all participating teachers received a Certificate of Appreciation for Outstanding Service to Music Education at the conclusion of the program (Madura Ward-Steinman, 2006).

PRESERVICE TEACHER REFLECTIONS

The 14 teachers rated their individual success in reaching each stated musical, creative, and teaching goal of the after-school program, using the following scales: "1 = no, not at all; 2 = no, not enough; 3 = yes and no, mixed feelings; 4 = yes, adequately so; and 5 = yes, exceptionally well" (see table 10.1).

The highest means for the musical goals indicate that the teachers adequately presented experiences for children to move to music and to perform/listen to a variety of music. They reported that they were inadequate in their teaching of composition. Although the mean for improvising is rather low,

Table 10.1. Means and Standard Deviations for Teacher Ratings of Met Goals

	Mean	SD
Musical Goals		
Moving to music	3.79	1.31
Performing or listening to a variety of music	3.71	1.07
Listening to and analyzing music	3.00	1.30
Singing alone and with others	3.00	1.41
Playing instruments alone and with others	2.86	1.17
Reading music	2.86	1.17
Improvising music	2.21	1.05
Composing music	1.64	.85
Teaching Goals		
Were you a positive force?	4.43	.51
Did you make the classes "interesting and extraordinary"?	4.29	.73
Did you make the experience enjoyable enough?	4.29	.61
Did you use age-appropriate teaching materials?	4.14	.86
Were you flexible in your teaching?	4.00	.39
Did you make the experience challenging enough?	3.93	.83
Did you let the children play and blow off steam?	3.79	.97
Were you a musical mentor?	3.71	.82
Did you learn their names fast?	3.50	1.29

one teacher taught call and response blues scale improvisation, and several included basic percussion (including body percussion) improvisation. The remaining musical goals were only moderately reached.

Teachers did feel that they adequately reached all of the teaching goals of successful outreach programs, especially in acting as a "positive force" and for making the experience "interesting and extraordinary" and "enjoyable" for the children. They also felt that they were successful in being flexible, in making the musical experience "challenging enough," in letting the children "play and blow off steam," and in being a musical mentor (Madura Ward-Steinman, 2006).

It is not surprising that many of the musical goals were inadequately reached due to a number of obstacles to those goals, including the short duration of teaching opportunities (once a week for six weeks, not including the orientation and concert dates) and the inexperience of the student teachers working in teams to create curricula. A limited focus on one or two skills would likely have produced greater achievement.

However, the fact that all of the teaching goals found to be related to successful after-school programs for at-risk children were met is admirable and a real achievement for the young teachers. Evidence of their success in this area was the children's consistent attendance throughout the program.

Although the administrators encouraged weekly attendance by contacting parents when children were absent and by sending reminder flyers home with the children, the student teachers played a vital role in motivating students to return each week. Analysis of attendance records indicates that, except for a significant drop for first graders, the total number of participating children in grades two through five actually increased by four during the nine-week period.

It was a tall order for the music education majors to concentrate on the program goals, design the curriculum, and then team-teach the children for nine weeks, but they benefited from this experience far more than they could have from a lecture-style course with minimal contact with real children. It was truly a collaborative effort for all involved, and flexibility was the key.

Perhaps most inspiring for music teacher educators are the college students' reflections on the main things they learned by teaching in the after-school urban outreach program. While these lessons might be learned in a well-structured general music class with adequate field experience at the core, it is nonetheless heartwarming to see the depth of the students' emerging realizations about teaching. Here are some of the students' insights:

1. "how to write organized lesson plans and then carry out the lesson,"
2. "the importance of planning ahead,"
3. "I learned to look ahead for big events coming up, like a performance,"
4. "all activities need to be kept short, and the more body movement with the songs the better,"
5. "if you keep the children busy, they are much easier to manage,"
6. "that it's tough to teach singing with a male voice,"
7. "that it is better to choose familiar songs over unfamiliar songs when they are reluctant to sing,"
8. "with care and positive output, children will respond to me,"
9. "kids are eager to hear what I have to say,"
10. "students *want* to learn,"
11. "kids love to sing,"
12. "I really do enjoy teaching at the elementary level,"
13. "that even though students act like they don't care very much, they still learn and remember,"
14. "the fantastic individual personalities such young students can have,"
15. "the balance between fun and discipline,"
16. "the importance of staying flexible,"
17. "the importance of communication with team-teachers,"
18. "how to succeed under pressure, with the help of supporting staff, co-teachers and faculty,"

19. "that the other music majors do actually contain a sensitive side which shows through in their involvement at the elementary school,"
20. "that our time was really valuable and appreciated by our students when they were sad over the last day of class,"
21. "that teaching is fun and rewarding,"
22. "teaching requires confidence,"
23. "that it takes years of experience to be a good teacher,"
24. "the power of teaching."

And last,

25. "I learned that kids are kids no matter where you are. It doesn't matter where they are from because they enjoy kids' songs and singing and basically all just want to be included and have a good time."

CONCLUSION

It began with one passionate outreach program director seeking a university partner to help garner financial support to bring music education to the urban neighborhood in which she was raised in order to "give back to the community." She found a music education professor who could imagine the benefits for both the children and the university students and agreed to be that partner. The result was nine weeks of a music teaching collaboration between 14 privileged university preservice teachers and just fewer than 100 underprivileged children in grades one through five. They learned much from each other, and hopefully were left with indelible impressions.

The partnership that began in the fall of 2003 continued throughout the remainder of the academic year, and due to its documented success was then funded by the university for a second year. By the third year, the outreach efforts involved even more university music majors and more local schools. The continued financial support from the university to enhance its neighborhood's artistic and intellectual life is a model for all universities, and its help in providing good instruments, sound equipment, and guest musicians was critical to the overall quality of the program.

Aside from all of the organizational details required for a successful after-school outreach program as described earlier, what became clear is that a successful partnership between a university music education department and an urban elementary school is due to the commitment of all the adults involved—the outreach director with the vision, the university music education professor, the graduate student staff, the undergraduate preservice teachers, the public school staff, the classroom teachers, and the parents of the children. While it would have been much easier to postpone a decision to be a partner, to forward the invitation to someone else, to decline to share space or time, or to cancel the project when it failed to progress as planned, it was the dedication and unique contribution of each person or group above that made this partnership workable.

What provides that intangible impetus for commitment to such a project? Is it only to provide the children with an alternative to wandering the streets unsupervised during the hours after school? No; it is more so to see the joy on their faces as they recognize the instruments in a Duke Ellington recording, or when they dance and sing a new song together despite ethnic, language, or intellectual differences. And, especially, it is the hope that these moments and memories will sustain the children in times of life's turmoil, as well as sustain the music education majors when occasional moments of doubt arise about the meaning of their chosen profession.

REFERENCES

O'Connor, S., & McGuire, K. (1998). *Homework assistance and out-of-school time: Filling the need, finding the balance*. Wellesley, MA: National Institute on Out-of-School Time.

Otterbourg, S. D. (2000). *How the arts can enhance after-school program*. Washington, DC: National Endowment for the Arts (ERIC Document Reproduction Service No. ED446829).

Pierce, K. M., & Vandell, D. L. (1999, March). *Safe haven program evaluation*. Madison: University of Wisconsin Center for Educational Research.

Roman, J. (Ed.). (1998). *The NSACA standards for quality school-age care*. Boston: National School-Age Care Alliance. Elementary and Early Childhood Education (ERIC Document Service No. ED458010).

Ward-Steinman, P. Madura (2006). The development of an after-school music program for at-risk children: student and preservice teacher reflections. *International Journal of Music Education: Research*, 24(1).

11

Musical Heritage: Celebrating Families through Music

Randall Everett Allsup, Amylia C. Barnett, and Emily J. Katz

What does it mean to be a citizen-educator—or a citizen-student—in a multicultural, global, urbanized world? What would music education look like, specifically music teacher education, if families and neighborhoods were placed at the heart of what was learned and taught? These questions and others led to the creation of a neighborhood program in East Harlem, New York, called "Musical Heritage" that brought public school students and their families together with music teachers and student teachers to make and perform music.

The project that follows was an example of a "give-and-take between minds." Teachers, students, and their parents who were strangers to each other created and performed music across difference. Assumptions were challenged, the strange was made common, and as a result, something new was known. Emily Katz, a student teacher working in the project, described it as follows: "It's difficult to prepare meaningful activities when your students are strangers. I feel like there is an importance to sharing experiences."

THE MUSICAL HERITAGE PROJECT

The Musical Heritage Project began as a reaction by preservice teachers at Teachers College Columbia University to a perceived deficiency in their preparation to teach in an urban setting. "Several students approached me with a pro-active plan. Not a formal research study, but an outreach project that would connect what we were studying in class to real neighborhoods and real students," recalled Professor Randall Allsup, a coauthor of this chapter. "I signed on as advisor, cautiously optimistic that we could do this in an honest partnership."

The point was, Allsup explained, to do more than simply "expose" beginning teachers to students and a neighborhood they didn't know. We wanted to "uncover the common," to build bridges between people, families, and cultures—to set a stage for dialogue. As such, Musical Heritage had to be much more than a quest for superficial "exposure." We needed to be careful that it did not become a kind-hearted outreach program in which graduate students are given the opportunity to "understand" people they presuppose as underprivileged. It was important to the organizers foremost, that we did *not* create a detached or disinterested laboratory with which to experiment with "strangeness."

The Heritage School, a high school in East Harlem, provided the setting, and with the assistance of the school principal, the music education students from Teachers College designed a program that focused on the educational needs of the students, family, and community. Musical Heritage was created with the following aims:

- Integrate school, neighborhood, and family through instrumental music;
- Provide an entryway for parents and students to get involved and feel comfortable at the school;
- Help participants express their personal narratives or histories through the creative and performing processes;
- Organize a culminating concert for the local community;
- Create a program that helps preservice music education students learn about and get involved in an unfamiliar large-city environment.

The preservice college students met monthly at the Heritage School on Saturday mornings beginning in September and continuing through June when they presented a public concert. Participants came from the neighborhood and ranged in age from three to 60 years old.

For the preservice college students at Teachers College, the Musical Heritage Project provided a site for both observation and field experience. The preservice teachers who volunteered to participate worked with the high school music teacher and local music educators to share in practice, planning, and teaching. They were allowed to record their time at Musical Heritage to fulfill the observation hours required for New York State certification. Finally, they were expected to keep a journal and meet with an advisor. The Musical Heritage Project serves as a possible model for how urban music education can provide a nonexploitative, reciprocal environment for understanding people and places that may appear different, even strange for the beginning teacher.

MULTIPLE CULTURES AND THE STUDENT TEACHER

The neighbors in East Harlem who elected to participate in the project spoke English and Spanish, but reflected in practical terms the entire African diaspora. Viewed in this light, the challenge for music teachers working in such a neighborhood had as much to do with the *collapse of distance* between people and places as it did with the identifiable individual differences that seem to separate us from one another.

The discrete categories that defined Western culture during much of the 20th century—race, class, language, nation-state, or religion—have dissolved, expanded, or mutated. In spite of this highly diverse, global world, "teacher education programs often fail to provide access to neighborhoods that are unfamiliar to the student-teacher," says Emily Katz, a preservice candidate and chapter coauthor. "We may expect to teach in a particular environment, but not end up there." Without some kind of intervention, many student teachers "are left with stereotypes about urban neighborhoods, their students and their families," observes Amylia Barnett, a cooperating music teacher at the High School of Environmental Studies in midtown Manhattan and chapter coauthor. "Without giving new teachers experiential knowledge in diverse environments, they are left without the tools to succeed, and as a consequence they will make generalizations and assumption about what they think they see."

UNDERSTANDING STUDENTS

Programs that prepare music teachers could do a better job to help teachers understand their urban students. "Understanding" is never given, but must be produced or, as philosopher John Dewey would say, *reconstructed* through forms of participation. Unfortunately, novice teachers sometimes confuse understanding their students with *identifying* their students. This is an important point to address when well-intentioned educators try to make sense of student cultures that are new to them. The problem with trying to identify students is that our attempts are almost always wrong.

An excerpt from a poem called *Among School Children* by W. B. Yeats (1996/1927) goes like this:

> O chestnut tree, great rooted bloomer,
> Are you the leaf, the blossom or the bole?

O body swayed to music, O brightening glance,
How do we know the dancer from the dance? (p. 44).

What or who do we see when a new student stands in front of us? We can
rely on empirical evidence—skin color, clothing style, even tattoos—but we
would be missing out on something beautiful if, as the poem suggests, we
saw only the leaf, a blossom, or scarred gray bark. As Yeats suggests, understanding others, understanding ourselves, understanding our world is far
more than *seeing*. Understanding disavows separation—identifying the parts
and portions, the leaf and bark. It is impossible to see only the dancer in the
presence of a dance—to see only a leaf and not the tree. Like the world we
live in, we are an entangled and contradictory history. It is hard enough to
know ourselves, let alone our students. "Any self," Dewey (1983) said, "is
capable of including within itself a number of inconsistent selves, of unhar-
monized dispositions" (p. 96). Human nature, he suggests, is a messy collage
of identities and cultural referents that may or may not make sense to an
outside observer (p. 96).

UNCOVERING THE COMMON

Creating a curriculum was an evolving process, one that always honored the
cultural heritage of the neighborhood we were in: Spanish Harlem. Since our
intent was to learn about our students and also to share and teach as a community, we could hardly "implement" a curriculum without including
everyone in the process. Yet, this posed a number of problems. When we
asked the project participants to share their likes and dislikes, they were hesi-
tant. Most did not have access to formal music training prior to Musical Heritage, and working with teachers and graduate students who had spent years
studying music as a profession was intimidating. Some felt that they did not
have the "proper" language to describe what they liked. The perception of
formality that accompanies the work of schools and teaching took some time
to dispel, as well. We discovered that an open exchange of ideas depended
upon *proven* trust. As a result, our curriculum developed in tandem with our
mutual understanding.

Multiculturalism as a generic pedagogical concept was less helpful in creating a curriculum than the process of pooling our individual talents. Evidence
that diversity *really is* a community's greatest strength was uncovered in our
planning. We shared lesson strategies and learned to take criticism and adapt.
This vigilant negotiation of difference, even across conflict when it occurred,
required a constant "stepping out of your comfort zone," recorded Amylia
Barnett. "You had to examine musical styles that you were unfamiliar with
and develop 'good enough' teaching strategies so that participants would feel

proud of what they did." Both the experienced teachers and the student teachers took turns as teacher or facilitator. When we were not teaching, we sat within the ensemble among the families, sometimes performing on our primary instruments, sometimes on percussion, keyboards, or voice.

"This is the hardest way to teach," says Professor Randall Allsup. "There is an incredible tension between preparing clear lesson objectives and looking for spontaneous teachable moments." We rejected any singular approach or method in favor of an eclectic curriculum that had to be first and foremost, engaging and relevant. We searched for music that reflected the participant's heritage but also developed skills and musicianship. Herbie Hancock's "Cantaloupe Island" lent itself well to this task. The tune had only two chord changes upon which to improvise, and everyone recognized the style.

TIMELINE

September: Recruiting and Organizing

Organizers met with the school principal to discuss the philosophy of Musical Heritage. We distributed flyers and attended PTA meetings to recruit participants. We applied for funding to allow us to implement the program at The Heritage School. We received and found funding for small percussion instruments and hand drums.

October: Exploring and Experimenting

The Sound Exploration Strategy: "Think of the first sound you heard when you woke up this morning." "How did the sounds of the neighborhood change during your journey here?" Percussion instruments were used to capture the sounds and feelings evoked. This exercise led to a discussion of the individuals' lives, their neighborhood, and life in East Harlem.

November: Re-Viewing Latin Jazz

Participants experimented with Latin rhythmic patterns. Rhythms were studied in the context of a basic *montuno*. Using this rhythm as a stepping-off point, we created original compositions in small groups.

December: Composing in Small Groups

We extended and refined our November exercises. Recording, playback, and analysis helped participants focus on what they liked and what they wanted to improve.

January: Expressing Visual Images and Words through Music

We studied the lyrics to Louis Armstrong's "What a Wonderful World." We pulled words from the text and described them musically on an instrument. We began watching an excerpt from *Blue Crush* and experimented with different ways to express our ideas.

February: Creating a Score to *Blue Crush*

Participants were asked to compose their own music to *Blue Crush*. We agreed that the clip had three definitive parts or sections. The spontaneous topic of transitions was discussed.

March: Arranging a Jazz Standard

We listened to several versions of "My Favorite Things," representing various styles. We discussed what we liked and disliked. We decided that "My Favorite Things" had too many chord changes to perform and created an arrangement of "Cantaloupe Island."

April: Notating Music

We discussed traditional and nontraditional methods of notating compositions. Participants discussed which selections of music would best represent us during our upcoming concert.

May: Refining Compositions

Participants finalized which instruments they would play in the concert. The group made decision about transitions, tempo, and nuance. We began to rehearse large sections and transitions.

June: Performing the Concert

The concert was announced at the PTA meeting and flyers were placed within the community. The performance included program participants and local musicians. We involved the audience in a jam session.

DISCUSSION OF EVENTS

Viewed from the past, the preceding timeline suggests a clear sequence of learning objectives. In truth, it took some time and much debate to determine how to proceed from session to session. The task became easier as we got to know and trust one another. The key, of course, was participation, a sort of continual negotiation of relationships. Dewey's (1916) suggestion that "each has to refer his own action to that of others, and to consider the action of others to give point and direction to his own," came to describe how trust helped our curriculum unfolds.

We began Musical Heritage with a basic sound exploration where we discussed the listener's experience from their time of waking until their arrival at Musical Heritage. Our Sound Exploration lesson plan asked participants to describe the musical and ambient sounds of their own lives and to discuss the sounds of East Harlem. This simple exercise, liberally borrowed from *The Soundscape: Our Sonic Environment and the Tuning of the World* by R. Murray Schafer (1994), helped all to relax and to learn about one another.

Rian Wilkinson, the high school music teacher who was familiar with the school, students, and neighborhood, was an important asset. His curriculum emphasized jazz, Latin jazz, and popular music. Wilkinson shared teaching strategies that worked with his own classes, but nothing was ever guaranteed. A song that worked with his high school students did not always excite the participants of Musical Heritage. One example of a surefire hit was a lesson plan entitled Muy Caliente! Participants enjoyed learning basic Latin rhythms and felt free to express individual rhythmic ideas within the context of a *montuno*. Sometimes positive experiences involved the use of popular culture. Creating a soundtrack to the surfing movie *Blue Crush*, a big success for all involved, suggested a global understanding of multiculturalism more than a local one. (For a sample lesson plan of Muy Caliente! and *Blue Crush*, see below.)

One continuous challenge was consistent attendance. Since the program was on Saturdays, participants did not attend regularly and absenteeism was generally high. But the culminating performance in June provided a clear end-goal that kept everyone increasingly focused and encouraged. When the day of the final concert arrived, we looked out at an audience of friends, family members, and school officials. The performers and the audience were proud of the accomplishments and this served to strengthen ties between the school and community. The jam session that concluded the concert gave everyone a chance to show off a little bit. We recall our shyest member, Terrance, played the drum set with confidence, and Antonia, who was convinced she couldn't make music, jammed on the djembe. Delene was delighted to play the flute, an instrument she hadn't touched since high school.

CONCLUSION

We learned much about music, and we learned more about each other. In our exit interview (perhaps the term *end-of-year discussion* is more accurate), many of the families reported surprise at the hidden talents in their midst. "I just had no idea how talented my son was on the drums!" remarked one father. Making music together also broke down the typical roles that are present in families. Family members had the opportunity to interact with each other in a unique way. Because parents often had less musical experience than their children, they were suddenly placed on an equal playing field with them. The school setting was demystified—a place for parents and grandparents, as much as for children.

The organizers of Musical Heritage wish to avoid the against-all-odds cliché of urban education. We take satisfaction, but not credit, for what we've done. The joys we celebrated with our students are common when caring teachers teach *with* and not *to* their students. Our hopes are already on the upcoming school year. As we make plans for expanding the project to include more schools and involve additional teachers, we hope that we can provide comfortable environments for preservice teachers to question, explore, and examine. But most importantly, we hope to give families a chance to come together to realize something new about themselves and their community.

SAMPLE LESSON PLAN FOR
MUY CALIENTE! STRATEGY

Warm-up:
Participants will:

- Choose a percussion instrument.
- Listen to teacher play rhythm on percussion instrument in 4/4 time.
- Mimic rhythm.
- Individuals create rhythm in 4/4 time.
- Class plays rhythm of individual.
- Teacher plays Javier Vasquez's "Alto Songo."
- Class chooses rhythms of those previously played and accompanies recording.
- Discuss rhythmic choices made. Question to lead discussion: Which rhythms worked? Was it challenging to make your rhythm fit with the song? Did you have to change your rhythm to make it work with the recording and the ensemble? Did you notice anything unusual about the selection played?

Objective:
Students will create an original composition based on Latin rhythms.

Materials:
pp. 33–34, #15, Section C & A from Mauleoón, R., & Sher, C. (1999). *Muy Caliente! Afro-Cuban Play-Along CD & Book*. Petaluma, CA: Sher Music Company. Javier Vasquez's "Alto Songo," Latin percussion instruments, i.e., recording equipment.

Learning Traditional Latin Rhythms

Participants will:
- Introduce 3-2 clave, 2-3 cascara, cowbell, tumbao, guiro rhythms.

Figure 11.1.   3-2 clave

3-2 Clave

Note: On the tumbao rhythm, O and P denote an open strike on the head of the drum, H denotes using the heel of the hand, T denotes using the toe (closed fingers) of the hand, and S denotes slapping the head of the drum.

Figure 11.2.   2-3 clave

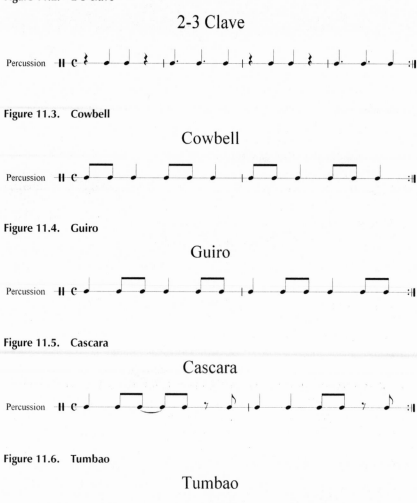

Figure 11.3.   Cowbell

Figure 11.4.   Guiro

Figure 11.5.   Cascara

Figure 11.6.   Tumbao

The left hand plays the H and the T while the right hand plays the O, P, and S.

- Practice each rhythm separately until confidence and rhythmic integrity is developed. Teacher plays Section A, a *montuno*, from *Muy Caliente! Afro-Cuban Play-Along CD & Book*.
- Students play rhythm while teacher plays Section A, a *montuno*.

Figure 11.7. Section A, #15

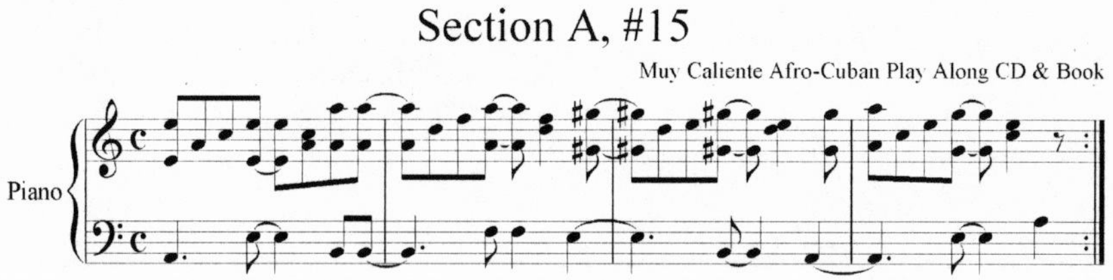

Section A, #15

Muy Caliente Afro-Cuban Play Along CD & Book

- Assign small group and individuals to specific rhythms.
- Practice staggering entrances of rhythms while teacher plays *montuno*.

Creating Music

- Ask students how they would create a composition based on the rhythms learned.
- Questions for discussion: How will we begin the piece? How will we end the piece?
- Have students listen to Section C from *Muy Caliente! Afro-Cuban Play-Along CD & Book*.

Figure 11.8. Section C, #15

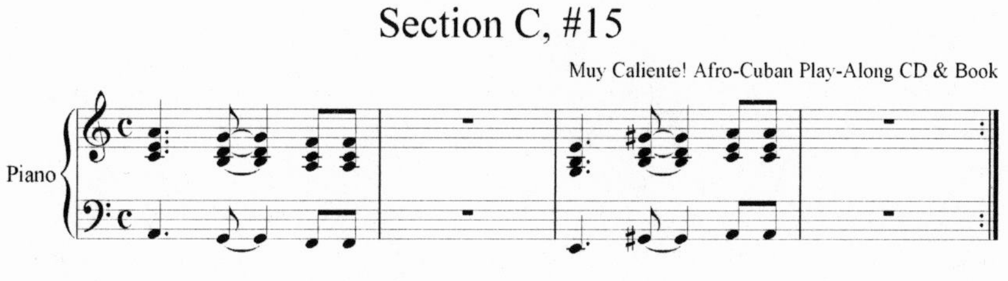

Section C, #15

Muy Caliente! Afro-Cuban Play-Along CD & Book

- Ask students if they think Section C could be used for an introduction or ending. If students do not think Section C is appropriate for their composition, ask for alternatives.
- Have students rehearse their composition.
- Record composition.
- Discuss the composition. Questions to lead discussion: What did you think worked well in your composition? What would you do differently next time? Was the beginning and ending effective? Where our intentions obvious musically?
- Discuss possible arrangements of the piece using elements such as repeated sections, layered rhythms, climax, solos, ending.

Extension

Have students listen to a variety of Latin pieces that incorporate *montuno*. Students discuss differences in selections and what they learned from their listening experiences. Students use what they learned from listening to music to enhance their own compositions.

SAMPLE LESSON PLAN FOR
BLUE CRUSH STRATEGY

Warm-up:
Participants will:

- Look at a picture of a surfer.
- Imagine what the surfer might feel, hear, and see while in the ocean.
- Discuss insights.
- Capture on a musical instrument the feeling of a wave, the ocean, or what it's like to surf.
- Share musical ideas with group.

Objective:
Students will create a musical soundtrack based on a video clip of *Blue Crush*.

Materials:
Blue Crush, picture of surfer, variety of instruments, audio equipment, Miles Davis's "Kind of Blue," Debussy's "La Mer," and Willie Nelson's "Blue Eyes Crying in the Rain."

Listening and Analyzing Music

Participants will:
- Watch a two-minute video clip of the film *Blue Crush*.
- Watch the clip while listening to Miles Davis's "Kind of Blue," Debussy's "La Mer," and Willie Nelson's "Blue Eyes Crying in the Rain."
- Discuss the different ways music affects the same clip.
- Questions to lead discussion: How did the music relate to the images? What type of mood does the music depict? Is the music convincing? What type of music do you think fits best?

Creating Music
- Students return to the musical idea they created in the warm-up.
- Watch clip and play ideas as seems musically appropriate.
- Discuss which musical ideas work with the selected clip and which work less well.
- Create a groove by using a simple chord pattern, repeating rhythm, or drone.
- Students perform musical ideas within grooves, as they deem appropriate to *Blue Crush*.

Extension

Students think about the clip in sections. What are the different moods evoked in the clip? Can the video clip be divided into different sections? If so, how will the sections differ musically? How do we transition between musical ideas?

REFERENCES

Dewey, J. (1916). *Democracy and education*. New York: Macmillan.

———. (1983). Human nature and conduct. *John Dewey: The middle works, 1899–1924*. Carbondale: Southern Illinois Press.

The Heritage School. (n.d.). New York: Author. Retrieved on September 1, 2005, from www.heritage-school.org.

Mauleoón, R., & Sher, C. (1999). *Muy caliente! Afro-Cuban play-along CD & book*. Petaluma, CA: Sher Music Company.

Schafer, R. Murray. (1994). *The soundscape: Our sonic environment and the tuning of our world*. Rochester, VT: Destiny Books.

Yeats, W. B. (1996/1927). "Among school children." *The collected works of W. B. Yeats volume I: The poems: Revised second edition*. New York: Scribner.

III

PARTNERSHIPS

12

Creating and Sustaining Urban Music Education Collaborations

Mitchell Robinson

This chapter will examine the nature of and interrelationships among issues that contribute to the creation and sustainability of partnerships between educational institutions or organizations, especially those in urban settings. A feature missing from most hierarchical structures in educational institutions is an understanding of the dynamics between the components of the structure and the integrity of the whole. Using the concept of *tensegrity*, or tensional integrity, as an organizational schema, I will show that tension between opposing individuals or groups is a fundamental issue in policy making. I will also argue that it is these very tensions, and the creative energies that they produce, that are the "engines" that drive successful collaborations between schools and colleges. Current work in the discipline of architecture also sheds light on the notion of tension as a factor in creating the energy required for effective collaboration.

URBAN CHALLENGES

Although the ideas discussed in this chapter are not specifically designed to be applicable to urban settings, the unique nature of the challenges present in urban schools involved in educational collaborations may be of heightened interest to educators in similar situations. While the obstacles for urban schools are not entirely dissimilar to those faced by rural and suburban districts,

In the inner cities, these challenges are often intensified. Our urban schools are frequently underfunded, understaffed, and overpopulated. The campuses are often located in economically depressed areas where hope has become little more than a word and where neglect, indifference, decay, and even hatred—toward others and even toward oneself—are such daily realities that some might consider them to be part of a normal existence. Sometimes these urban areas are little more than incubators of indifference; they can scarcely be said to be an appropriate environment for children's education. (Hinckley, 1995, p. 32)

Hinckley (1995) offers three suggestions for those interested in reshaping today's urban music programs. "Relevance, high expectations, and variety are part of the secret of the success and survival of music programs in many urban areas" (p. 33). The author also describes the music program that might be offered in the "ideal urban school":

- Facilities would be attractive and well-equipped.
- The teachers would be the best available, and would have a clear understanding of the various cultures present in their community.
- There would be regular visits by school and community leaders.
- Music making would be an ever-present aspect of the educational process, and would serve as a bonding agent for the diverse interests and backgrounds of students.
- Students would be curious, and select music from many styles and periods for their personal listening.
- An eclectic repertory would be performed by diverse and alternative ensembles (i.e., gospel choirs, salsa bands, synthesizer ensembles), in addition to traditional performing groups.
- Students would be composers, and peers would perform their compositions.
- Course offerings would be rich and varied, complete with technological support.
- Music, theater, dance, graphic and plastic arts, and language arts would be involved in collaborative activities.
- Teachers would have ample preparation and visitation time, as well as extensive professional development opportunities. (p. 35)

To be sure, Hinckley's suggestions could be understood as a set of recommendations appropriate not just for urban music education, but for effective music teaching and learning in all settings. My experience working in urban schools and with urban music teachers has also led to the identification of a number of structural challenges often associated with inner-city school systems, such as:

- Inefficient administrative structures;
- Unwieldy budgetary and financial procedures;
- Ineffective communications systems; and,
- Inadequate staffing patterns and assignments.

While these characteristics are not limited solely to urban school systems, it seems clear that further discussion of issues of administrative and organizational structures may be helpful in our examination of educational collaborations.

HIERARCHICAL VS. NONHIERARCHICAL MODELS

Although the distinctions between organizational structures in education and industry are becoming less sharply defined, most business models are characterized by distinct levels of authority (i.e., grades, tiers, classifications) and clear channels of command: assistants report to managers, who report to vice presidents, who in turn report to presidents. Schools, it would appear, employ a more nebulous system of distinctions to separate employees.

Organizational structures built on strict hierarchies have long been a staple of business management, but are now being reconsidered by some researchers in the field of organizational theory, especially in respect to new configurations of multi-organizational and multinational structures brought about by a widening global economy. Some of these nonhierarchical models offer new insights into the complexities of human behaviors and relationships.

> The non-linearly structured interrelationship of decision arenas here contrasts with the linear listings and checklists to be found in standard management textbooks. In the latter it is assumed that functional integrity is maintained by top-down decision making. The weakness of this is evident from the increasing number of constraints (e.g. in personnel relations) to which top-down management is subject. (Judge, 1979, p. 590)

Traditional "top-down" management styles and structures often prove inadequate for handling the intricacies of interorganizational relationships (IORs), such as collaboratives. Partnerships require creativity and flexibility in structure—rather than a blind adherence to formal channels—traits not always nurtured in hierarchical organizations. IORs need to be managed in such a way that the pressures that often prove damaging to traditional management structures instead become sources of growth. The IOR structure as a whole needs to be dynamic, adaptive to constant change, and able to not only survive constant tension, but to turn that tension into a useful commodity.

The ideal partnership organizational structure, then, is one that

- is nonhierarchical (both top-down and bottom-up) in form.
- represents the activities, functions, communications, and behaviors of individuals within partner organizations and the interorganizational relationship, rather than merely organizational schemes and formal chains of command.
- can withstand immense stresses from outside—and inside—forces.
- absorbs and diffuses tension equitably among its members.
- transforms tensions into usable, positive energy.
- consists of members of different kinds who can fill multiple roles.

TENSEGRITY

The relationships that form the core of partnerships cannot be represented by static, linear forms. A model that characterizes such relationships needs to be fluid, dynamic, sturdy, and able to handle tremendous tensions—applied both from outside forces and from within the structure. This model also needs to accommodate change, in form and behavior, in ways that traditional hierarchical organizational arrangements cannot.

In my attempts to find an appropriate structural model for representing collaborative organizational relationships, I came upon the concept of *tensegrity*. The word *tensegrity* is a contraction of *tensional integrity*, first popularized by the American architect and engineer R. Buckminster Fuller (1895–1983). Tensegrity is based on principles of continuous tension and discontinuous compression. For Fuller, the concept manifested his philosophy that nature uses tension primarily and compression secondarily, whereas humans often misguidedly do the reverse. (For examples of tensegrity structures, please see: www.georgehart.com/virtual-polyhedra/straw-tensegrity .html.) Tensegrity structures are systems that stabilize themselves by balancing counteracting forces of compression and tension; stress is balanced and distributed by tension, not just by the strengths of individual structural members. An increase in tension in one member results in increased tension in all members. This increase in tension is balanced by an increase in compression within certain members, typically the structural components most adjacent to the affected member. "Transmission of tension through a tensegrity array provides a means to distribute forces to all interconnected elements, and to mechanically 'tune' the whole system as one" (Ingber, 1998, p. 56).

Donald Ingber, associate professor of Pathology at Harvard Medical School, has extended the tensegrity metaphor to the study of living organisms, positing a "universal set of building rules (that) seems to guide the design of organic structures—from simple carbon compounds to complex cells and tissues" (p. 48). Ingber pioneered the concept that living cells and tissues stabilize their shape and structure through tensegrity architecture. Synthesizing previous study in cell biology and sculpture, he combined the methods of molecular cell biology with mechanical engineering approaches to analyze molecular and cellular structures and developed a mathematical basis for cellular response to mechanical stress.

COMPONENTS OF TENSEGRITY STRUCTURES: *PULLERS, PUSHERS, AND INTEGRATORS*

Ingber also identified several known components of living cells and defined their functional roles in a tensegrity model of cellular structure. Cells are made up of different types of structural members, each with specific, mutually complementary tasks and functions. Similarly, there are three basic roles that individuals may assume in partnerships structured on tensegrity principles: inside pullers, pushers (from inside and outside the partnership), and integrators. Like their counterparts in the cell, each of these roles plays a crucial function in the maintenance of the collaborative structure, and these roles are interwoven. A partnership made up of only pullers and pushers will lack the connectedness brought to the structure by the integrators, whose function is to link the other members to each other, to the nucleus, and to the outside environment. Similarly, a group overpopulated with integrators may appear solid but will miss the focus on institutional mission and product supplied by the inside pullers and the communication to those outside the group that is the domain of the pushers. Table 12.1 shows a comparison of properties of tensegrity components in cells and relationships between partner organizations. As in any model, the designations below are generalities and are included only for purposes of comparison and discussion.

There are two organizing principles of tensegrity that offer substantial assistance in the development of effective organizational models: the idea of *difference engines*, or acceptable levels of discord, and the concept of *pre-stress*. Both of these concepts speak to the importance that the notion of equilibrium plays in developing and maintaining healthy, productive collaborative relationships.

DIFFERENCE ENGINES

The tension between opposing factions or options is a fundamental issue in partnerships. Again, architecture points to the importance of appropriately interrelating tension and compression elements (Judge, 1991). Judge advances

Table 12.1.   A Comparison of Properties of Tensegrity Structure Components in Cells and Partnership

In a Cell	In a Partnership
Nucleus	*Leader(s) and/or Core Values of Each Partner*
Contractile microfilaments: pull the cell's membrane and its internal parts toward the nucleus, respond to anchorage by shortening and increasing isometric tension within the lattice	*Inside pullers*: respond to tension by increasing tension *Inside pushers*: respond to tension by compressing within the structure
Compressive elements (microtubules): two types: inside the cell (compressive "girders" of either microtubules or bundles of cross-linked microfilaments), and, outside the cell (extracellular matrix)	*Outside pushers*: the outside environment, marketplace, community
Intermediate filaments or Integrins: connect contractile and compressive elements to one another as well as to surface membrane and nucleus (guy wires)	*Integrators*: connect inside pullers and inside/outside pushers, provide internal stability, keep opposing forces in equilibrium within the structure

the concept of a *difference engine* that helps drive a *sustainable community* (1998, p. 1). Contrary to traditional models of group dynamics that strive to produce agreement through consensus, organizations driven by a difference engine acknowledge a certain level of discord as a necessary, even desired, prerequisite of healthy growth. "The greater the mutual incompatibility, the greater the tendency of the compression elements to avoid confrontation and proximity to the centre, the greater the tension required to maintain them in position, and the greater the energy inherent in the system" (Judge, 1978, p. 263).

Judge cites many traditional social systems as *difference-oriented*, or driven by variance between opposing factions. These include:

- Families
- Religions
- Gender relationships
- Immigration trends
- Intergenerational conflicts

This is not to suggest that disagreements between group members are to be encouraged as a normal mode of doing business. But it does propose that learning how to function efficiently in a collaborative climate marked by elements of tension, stress, and even controlled chaos can eventually lead to deeper levels of fulfillment and actualization. Individuals skilled at such interactions can use disagreements as catalysts for even greater levels of growth. According to Judge:

> Clearly both natural and social communities, as well as cultural life in general, benefit from different ways of doing things. In the natural environment, these differences create niches in which other things can happen. Both natural and social environments abhor monotony as much as a vacuum. Perhaps it is that logic is simply inadequate to detect what is engendered by difference and disagreement. Faced with disagreement, a person can be challenged by it, or can appreciate the drama of it as a happening. Like a volcano, it disrupts the static environment. (1998)

How then can differences be used to drive tensegretic organizations? The key issue here is understanding. First, those involved in such organizations must seek to understand the nature of the differences within the group or between competing approaches. This may be accomplished by creating some type of ordering system that attempts to delineate categories among the various differences within the organization. As scientists respond to the variety of chemical elements, species, or other observable natural phenomena by developing typologies—such as the periodic table or taxonomies of species—so are we also naturally confronted by a panoply of colors, textures, tastes, and experiences in our everyday lives. We instinctively reject any overgeneralizations of these experiences implied by simplistic, abstract typologies, and are unwilling to cram the differences we experience in daily life into crude categories. Indeed, it is often our ability to deal with subtle differences that ensures both our survival and our ability to thrive in a society that becomes increasingly more diverse and complex.

Second, a degree of sensitivity regarding variety and diversity when ordering differences must be observed. In other words, we must appreciate the nature of the differences inherent among groups. Judge identifies the following approaches:

- Recognize only the minimum number of differences, namely only gross variations (e.g., carnivores, herbivores, and omnivores).
- Focus on the dominant type, or possibly types, treating the remainder as ancillary or marginal.
- Focus only on a limited number of categories (e.g., animal, vegetable, mineral, or abstract) to form an abstract typology or model through which the world may be perceived.
- Adopt a particular typology through a dominant institution, declare it to be the most appropriate, and then require that people adhere to it in subsequent transactions, or else face penalties (e.g., the approach of major religions, scientific disciplines, and government agencies). (1998)

Not all of these approaches are satisfactory, or even acceptable, in dealing with educational collaborations. Allowing the ethic of a *dominant institution* to become the superior approach, for example, would obviously create unacceptable inequities in power between member organizations. Unfortunately, this condition is quite common in educational collaborations, with the university partner often assuming the leadership role while the school partner assumes the role of receiver or follower. This imbalance is all the more reason to advocate for models of collaboration that recognize this situation, and ensure equity between partners.

Appreciating diversity is crucial to comprehending how competing ideas and approaches can be incorporated into the whole. Recognizing variance and being sensitive to the opinions and ideas of others, is fundamental to creating difference engines in tensegretic organizations. Unless opposing factions are given a voice in group debates, the results of this dialogue will lack the richness and complexity of more inclusive discussions.

Finally, polarities or differences of opinion within the interorganizational relationship must be secondary to an underlying sense of unity or oneness. This central idea is expressed in the literature on educational collaboration as the importance of each partner sharing a common mission or goal, typically the improvement of student learning. Indeed, most examinations of problems within educational partnerships point to fundamental disagreements between partners on the IOR's shared goals.

In tensegrity-based partnerships, these common beliefs must reside not just within the group's nucleus or core but also within each individual involved in the collaborative. It is the shared understanding of the partners' mission that sustains the collective members through the inevitable differences of opinion and changes in personnel that plague all such collaborations. One of the unique abilities of tensegrity-oriented organizations is the willingness to incorporate difference as an accepted means of doing business, and as a way of honoring the diversity of its membership. It is this quality that distinguishes these organizations from the desperate quest for consensus and common ground that characterizes traditional, hierarchical management structures.

PRESTRESS

Fuller and Ingber acknowledge the role that prestress plays in ensuring the stability of tensegrities. Prestress means that structural members that can bear only tension are distinct from those that bear compression, so that even before a tensegrity structure is subjected to an external force, all structural members are already in states of tension or compression. "Within the structure, the compression-bearing rigid struts stretch, or tense, the flexible, tension-bearing members, while those tension-bearing members compress the rigid struts. These counteracting forces, which equilibrate throughout the structure, are what enable it to stabilize itself" (Ingber, 1998, p. 49).

Most theories of group dynamics recognize that the lifespan of each group encompasses a finite period, during which several distinct stages can be observed (i.e., engagement, differentiation, individuation, intimacy, disillusion) (Brossart, Patton, & Wood, 1998, p. 1). Several studies in the literature included process models. These models identified

- four characteristics of collaboration—environmental, relational, procedural, and structural (Intriligator, 1986, p. 5);
- four domains of collaboration—engagement, negotiation, performance, and assessment/evaluation (Uhl & Squires, 1994, p. 3);
- six steps for systemic change—awareness/readiness/commitment, collection of baseline data, development and approval of master plan, implementation and monitoring of action plans, evaluation, reassessment (Hackmann & Barry, 1994, pp. 4–5); and,
- eight stages of development of collaboration—hostility and skepticism, lack of trust, period of truce, mixed approval, acceptance, regression, renewal, and continuing process (Trubowitz, 1986, pp. 19–21).

In a prestressed tensegrity, tension is continuously transmitted across all structural members. All entities stabilize themselves by arranging their parts to minimize energy and mass through continuous tension and local compression. The transmission of tension through a tensegrity array provides a means to distribute forces to all interconnected elements, and to tune the whole system as one (Ingber, 1997, p. 575).

In human systems, we can think of this increase in tension on a particular individual being balanced by an increase in compression by another person, who picks up the slack within the structure. This might be accomplished by sharing resources, increasing communications, or offering assistance between individuals or groups. Tuned, or prestressed, organizations, then, tend to work more efficiently than those that are not already stressed, because members are more aware of the needs of their coworkers, and are always ready to respond when the group is stressed.

PARTNERSHIP PARADOXES

Educational partnerships are, by their very nature, full of contradictions. In school/college collaborations, differences often occur in the form of tensions—between opposing viewpoints, opinions, approaches, organizational structures, and among people. These differences are mediated in human systems through careful negotiations between individuals and groups of people. In tensegretic terms, organizations and the people that work in them exist in a climate of tension. In order to operate effectively these groups maintain a state of prestress, which depends on each structural member functioning according to its assigned role within the organization.

Tensegretic organizations respond to tension by diffusing pressures across the entire array in an effort to maintain equilibrium. The fact that tensegrities naturally seek a state of equilibrium does not mean that these structures attempt to create climates that eliminate tension altogether. In fact, organizations operating according to tensegretic principles embrace tension as a necessary component of collaborative work: "Initially we saw the differences between schools and universities as potential sites of conflict; we conclude with the position that tensions cannot be resolved and are instead to be cherished as potential sites for our learning and growth" (Johnston, 1997, p. 12).

How can educational collaborators reconcile the tensions that seem to be intrinsic elements of these relationships? The answer may be in how we view these differences. Rather than considering points of tension as sources of friction, these differences can be examined as opportunities for learning and understanding diverse thoughts. John Dewey considered dualisms as interrelated parts of the same whole, and not as separate ideological constructs. His idea of "social negotiation in the shaping and learning of a community underlies" this approach to "working across differences in productive ways" (Johnston, 1997, p. 13).

Looking at differences as potentially productive sources of energy is key to functioning in a climate of tension. A useful metaphor for understanding how learning can be generated through difference can be found in the study of the pedagogical process itself. Learning theorists have argued that "what is not known is identified on the basis of what is known" (Gordon, 1984, p. 48). In music, we learn an unfamiliar tonal or rhythm pattern by comparing the new pattern to one previously learned, and give meaning to the new pattern on the basis of its similarities to and differences from the one already learned. In this example, learning comes from observing and cataloguing the differences between patterns; in the process, new meaning is created out of difference.

In the earlier discussion of *difference engines*, a three-step process was outlined for channeling energy produced by creative tension in a productive manner. It is worthwhile to revisit this process now:

- Understanding and ordering differences;
- Observing a degree of sensitivity regarding diversity when ordering differences;
- Basing differences on an underlying unity of mission.

Participants in educational collaborations who follow these steps will notice improved communications, although not necessarily decreased levels of disagreement. The purpose of this process is not to eliminate discord, but to stimulate meaningful dialogue and take advantage of conflicts as potential sources of learning. This type of discourse, as discussed above, is often frustrating and always time consuming. It does produce, however, a quality of interaction that is difficult to recreate through hierarchically governed systems.

These interactions give rise to a rich climate in host groups that is conducive to risk taking, and personal and professional growth. The sense of empowerment generated among those participating in such work is a necessary counterbalance to the natural inequities in power, resources, and prestige often found in school/college partnerships. This check and balance apparatus is a built-in advantage of tensegretic organizations, but requires awareness and sensitivity on the part of all members in order to be effective. It is the obligation of those traditionally lacking in power within educational institutions (i.e., teachers, students) to demand an equitable role in both decision making and responsibility in their organizations, while it is incumbent upon administrators and other school leaders to welcome these individuals as equal stakeholders in the collaborative process.

Johnston terms differences in collaborative groups *productive tensions*, and acknowledges that not all differences work in a climate of productive tension. "Some differences are destructive and . . . cannot . . . be made productive. How we use this concept of productive tensions while we continue to be critical of both the categories and assumptions [of new participants] is our ongoing challenge" (1997, p. 16). Consider the following apparent contradictions that characterize collaborations between schools and colleges:

- We intuitively know that working together is preferable to working separately, but also understand that producing tangible results via teamwork can be harder and more time consuming than going it alone.
- Collaborators know that differences in opinion and approach provide the creative energy and tension that fuels sustainable relationships, but are equally aware that these relationships must be built on a foundation of shared visions, missions, and goals.
- The equitable allocation of resources from each partner is a prerequisite for effective collaboration, yet school/college partners are rarely equals in issues of power, prestige, or resources.
- Partnerships are inherently egalitarian in structure and practice, but strong leadership is an acknowledged requirement for success.
- Traditionally, the domains of theory and practice have been associated singly with higher education and K–12 schools, respectively. School-

college partnerships attempt to blur these lines by developing new models of instruction, professional growth, and teacher empowerment.

All of these examples feature an inherent dualism or dichotomy of difference. This kind of contradiction is in contrast to the ethos of traditionally structured organizations, which struggle to seek accord, agreement, and consensus in order to sustain themselves.

CONCLUSION

Perhaps the most compelling characteristic of the tensegretic theory of educational collaboration advanced here is the recognition that it is people, not structures that make partnerships work. Tensegrities consist of both *roles* and *functions*, and it is the interaction between them that produces the energy necessary for effective collaboration. Unlike traditionally structured groups that depend on agreement and uniformity of opinion, tensegrity organizations thrive on the differences between people, ideas, and strategies, and on the contributions that committed people and partner groups connected by a shared vision make to attain outcomes that they could not achieve alone.

The process of collaboration is in many ways a living, cyclical enterprise. The theory of collaboration offered here may be used to analyze and assess other models of educational partnerships, creating an organic cycle of generation, evolution, evaluation, and, eventually, renewal. As the models evolve, the lessons learned from the perspectives and contributions of the participants will doubtlessly inform the theoretical framework.

LAST WORDS: A PARTNERSHIP PRIMER

People involved in educational collaborations often look for guidelines or models to assist them in developing approaches to doing collaborative work in their own settings. Unfortunately, many of these lists provide suggestions that prove to be of more harm than good, as the study of collaboration stubbornly resists generic classifications and categorizations. There are, however, some common elements to these kinds of relationships that may prove useful to those interested in collaborative initiatives, and can be used to see if all of the necessary elements are in place in your setting for an effective collaboration. Applied to specific situations, these questions can help generate an institutional or community-wide self-assessment that organizers can then use to identify potential partners, formulate shared missions and objectives, locate resources, and design an effective action plan.

Leadership and Vision

- How will your music education community assess its needs?
- Is top-level institutional support and cooperation present from each member organization?
- Is the institutional climate of each member organization conducive to risk taking?
- Are the goals of each member organization clearly defined and congruent?
- Do the partners share a common vision and goals for the collaboration?

Resources and Structures

- What resources (i.e., musical, human, financial, time) are available in your community?
- Are the member organizations willing to allocate sufficient resources toward partnership initiatives?
- How will key people (i.e., visionaries, leaders, potential adopters) be identified?
- Will your partnership invite other community music organizations as potential collaborators?
- Will your partnership involve:
  - preservice teacher education?
  - professional development opportunities for teachers?
  - defining music literacy for the community?
  - curriculum development or revision?

Assessment and Evaluation

- How will you document and communicate the activities of your partnership?
- What kinds of documents and artifacts will be collected throughout the evaluation process?
- Who will do the evaluation (in-house participants or outside consultants)?
- How will you design your assessment to measure music learning authentically?
- How will you know your partnership is successfully meeting its goals?

REFERENCES

Brossart, D. F., Patton, M. J., & Wood, P. K. (1998). Assessing group process: An illustration using Tuckerized growth curves. *Group Dynamics Theory, Research, and Practice*, 2(1), 3–17.

Fuller, R. B. (1961). Tensegrity. *Portfolio and Art News Annual,* 4.

Gordon, E. E. (1984). *Learning sequences in music.* Chicago: GIA Publications.

Hackmann, D. G., & Barry, J. E. (1994, November). A university/school collaboration model for systemic change through site-based management. Paper presented at the fifth annual meeting of the National Conference on School/College Collaboration of the American Association for Higher Education, Washington, DC.

Hinckley, J. (1995). Urban music education: Providing for students. *Music Educators Journal,* 82(1), 32–35.

Ingber, D. E. (1997). Tensegrity: The architectural basis of cellular mechanotransduction. *Annual Review of Physiology,* 59, 575–599.

———. (1998, January). The architecture of life: A universal set of building rules seems to guide the design of organic structures—from simple carbon compounds to complex cells and tissues. *Scientific American,* pp. 48–57.

Intriligator, B. A. (1986, April). Collaborating with the schools: A strategy for school improvement. Paper presented at the annual meeting of the American Educational Research Association, San Francisco, CA.

Johnston, M. (1997). *Contradictions in collaboration: New thinking on school/university partnerships.* New York: Teachers College Press.

Judge, A. J. N. (1978). Transcending duality through tensional integrity: From systems-versus-networks to tensegrity organization. *Transnational Associations.* Available at www.laetusinpraesens.org/docs/systen2.php.

———. (1979). Implementing principles by balancing configurations of functions: A tensegrity organization approach. *Transnational Associations.* Available at www.laetusinpraesens.org/docs/implprin.php.

———. (1991, December). Metaphors as transdisciplinary vehicles of the future. Paper presented at the Conference on Science and Tradition: Transdisciplinary Perspectives on the Way to the 21st Century, organized by UNESCO, Paris.

———. (1998). Living differences as a basis for sustainable community. *Transnational Associations.* Available at www.laetusinpraesens.org/ docs/quenchin.php.

Robinson, M. (1998). A collaboration model for school and community music education. *Arts Education Policy Review,* 100(2), 32–39.

———. (2005). A tensegretic theory of school-college collaboration in music education. *Arts Education Policy Review,* 106(3), 9–18.

Trubowitz, S. (1986). Stages in the development of school/college collaboration. *Educational Leadership,* 43(5), 18–21.

Uhl, S. C., & Squires, S. E. (1994, April). Enhancing systemic change through effective collaboration: A formative perspective and approach to collaboration. Paper presented at the annual meeting of the American Educational Research Association, New Orleans, LA.

13

Collaboration: The Key to Successful Professional Development for Urban Music Teachers

Al D. Holcomb

The grant project training has made an incredible difference in my teaching this year! The seminars have brought focus to my curriculum planning and teaching and given me valuable materials. The enthusiasm and emphasis on musicality has reminded me every month why I do what I do! However, the skills I have learned in technology training have been my greatest area of achievement. The opportunity to collaborate and learn from other teachers has been wonderful.

(Project participant)

There are many reasons this grant project worked, but one in particular that makes it different is that we have a regular group that consistently gets together. Knowing we have a regular group of people working for the same goals and sharing many of the same experiences has helped me to have trust in other teachers and "the system" in general. For me, the group became very important because I knew I would be seeing people who understood my situation. This kind of group is very important for music teachers because we have all grown up being in musical groups and in general, that kind of social environment gives us security. The most important thing I received was the support and security of being with the other teachers.

(Project participant)

OVERVIEW

In the fall of 2001, Orange County Public Schools (OCPS) joined with the University of Central Florida (UCF) to create a four-year professional development program for music teachers in the OCPS schools that receive Title I funding. Four years later, this project provides an interesting study in the development of an effective partnership.

The collaboration began when the OCPS Fine Arts coordinator approached two UCF music education faculty members about designing a federally funded professional development program for music teachers in Title I schools. The UCF faculty members then worked with the OCPS Fine Arts coordinator and the director of Grant Services to write a grant application for the Professional Development for Music Educators Project (CFDA No. 84.351C). The following five objectives were specified in the proposal:

1. To develop high-quality in-service professional development modules for music teachers
2. To train teachers with up-to-date research-based information to better prepare them to teach music
3. To establish sustained and ongoing collaboration between teachers, cohort groups, mentors, local universities, and arts organizations
4. To implement use of technology in the daily instructional routine and
5. To create materials and models to be easily replicated.

In accordance with the grant rationale, the proposal supported the strengthening of music education toward Florida Sunshine State Music Standards (Florida State Department of Education, 1996). In an attempt to provide national relevance, the proposed project was designed to align with National Staff Development Council Standards (National Staff Development Council, 2001) and National Board Certification (National Board for Professional Teaching Standards, 2001). By engaging in research-based professional development in the areas of reflective practice, collaboration, mentoring, technology education, and best practices in music teaching, teachers would be better equipped to address the challenges of teaching a highly diverse and frequently large student population. The grant was awarded to OCPS in the fall of 2001 with annual funding provided for three more years. Grant money was used to fund guest presenters; conference attendance; release time for teachers to attend grant activities; technology equipment, resources, and training; external evaluation of grant activities; and stipends for project leadership, implementation, and research by university faculty.

PROJECT FRAMEWORK

Between 25 and 40 general, choral, and instrumental music teachers participated over a four-year period in the comprehensive program of training, support, and assessment that was developed to address project objectives and perceived areas of need by participating teachers. Primary components included monthly seminars, a support network that included mentoring and cohort group interactions, curriculum and assessment development projects, artist-in-residence projects, technology training, and portfolio development. In addition, teachers received funding to attend music conferences and summer development projects. The OCPS Fine Arts coordinator and two UCF music education faculty members served as project leaders who met regularly to plan project activities. External evaluators were used each year to assess program effectiveness.

Seminars

Over a four-year period, monthly seminars provided regular opportunities for training and collaborations among participants. During the first three years, the primary focus areas of the project included building community and trust among participants; enhancing teacher musicianship; and improving skills related to planning, teaching, assessing, and reflecting on music learning. Nationally recognized music educators, project leaders, and curriculum specialists from the Florida Department of Education presented seminars in the areas of African and Latin American folk music, solfège training, standards-based music education, classroom management, and sequential planning. Other seminars were used to address current issues in music education, including arts advocacy, music assessment, literacy connections through music education, brain development, and technology training. Teachers received instructional resources for each seminar topic, completed relevant individual and group assignments, and analyzed instructional process and techniques used by each presenter. Project leaders and mentors assessed participant understanding of seminar content through written assignments, surveys, discussions, and teaching observations.

Mentors and Cohort Groups

In addition to the informal support participants provided to one another during seminars, a system of peer support through mentors and cohort groups was initiated during the second year of the project. Selected by project leaders, OCPS music teachers served as mentors to cohort groups of three–four teachers. Mentors were selected for various reasons, including expertise with Orff or Kodály methodologies, National Board certification, proven success with student interns, consistently high ensemble evaluations, and/or proven success in an urban setting. In addition, an attempt was made to include successful minority teachers from the district. During seminars, mentors met with their cohort groups to discuss classroom applications of seminar content, address common problems, and organize classroom visits. Mentors received specialized training to work with adult learners and facilitate discussion through reflective questioning. An informal network of support among mentors evolved as they collaborated to develop effective mentoring strategies.

In addition to completing projects during seminars, cohort group members were given opportunities to visit each other's classrooms. Grant money provided funding for release time for cohort group members to observe each other, plan units of instruction, coteach lessons, and attend workshops together. Cohort group members maintained regular communication during the school year through seminar interactions, after-school meetings, phone calls, and email exchanges. Mentors prepared summative reports of all cohort group interactions that occurred during the year.

Curriculum and Assessment Development

Project participants and mentors participated in various grant-funded curriculum and assessment projects throughout the four-year project. At the end of the first year, a team of OCPS elementary teachers, including project participants, developed assessment tools and resources for the district music standards. During the second year, grant project teachers helped to develop instructional resources and essential learning outcomes from district music benchmarks. After the fourth year of the grant, project participants elected to meet during the summer to continue the development of curriculum resources.

Technology Training

The project goal of incorporating technology into the daily instructional routines of participating teachers became the focus during the third and fourth years of the program. In the spring of 2004, each participant received a music technology workstation, including a computer, printer, keyboard, video camera, and a selection of music software applications. National and local experts provided training and support to assist teachers in using the equipment for notating compositions and arrangements, making accompaniment tracks, recording video and audio tracks, and providing music instruction. OCPS technology staff provided district-wide training and site support for computer and web-based projects. Project participants with technological expertise provided individual support to colleagues upon request. Ongoing technology training provided teachers with the skills for capturing and editing video excerpts of teaching and learning and for creating class compositions, accompaniments, and arrangements for student performance. By the end of the fourth year, most teachers had created a web page to communicate information about their music program and educate readers about the role of quality arts education.

FINAL FOCUS: DOCUMENTING EVIDENCE OF TEACHING EFFECTIVENESS

During the fourth year of the project, participants began the process of developing electronic portfolios. They used these to document performances of best practice related to planning, teaching, and assessing music learning; demonstrate their ability to accurately reflect on teaching and learning; display a high level of personal musicianship; and demonstrate student achievement. Working individually, with mentors, and in cohort groups, participants reviewed and evaluated video excerpts, lesson plans, lesson reflections, and student work to include in the online portfolios.

OUTCOMES

At the conclusion of the fourth year of the professional development project replicable training modules and resources based on researched-based strategies were developed. University of Central Florida music education faculty continued to be involved in planning activities and developing future programs. Participants expressed a strong interest in maintaining collaborative activities with other participants, cohort group members, and mentors.

Project assessments indicated significant changes in participant attitude, professional activity, and classroom practice. Participants interacted more frequently with one another to strengthen teaching and learning and demonstrated increased enthusiasm about teaching and professional development. Because of their involvement with the project, an increased number of teachers elected to stay in their schools, enroll in master's degree projects, attend state and national music conferences, and pursue National Board certification. Participants were observed teaching African and Latin American music with increased understanding and authenticity and assessing students individually more often. Teachers were regularly using technology resources to improve music teaching and learning.

The grant project made an impact on music teaching throughout Orange County. As a result of their participation in the project, mentors demonstrated improved music teaching and leadership skills. Current districtwide curriculum and development projects now reflect the language, structure, and content of grant project training materials. Mentors have incorporated grant project strategies into the mentoring of all new music teachers in the district. Choral directors in the district are being encouraged by their general music peers to create electronic music teaching portfolios next year.

The music education department at the University of Central Florida benefited from the university–urban school partnership. As a result of attending grant project seminars, UCF students were exposed to national and local educational experts. A special topics course with a focus on music teaching in an urban setting was developed to allow UCF students to have authentic learning experiences in the classrooms of grant participants. As a result of successful interactions with grant project teachers, an increased number of music education students observed, assisted with instruction, and pursued employment in urban schools.

INSIGHTS

The opportunity to collaborate with other urban music teachers was a highly valued professional development experience. A sense of community developed over time that allowed participants to feel comfortable asking questions, sharing strategies and lesson plans, and having peers observe their teaching. Since they are often the only music teacher in their buildings, many participants lacked opportunities for collaboration with music teacher colleagues prior to this project. Being part of a learning community where their needs were understood motivated teachers to participate more fully in professional development experiences.

Although the completed portfolio provides a tangible product for evaluating teaching effectiveness, the collaborative processes of planning, developing, and reviewing the portfolios actually provided the learning opportunity that led to improved practice. Engaging the participants in portfolio development was one of the most challenging aspects of the program. While the majority of the teachers had started or completed their portfolios by the end of the fourth year, a few teachers had not, reporting a lack of time as their main reason for not starting portfolio development. It is possible that these participants were not comfortable sharing lesson plans or video excerpts with their colleagues or lacked technology skills.

CONCLUSION: DESIGNING FUTURE PROJECTS FOR URBAN MUSIC TEACHERS

The urban music teachers in this project valued opportunities for collaboration with their peers over all other activities. Thus, release time for peer observation, problem solving, coteaching, and planning provided a valuable learning experience for teachers. Mentors enhanced these cohort group collaborations by facilitating discussions, identifying areas for group and individual growth, organizing future cohort group interactions, observing lessons taught by participants and providing feedback, coteaching lessons, and providing curricular resources. Mentoring worked best when there was flexibility in how mentors were assigned, as teachers preferred to choose their mentor or have multiple mentors. Ongoing training and support was needed to help mentors feel comfortable and competent with mentoring skills.

The technology training was also considered valuable. This project provided increased opportunity for teachers to collaborate on lesson design and portfolio construction. We found that teachers needed to have the appropriate equipment as well as ongoing training and support to give them an understanding of how technology can improve teaching and learning. It was possible to raise teachers' level of comfort with additional training experiences and individual support.

The impact of this project on participant attitude and classroom practice suggests that school–university collaborations are a viable model for the professional development of music teachers, especially those in urban areas. Such partnerships can provide effective leadership, implementation, and continuous improvement for music programs in urban schools.

REFERENCES

Florida State Department of Education. (1996). *Florida sunshine state music standards*. Tallahassee, FL: Author.

National Board for Professional Teaching Standards. (2001). *Music standards*. Washington, DC: Author.

National Staff Development Council. (2001). *National Staff Development Council standards*. Washington, DC: Author.

14

Restructuring and Partnering in Urban Schools: Change, Cooperation, and Courage

Herbert D. Marshall

In the often bleak landscape of urban music education in the United States there are islands of success—programs where teachers and administrators strive persistently to improve their students' music learning through changes in scheduling, cohorts of cooperating teachers, collaborations with business or higher education, revisions of curriculum, and so forth. These improvements are attainable by any determined faculty, and are sufficient to change the course of ailing schools or, even better, serve as preventative medicine to avoid a critical condition.

With the intent of improving music education opportunities for urban students, this chapter documents the contributions of visionary music educators in schools from three cities in different regions of the United States. Each city has a different population (as per the 2000 U.S. census): Jackson, MI (36,316); Hartford, CT (121,578); and Atlanta, GA (416,475). None of these schools sees itself as a "model," but each team of educators consented to discuss how their experiments and achievements have helped them use music to meet the idiosyncratic needs of their communities.

Music is valued at each of these sites; in these communities and schools music is an essential part of the learning environment. Teachers and administrators offer opportunities for music study to all students, regardless of income, and individualized instruction is available to meet the needs of diverse students. Music specialists in these schools serve as mentors, colleagues, and arts liaisons. They have met challenges with creativity, courage, and cooperation. It is hoped that through their example, others may identify needs, examine current practices and structures, seek collaboration, and continue to serve music learners to the best of their ability.

METHOD AND ANALYSIS

The three settings included here were brought to the author's attention by colleagues, educators, and students. Patton (2002, p. 243) refers to this process as "Snowball sampling." Naturalistic inquiry methods were used to construct a case study of each setting. The author served as the primary researcher.

Data collection began in the fall of 2002. Site visits occurred at all three sites over the course of two school years. These visits included interviews and observations with at least one administrator and music educator in each school. Music classes and other events were observed, along with the schools and surrounding neighborhoods. Students were observed but not interviewed. Whenever possible, interviews were tape-recorded and transcribed.

Interviews, which were scheduled at the convenience of the participants, incorporated a blend of structured and unstructured questions. All participants were asked about the evolution and process of their contribution, but their intent, goals, preparation, and inspiration emerged as they became more engaged in the interview. Periodically, schools were contacted via phone and email to update information.

The aim of this research was to observe and disseminate information about incremental success, not to evaluate or critique the programs. Within this context, data triangulation was achieved by blending information gathered from observation, administrator interviews, music specialist interviews (independent from the administrator), nonmusic specialist interviews, and document analysis. Mindful of time and space constraints, and guided by input from participants at focus sessions at the 2005 MENC Eastern Regional Conference in Baltimore, Maryland, the final case study narratives are built around the following emergent themes:

- The need and motivation to affect change;
- The role of the administrator as advocate and leader;
- The relationship of the music specialist to learners, peers, and community;
- The role of music and the arts within the school and community;
- The relationships between the school and community musicians and educators; and
- The effects of institutional change on learners.

THREE CASE STUDIES

Centennial Place Elementary School
(www.centennialplace.net/)

Introduction

Centennial Place Elementary School (CP) is relatively new, having been built in 1998 to replace an older building during a time of neighborhood renewal immediately following the 1996 Summer Olympic Games in Atlanta, Georgia. The entrance atrium resembles an airport hangar—high, curved, and sunny. Upon entry, one sees color, foliage, and comfortable furniture in all directions. Down the central hallway is a large wall display made up of student-notated ostinati to accompany the "Dance of the Sugar Plum Fairy." The instrumentation includes soda bottles, paper bags, cardboard tubes, and clothes hangers. Just as these sound sources are creative variations on Tchaikovsky's original masterpiece, Centennial Place Elementary School (CP) is a variation on urban education.

In the first experiment of its kind in the United States, a low-income housing development that had become a magnet for poverty, drugs, and violence was replaced with a development for mixed income residents with mixed ownership units. A public–private partnership built 950 units to service families, offering 40% of the units at market rate, 40% at a subsidized rate, and 20% on tax credits—most for rent, some for sale. The school is situated among these housing developments—Centennial Place Apartments and Centennial Park North—surrounded by an urban blight area, in the long shadow of the Coca-Cola Company's national headquarters, and across the street from Georgia Institute of Technology. The 1996 Olympic Village, now dormitories for Georgia State University, is a few blocks away. CP serves a student population that is 93% African American, with 62% of students on free or reduced lunch.

Dressed in uniforms of blues, whites, and yellows, about half of the students come from the immediate urban neighborhood, while the other half come from around the city of Atlanta. CP is a popular choice. Enrollment is based solely on parental requests—which means getting to the district office early to get a place in line each spring. Dr. Cynthia Kuhlman, principal, attributes this to the school's strong record of success in its brief lifetime—all under her leadership—and its focus on science and math, project-based learning, and strong emphasis on the arts.

Structure

Several initiatives make CP an interesting learning and teaching environment. *The principal schedules all music classes and rehearsals during the school day.* These are led by a full-time general music/choral specialist and two instrumental specialists, band and strings, who are shared with two other schools. *Instruction takes place year-round. The school is a partner in Georgia State University's (GSU) Sound Learning program.* This program brings a GSU facilitator and several performing artists into the school for a yearlong residency of demonstrations and performances. Underpinning these innitiatives is a community, staff, and principal who share a commitment to learning and a belief in the arts as essential in the education process.

Approximately 50 fourth- and fifth-grade students sing in chorus; they rehearse one hour each week. In most Atlanta Public Schools, instrumental instruction begins in fourth grade. The principal at CP supports an enhanced program with instruction before grade four as teaching time permits. Thus, students from kindergarten through grade five may study stringed instruments, and all students in grades two and three learn to play the recorder.

When it opened in 1998, CP adopted a year-round calendar. Students attend classes in nine-week sessions, separated by three-week intersessions, and a full-month summer vacation (see specifics on the APS website: www.atlanta.k12.ga.us/). The first week of each intersession is used for remediation and enrichment through classes taught on a voluntary basis.

As part of the Atlanta Public Schools' comprehensive reform model, all schools selected Whole School Reform models. The year-round schedule is well suited to the school's reform design: Co-Nect (www.co-nect.net/). The CP website states that their reform model "uses technology and project-based learning." Faculty adopt broad school themes and a specific theme for each grade. Grade-level instruction is driven by a question teachers and students strive to answer through projects and research. The intercessions allow time for teachers to develop these broad themes and projects or to further develop a line of inquiry as an enrichment class.

In 1999 Dr. David Myers, professor of music education at Georgia State University (GSU), crafted an arts-based school reform model that involved the university, elementary schools in the Atlanta area, and professional musicians from the region. One senses from Myers's writing that this unique relationship evolved from the abundance of talent and creativity around Atlanta and Myers's dissatisfaction with other arts-based reform models. Myers writes, "If the systematic growth of developmentally appropriate musicianship and musical understanding is not at the core of music teaching and learning, then the activity should neither be labeled music education nor presumed to demonstrate broad values of the arts in the curriculum" (2003, p. 6).

GSU contracts various professional chamber ensembles to engage in a yearlong residency that includes in-service training, planning meetings with grade-level teachers, and at least four interactions with all students from the grade. Guest musicians (including members of the Atlanta Symphony Orchestra, freelance artists, and student ensembles from GSU) work colaboratively with grade-level teachers and music specialists. Presentations to students occur during class time, not in place of music class. These visits are organized and facilitated by the music specialist and a site coordinator from GSU. Site coordinators are always experienced teachers, either adjunct faculty or graduate students from GSU.

Sound Learning strives to provide a sense of equality and interdependence between performer, grade-level teacher, music teacher, and student (Myers, 2003, p. 9). All of the involved parties go to great lengths to speak the same language and educate each other in the process of teaching. Professional guest musicians, who in some programs might see their involvement as a chore, describe learning to communicate complex musical constructs to children and mentoring university musicians as highly satisfying. Grade-level teachers are viewed as the big-picture learning experts who can help students connect musical content to all other aspects of their curricula. The presence of the music teacher is pivotal—Sound Learning will not partner with a school without a certified music specialist—and the program supplements rather than supplants his or her efforts. Students also have an active voice in the process. Through projects and reflection, the partners gather evidence to evaluate the degree of success of their collaboration.

Observations

It was Cynthia Terry who brought Sound Learning to Centennial Place when she transferred to the new school in 1998. Since that time, Sound Learning has become an essential component of the overall culture of the school. GSU and CP make the partnership available to grade-level teachers by choice. The teachers, facilitated by the music educator and site coordinator, choose a theme. They discuss the theme, and with the guest musicians, and with the music teacher, they determine how music might help meet their goals for the students.

Visits to Centennial Place are intimate and interactive. Sound Learning events are often held in the library, with the musicians in a small open space and the students seated around them. Through music making, lecture and demonstration, and lively discussion, the adults (teachers and guests) illuminate connections between the music and the grade-level curriculae, such as form or history or acoustics or texture. To use one of Myers's colorful terms, the program eschews the "drive-by performance" model of arts education. Periodic visits during the school year indicate that relationships have developed between students, teachers, and musicians. In fact, the musicians begin to feel like teachers and the teachers feel like musicians. Musical offerings include tunes that are familiar to the students, letting the students feel that they can be experienced musicians along with the guest artists. Because the program does not promote a certain genre of music, the content and repertoire is flexible to meet the needs and interests of students.

Now in its fifth year at CP, Sound Learning is funded primarily through grants from the National Endowment for the Arts, the Fund for the Improvement of Postsecondary Education, and GSU (Georgia State University School of Music, 2004). Schools in the partnership generally contribute $1,000 per participating grade level to help defray costs. This partnership truly alters the environment of the school and enhances grade-level teachers' view of music as an integral part of learning and the music educator as essential in the school community.

Outcomes

A positive outcome from arts integration was on display while data were being collected for this chapter. A large display area was festuned with found objects-turned-percussion instruments—food containers, paper towel tubes, paper sacks, and so forth. A project, primarily coordinated by the art teacher, featured students listening and moving to Tchaikovsky's *Nutcracker*. Students identified patterns in the form of rhythmic ostinati. Students then used found objects-turned-instruments to perform these ostinati, which ultimately became a large mixed-media collage to document their experience. It would seem that when you make a school attractive to artistic teachers, and create an artistic and supportive environment in which to teach, the outcome is conceptual and creative experiences with the arts and learning. When projects such as this grow too large for the daily schedule, the year-round calendar intercessions provide extra time. During one fall, music teachers invited students to plan the winter concert during intercession. Students were involved in selecting themes and repertoire for the concert.

One constant in urban education is change. Students are mobile and teachers are mobile. Principal Kuhlman enjoys an ample pool of new applicants and potential transfers when teaching openings arise, attributable in part to Sound Learning and other exciting partnerships. Recent faculty turnover at Centennial Place means that none of the original music educators still work there and many grade-level teachers are new. Because of their belief in Sound Learning, and willingness to constantly assess and revise, the partners met to organize an in-service for the whole school in the fall of 2005, to reestablish goals and procedures and help new faculty learn about the opportunity to participate in this exciting collaboration. Thus, change does not have to be feared; it can lead to evolution and growth.

Myers and Kuhlman view Sound Learning as a process, not a program, and continually reevaluate their work. Because it strives to be inquiry- and project-based, it is well suited for Centennial Place's reform model. First-grade teachers wrote Sound Learning into their curiculum. The science curriculum features a sound unit in which students create and perform on original instruments, and less-formal applications are integrated into the social studies and language curricula. Other grades come in and out of the partnership as suits their needs. Students involved in Sound Learning complete a project, for example, a performance or portfolio, as a culminating experience and an opportunity for adults to assess learning. "Project Day" features participation by all students in grades 1–5, celebrating the year's music learning with faculty and parents.

Implications

Because of the opportunities provided by the joint efforts of guest musicians, facilitators, and the music specialist, grade-level teachers gained insights into the possibilities of arts-based learning for students. As students were called upon to be musical and respond to music, these teachers could observe the results of the music curriculum in an authentic setting. Whatever preconceived notions they might have had about music education were revised because of firsthand observation of learners they knew, exhibiting skills learned from a colleague. When students are being musical *and* using higher order thinking skills to explain and evaluate musical concepts, grade-level teachers have a new opportunity to see music education as an ally in producing thinkers and problem solvers. Music educators cannot discount the beneficial effects of teachers bonding through positive outcomes for students and building trust and collegiality. Other implications include the following:

- An effective administrator who believes in the power of arts education can see that belief manifest in his or her school. Music instruction during the day sends a strong message of music's role in the school.
- Parents and faculty will support music and the arts as essential parts of education when there are clear integral roles for them in the daily life of the school.
- Music partnerships that are truly content-driven and collaborative have a profound effect on music teaching and learning.
- With vision, courage, and cooperation, schools and neighborhoods can revise, renovate, and rebuild to the benefit of all.

University of Hartford Magnet School
(www.crec.org/uhms/)

Introduction

Between a foreground of snow and a background of forest preserve is nestled a two-story brick structure that resembles an Olympic village. A cluster of buildings, each housing a classroom, with peaks, bay windows, and doors to outside play areas, make up the village. Inside, the hallways are angled paths, not straight lines. It is a labyrinth with puzzles and discoveries around every corner. Windows and skylights help students maintain a connection with the environment outside. Each classroom has a separate office for the teacher that doubles as an observation room, where observers can see and hear the class without intruding.

The focal point of the school is the *Agora*, an ancient Greek word for "meeting place" that resembles an intimate amphitheater. As some urban schools become more homogenized, this school houses a remarkably diverse multicultural family—both students and staff—who assemble daily to sing, read poems, solve math problems, present environmental lessons, and celebrate. There is much to celebrate.

The University of Hartford Magnet School (UHMS) is one result of a rancorous lawsuit that forced the State of Connecticut to find creative solutions to the inequities between learning opportunities for urban and suburban students (*Sheff v. O'Neill*, 1991). Students from seven districts in the environs of Hartford, Connecticut, under the umbrella of the Capital Region Education Council (CREC) are chosen by lottery to attend the school. One goal of the school is to blend urban and suburban students. The school serves students from prekindergarten through grade five. Eighteen percent of students receive special services, 48% are entitled to free or reduced meals, and over half come from urban neighborhoods.

Structure

The school is a result of collaboration between the State of Connecticut, the CREC, and the University of Hartford. It is located on university property, and the university, particularly the School of Education, Nursing, and Health Professions and the Hartt School of Music, has a strong presence in the building. After a long incubation period, the planning committee from the University of Hartford suggested that the school be organized around Gardner's multiple intelligences theory (MI). Professor John Feierabend, of the University of Hartford's Hartt School of Music, was on this committee and figured prominently in the decisions regarding music at UHMS. He suggested that UHMS try a variation of MI theory. In addition to educating the whole child through all the intelligences, he also wanted to develop each child's primary intelligence or interest to its fullest potential. Feierabend refers to this as a blending of "intelligences integrated and intelligences alone." In this model, *all teachers* teach verbal/linguistic and mathematical/logical intelligences, although for some, it is their primary focus. Others called essentialists specialize in visual/spatial, bodily/kinesthetic, and musical intelligence—roughly corresponding to art, physical education, and music in traditional schools. Pre-K through second-grade students see a music essentialist for 45 minutes every other day; third- through fifth-grade students see a music essentialist for 60 minutes every other day. An extended-day program allows time for choral and instrumental instruction.

Principal Cheryl Kloczko was hired a year before the school opened. Kloczko had met and interviewed Gardner and used MI during her tenure as a gifted/talented teacher. She supervised the completion of construction (the first building designed specifically to accommodate an MI school) and recruited the first student body (over 1,400 applicants for 276 seats, grades pre-K through 3). She evaluated 300 applications and eventually hired a faculty of 15 experienced educators who were interested in MI, and were risk takers. The school opened in September 2001 and has since expanded to include grades four and five.

Observations

I learned more about MI theory in my three days at UHMS—seeing it in practice—than in 20 years of reading books and articles on the subject. Briefly, the theory states that rather than teaching toward, and measuring, intelligence as a single dimension, there are multiple, discreet intelligences: verbal/linguistic, visual/spatial, logical/mathematical, interpersonal, intrapersonal, bodily/kinesthetic, musical, and naturalistic (Gardner, 1999). Recognizing unique intelligences both validates those whose potential is not traditionally measured or even utilized in school and reveals new pathways as effective means for learning. Thus, the faculty need to know their subjects thoroughly, understand their students' individual differences, and know how to facilitate multiple means of learning. For music educators it would seem that this theory is a panacea, as it places our subject on an equal plane with other academic subjects.

The best illustration of blended instruction and intelligences was the pair of rabbits in the visual/spatial room. While preparing for class, the visual/spatial essentialists explained that these two litter box-trained rabbits were the focus of a complex and long-term naturalistic unit on predators and prey. Students learned that animals that are near the bottom of the food chain view nearly everything as a predator. Thus, nature has instilled in them an acuity and aversion to noise, sudden movement, and aggression. The child with high naturalistic aptitude is highly stimulated around the animals and, thus, seems more likely to attend to visual/spatial content. The high aptitude visual/spatial student is stimulated by the class content while concurrently strengthening other dimensions. While working on art projects at their desks, the students were aware of their noise level (interpersonal and intrapersonal), the types of movements they made (bodily/kinesthetic), and the impact of their choices on the rabbits (naturalistic). The students like to see and interact with the rabbits, so they learn to control their predatory—perhaps even carnivorous—tendencies to make the rabbits feel safe enough to interact with them.

Many teachers at UHMS are musical and use music in their teaching. In grade-level classrooms I heard students playing instruments, echoing rhythm patterns, and singing songs. I saw a song tree on which were posted all the songs known by the students. A kindergarten teacher used songs to transition between activities and adjust the noise level in the room. With a Lamb Chop puppet and a killer Bette Midler impersonation, she improvised an entire song around a poem she was presenting that day. The children had memorized the Gingerbread Man's lines in the story and sang his part "Run, run, run as fast as you can. You can't catch me I'm the Gingerbread Man." The students had a collective memory of the tune for the refrain and settled on a comfortable pitch on their own, as they might do on a playground. Students also led body percussion call-and-response patterns to signal cleanup. When students see the adults in their world making music and facilitating musical exploration, it is a powerful affirmation of music's essential place within education.

Essentialists (visual/spatial, bodily/kinesthetic, music) integrate other subjects and processes into their classes as well. Two music essentialists teach at UHMS: Lillie Feierabend and Laura Deutsch. Both deliver high-quality instruction incorporating moving, singing, playing, reading, and writing. They also teach parts of speech, body awareness, sense of self, responsibility for behavior toward others, and many more concepts from other classes. Ms. Feierabend also teaches music in the preschool program. In addition, the music essentialists offer musical resources to the staff and lead activities in the Agora. They are essential to the school and serve as mentors to the wider community, hosting observers and mentoring student teachers from the University of Hartford.

Outcomes

Students see and hear a consistent message that music is important, music is a normal part of daily life and, for those who are especially interested and adept at music, it can be the focus of their lives. I have seen no other school where music is integrated to this degree into every facet of the students' days and educators from different specialties are treated with such equality—as essential. As the UHMS faculty successfully blend multiple ways of learning, so too are children from disparate cultures and resources drawn together, enriching all involved.

The Agora or "meeting place" is a good metaphor for this blending. Here is a space, central in the school, reserved for gatherings—meetings of cultures, minds, and intelligences. Applause can be such a strong motivator, yet in many traditional schools, arts and sports activities are the only events in which young people garner applause. In the Agora, individual musicians may be praised, but community music making is also highly valued. Young people are also lauded for problem solving, poetry, and art. The school provides a meeting place where everyone and everyone's talents are appreciated. The school also provides instruction in interpersonal skills, so learners earn approval from their peers as well as adults, which promotes the feeling of community.

The one salient feature of the UHMS school that may be a challenge to replicate is the sense of unity and collective consciousness of the faculty. When it opened, resources were concentrated in full-time teaching faculty and outreach services to second-language students, at-risk families, and young mothers. The school opened with special education staff, but without area coordinators or curriculum specialists. Instead, funds were allocated for faculty in-service and curriculum writing projects that included essentialists.

While this may be a heavy responsibility for staff and principal, the result seems to be that everyone knows what everyone else is doing. Thus, it is logical that faculty know how to integrate concepts, because they helped write each other's curricula. My perception is that because all faculty are intellectually versatile and committed to teaching, they display a sincere interest in the whole school curricula and acknowledge each teacher's responsibility to teach the whole child. The most outstanding example of this came as I was finishing a kindergarten classroom observation and interview. The teacher, Mrs. Cassella, said, "Thank you for doing music research. Music is such an important part of my classroom and I love being in a place where I can use everything to help children."

Implications

- Inequity in educational opportunities is ubiquitous and insidious, yet when corrected, the momentum for equality can lead to a unique and positive coalition for learning and social change.
- Strong leadership and a schoolwide philosophy of multiple intelligences make this school a place where music and learning thrive. We often ask preservice teachers to write a philosophy statement and seek out an institution compatible with that philosophy. UHMS is proof of how powerful it can be to teach with a common sense of purpose.
- Music specialists can maintain strong programs and cross disciplines when given sufficient support and contact time.
- Urban schools are often required to adopt a curriculum or reform model to unify their approach. Why have we been so complacent in accepting reform models that undermine the role of the arts and arts specialists? The MI option at UHMS bolsters the arts and is projected

to show significant progress in standard mathematical and linguistic testing.

- UHMS benefits from a partnership with the university next door. This university assists with medical staff, counselors, musicians, and other professionals in exchange for opportunities for observation, internships, and insights into innovative practices. Many urban schools have colleges or institutions nearby that can be a source for partnerships. At UHMS, the benefit to preservice teachers, counselors, and nurses is significant.
- When there is music making at every level and from every corner of the institution, learners see that it is normal for music to be infused into life as another form of communication and creativity. In urban education, it takes a *musical* village to raise a child.

Jackson High School (scnc.jps.k12.mi.us/~jhs/)

Introduction

Jackson is a small city in Michigan with a diverse population. The school system includes nine elementary schools, two middle schools, one adult/ alternative education center, and one central high school. In a larger city, one might find two high schools, one with a reputation for performing and another with a reputation for sports or academics or technology. But in Jackson, the high school is the showcase for the musical experiences and outcomes of the district. Because Jackson has remained essentially a one high school city it is a good site in which to study issues and trends in urban education without the specialization or stratification that may occur with multiple high schools.

Jackson High School (JHS) has a population of 1,700. The intersection of the past and present is evident in the structure of the high school itself. The building dates from 1927 and is a large stone fortress, resembling an Ivy League college building. The spires and decorative masonry contrast with energy-efficient windows and handicap access ramps. Inside, there are stone and marble, high ceilings, and wide hallways. The library is a study in contrasts: it is equipped with a fireplace and a computer lab. Similarly, the auditorium still boasts a balcony and decorative plaster work, but a recent renovation equipped it with the latest lighting and sound equipment.

Within this environment, the music department could justifiably choose either a completely traditional performance-based program—band, chorus, and orchestra—or a contemporary music industry program—technology, composition, and a fusion of styles. Mirroring their surroundings, this department is growing and achieving with a blend of traditional and contemporary offerings.

Structure

In the 1990s the music department offerings consisted entirely of performance ensembles. There was a music theory course in the course listing, but it had not been offered in years. Half of the course offerings were band ensembles, due to a recent explosion in band enrollment. In 1990, enrollment in the high school band, chorus, and orchestra totaled 110; in 1999 it reached 307. At that time, an ambitious curricular expansion was proposed in an effort to reach a more diverse student body by providing entry-level ensembles and classes in percussion, guitar, keyboard, and theater technology. Thus, students who did not participate in performing music in middle school had multiple points of entry to reconnect with musical learning.

JHS operates on a traditional six-period schedule, but offers credit for courses taught during an optional seventh period (see table 14.1). In addition to the credit-bearing courses, the department fields a marching band and produces a musical in the spring. There are numerous chamber groups, such as flute ensemble, that provide opportunities to perform and create. When the administration noticed a significant rise in academically at-risk freshmen (students who failed at least math and language arts in their first semester) they formed a special group of faculty to focus on academic skills, life skills, and self-esteem. A group of after-school electives was created to engage the at-risk students in creative and practical skills, such as cooking and consumer education. The orchestra teacher—a musician of many talents—offered to teach a Korean drumming ensemble that became a popular option for the at-risk students.

Jackson schools employ four music educators whose primary responsibilities are at the high school. Offerings and enrollment in spring of 2005 are listed in table 14.1.

Observations

During my visits to JHS I devoted more time to the course offerings, less to the traditional bands, choirs, and orchestra. The instruction in these traditional ensembles seemed on par with instruction in many systems with a few exceptions: (1) to help the faculty individualize instruction the ensembles are scheduled in manageable sizes that can be combined when necessary for special events; (2) a percussion specialist was hired to teach a percussion class and provide specialized instruction for the percussion section during larger band rehearsals; and (3) there is a refreshingly high degree of coordination and cooperation among levels: for example, there is an emphasis on rote-before-note teaching of traditional folk melodies at the early grades that is continued at the high school in warm-up and creativity exercises, and all faculty, including elementary, are invited to marching band camp to assist in sectionals and show design. This provides an extended period for the faculty

Table 14.1. Jackson High School Music Courses

Course	Enrollment
Percussion Class	18
Guitar Class	18
Electronic Music sect 1	22
Electronic Music sect 2	21
Play Production	83
Orchestra	34
Jazz Ensemble	15
Jazz Band	15
Euphony Choir	25
Varsity Choir	43
Concert Band	13
Cadet Band	45
Symphony Band	45
Varsity Band	54
Varsity Wind Ensemble	38
Total Enrollment	489

to work together and assess the outcomes of many aspects of their instruction. It has become a tradition with the faculty and is perpetuated primarily by positive and respectful collegial relationships. Beyond the aforementioned elements, one hears appropriate literature and quality performance levels in the traditional ensembles.

Guitar class is designed for students from many backgrounds: those who play other instruments, those with limited guitar skills, and those with no prior experience. The school purchased a set of inexpensive acoustic guitars for class use. The diversity of learners creates a myriad of learning styles with preferences for rote-learning, note-learning, chord progressions, melodic playing, and a variety of genres. The instructor uses a combination of percussion and guitar teaching techniques and materials gleaned from world drumming and MENC workshops. It is anticipated that the growth in this class will necessitate beginning and advanced sections in the near future.

What was originally proposed as a keyboard class has become a sophisticated electronic composition, sampling, sequencing, and mixing course taught in a lab with PCs and keyboards. As with the guitar class, the students have a variety of backgrounds; most love music and the music business but have little formal training. It was evident that Electronic Music was the highlight of many students' day. They arrive at class early and immediately choose a workstation. There is some discussion of school events, but more conversation about projects they are working on for this class: "Check out this beat" and "Are you gonna use this track" and "Show me what you got done so far." The predominant genre is hip-hop. The instructor earns the students' respect by being current with both musical styles and technology. The chief management issue is pulling temporarily distracted students back from websites or email.

Because rap and hip-hop artists sample from many styles, the instructor has been successful at introducing students to repertoire from folk, jazz, R & B, and classical music as material to be remixed and morphed into contemporary styles. The instructor sets up projects and provides the necessary materials and readiness, then the students work independently (with headphones) for much of the time. The instructor monitors and assists. Every functional workstation was used. Student projects are shared with the class.

Outcomes

The high school demographic is one of significant buying power. Thus, you know you are engaging students—especially urban students with limited resources—when they invest in your subject. The guitar instructor finds that many students become highly motivated to continue learning, seek outside instruction, and purchase their own instruments. The instructor facilitates this by directing parents to reputable dealers who specialize in beginner instruments and advising parents on what to look for when purchasing a guitar. Likewise, students find the Electronic Music class so stimulating that they purchase software to install on home computers. In an age when the "technical divide" keeps some low socioeconomic learners from achieving their potential, the Electronic Music class was a factor in motivating some students and families to find funds to acquire equipment to continue their work at home.

While I am a staunch advocate for active music making and performing ensembles, I believe that music on the concert stage and athletic scene lacks appeal (or perhaps relevance) for some students in urban settings. By allowing for multiple points and levels of entry, and various means of expression, the music department at JHS is serving a broader cross section of its student population.

Here is one possible measuring stick. If you collect data on the ethnicity and socioeconomic status of the students in your secondary music ensembles and compare it to the demographics of your entire high school population, how similar are the two data sets? If they are similar, then congratulate yourselves. If they are dissimilar, then ask yourselves, as the faculty at JHS did, "Can we broaden our philosophy of music education and expand our vocabulary to appeal to different kinds of music learners?"

While that data is beyond the scope of this article, the faculty of JHS know they are moving in that direction and continue to make great strides. In so doing, they become eligible for more grants, touch more lives, and become more firmly rooted in the life of the school and community. In addition, they offer classes, many as electives, that fill needs and schedule requirements for students. If there is a threat of faculty layoffs, it is not economically advantageous to eliminate a music position because the students that were being served, particularly in guitar and electronic music classes, would need another option, requiring additional staffing elsewhere. When one considers the growth in Jackson High School music—nearly three whole positions added, an increase in enrollment of 345%, and greater equity in serving students—then their commonsense restructuring and refocusing would seem a worthwhile pursuit.

It appears that music educators can lead urban faculty in responding to different challenges and demographics in urban settings. They can meet the needs of a greater percentage of the student body without sacrificing enrollment or quality of their traditional performing ensembles. When you gather a faculty with diverse skills and a willingness to adapt instruction to meet the needs of learners—particularly at-risk learners—you have a resourceful and chameleon-like team able to react to the ever-changing landscape of urban education. In addition, the energy created by learning new repertoire and techniques is transferred to energize teaching and learning in the classroom. These observations are consistent with the results of Shields's (2001) study of urban adolescents in music classes.

Implications

- A unified faculty with a commonsense and compelling proposal can affect significant structural change.
- Educating administrators about the arts is a worthwhile pursuit, as is keeping abreast of current trends and technology. Being a team player when the administration launches a challenging pilot program raises your standing; being a stunning success makes you formidable.
- Good musicians have the skills to understand and embrace a variety of genres and styles; good educators are lifelong learners. Adapting instruction to diverse learners may keep the music department from appearing elitist and unapproachable to the general faculty, students, and community.
- If the music faculty is not culturally akin to the majority of the student body, they can somewhat mitigate this dissonance by being open and responsive to the lives and tastes of their students. There can be flexibility without compromising standards.
- This case is primarily a study in restructuring and benefits from reimagining a music department. There were no external partners present other than portions of funds from granting institutions for some equipment and staffing. Rather, the partnerships seem to be internal: within the JHS music department as well as faculty in theater and technology, and

among their music colleagues at the middle and elementary schools. These partnerships are next-door and across town. They are forged through cooperation and respect.
- Urban students are clamoring for arts offerings. Through enrollment, enthusiasm, and financial commitment, they assure us: If you offer and staff it, we will come.

CONCLUSION

Having spent years listening to the trials and tribulations of urban music educators and watching them (justifiably) flee to the suburbs or leave teaching, it was refreshing to interview successful teachers who liked their jobs. Having witnessed substandard support for music and the arts, and the shell game of showcasing arts magnet schools while most schools go underfunded and unstaffed, it was a joy to see students who did not have to audition to have high-quality musical opportunities in their schools. While these three case studies are unique, I firmly believe that their examples of courage and cooperative spirit can bring about much needed change.

- As neighborhoods and cities rebuild, so too should schools, with input and commitment from all local stakeholders. Teachers can be agents of change.
- It is not easy to be an administrator who fights for the arts—partially because the arts are complicated and costly, and sometimes benefits become apparent far into the future. We in higher education must do more to educate potential administrators. Arts advocates must join local search committees and demand that any potential candidate have an awareness of the importance of the arts in education.
- Although these three sites all have strict security and are in urban areas with real problems, within their walls there was a palpable sense of calmness and safety. One reason for this is harmony among the staff—respect and goodwill among teachers that extends to the music teacher. We underestimate the power of mutual respect. Students and parents follow the example of teachers. By being competent and cooperative, and engaging in beneficial partnerships, music educators, and by extension their subject, earn the respect of the school community. This may require stepping outside one's comfort zone and teaching in a manner that is different than one was taught, but these adjustments may yield great results.
- In order to educate the school and community about the value of the arts one must win them over one person and one family at a time with music that is recognized as masterful and music that is relevant. When major structural or curricular reforms begin, we must not abdicate our responsibility to advocate for our subject.

- Intrascholastic and extrascholastic music partnerships can be beneficial. It is important that all partners have a stake in the outcome and that the focus is music and music learning.
- While popular music and music reproduction devices may change, young people continue to have an endearing fascination and love for music. The more musical models, styles, and representations, the better. While music is the domain of music specialists, it does not belong to us. In these studies, the music educators were catalysts for a culture of music: not the nucleus, but part of a network of music teachers, learners, and makers.

REFERENCES

Gardner, H. (1999). *Intelligence reframed.* New York: Basic.

Georgia State University School of Music. (2004). Georgia State University School of Music Programs Earn National Recognition. Retrieved on September 1, 2005, from www.music.gsu.edu/articleview.aspx?id = 71.

Myers, D. E. (2003). Quest for excellence: The transforming role of university–community collaboration in music teaching and learning. *Arts Education Policy Review* 105(1), 5–12.

Patton, M. Q. (2002). *Qualitative research and evaluation methods.* Thousand Oaks, CA: Sage.

Shields, C. (2001). Music education and mentoring as intervention for at-risk urban adolescents: Their self-perceptions, opinions, and attitudes. *Journal of Research in Music Education* 49(3), 273–286.

SUPPLEMENTAL READING

Delpit, L. (1995). *Other people's children.* New York: The New Press.

Fiske, E. B. (Ed.). (1999). *Champions of change: The impact of the arts on learning* (Report No. SO-031-346). Washington, DC: President's Committee on the Arts and the Humanities; Arts Education Partnership (ERIC Document Reproduction Service No. ED435581).

Gardner, H. (1983). *Frames of mind: The theory of multiple intelligences.* New York: Basic.

Hoerr, T. (2002). *Becoming a multiple intelligences school.* Alexandria, VA: Association for Supervision and Curriculum Development.

Krueger, P. J. (2002). Breaking the isolation: Beginning music teacher views on collaboration. In C. M. Conway (Ed.), *Great beginnings for music teachers: Mentoring and supporting new teachers.* Reston, VA: MENC.

Myers, D. E. (1996). *Beyond tradition: Partnerships among orchestras, schools, and communities.* Atlanta: Georgia State University.

Oreck, B., Baum, S., & McCartney, H. (2000). *Artistic talent development for urban youth: The promise and the challenge* (Report No. EC-308-349). Storrs, CT: National Research Center on the Gifted and Talented (ERIC Document Reproduction Service No. ED451665).

15

Learning through Music Creates Learning for Life

Jonathan C. Rappaport

PREFACE

As a music educator with over 35 years of practical experience teaching music on all levels of public school education, I am delighted to be part of this important conversation. As a head of a school where I can make important decisions about the music program, I feel I bring a unique perspective to this dialogue. Often there is not much discussion between teachers, administrators, state departments of education, and teacher-training institutions. Music educators must stand up and be heard—it is not enough simply to do a great job as a music teacher or administrator. Music teachers must promote what is important and let others know that music education is critical for the full human development of the children of the world. I urge my colleagues to extend the conversation started in this important book in any way possible. Please join professional organizations and take leadership roles; become involved in writing state curriculum frameworks or local arts curricula; and make presentations to administrators, parents, and school boards. Together, we can make a significant difference.

LEARNING THROUGH MUSIC CREATES LEARNING FOR LIFE

Public education in the urban and rural areas of the United States has been in crisis for many decades. The evidence documenting these problems is overwhelmingly clear. Since the 1970s, the National Assessment of Educational Progress (NAEP) *Trends in Academic Progress* has provided data related to the nation's ongoing concerns about the achievement gap between affluent suburban schools and urban/rural districts (National Center for Educational Studies, 2000). While these results are often reported as disparities between whites and students of color, the issue is primarily one of enormous economic inequality. A study released in the fall of 2003 by the Educational Testing Service revealed that Black and Hispanic students are "disadvantaged" compared with White and Asian students in 14 indicators linked to learning (*Parsing the Achievement Gap*, 2003). This problem is not only an American one: A 2002 report by UNICEF found wide achievement gaps between students in some of the world's richest countries. The study found a correlation between children's family backgrounds—particularly socioeconomic status—and their achievement in school (A League Table of Disadvantage in Rich Nations, 2002).

Numerous "reasons" are given to explain this achievement gap. Many problems beset schools that serve at-risk students, including insufficient funding and a host of social problems surrounding poverty, malnutrition, and lack of adequate support systems. Fortunately, research from the past 10 to 15 years suggests promising methodologies and approaches that address the educational needs of impoverished children. For example, Clara Park, in several separate studies from 1997–2000, showed that a wide variety of immigrant populations (Asian, Mexican, Armenian American) often have a stronger preference for kinesthetic and tactile learning styles (Park, 2001). African American psychologist Barbara J. Shade cites Charles Keil's observation that "the prominence of the aural perception, oral expression and kinesic codes . . . sharply demarcate the culture from the white world" (Shade and Jones, 1991, p. 235).

Obviously one can never interpret this to mean that all children of any particular ethnic or national group learn only kinesthetically or aurally. However, it is essential that teachers acknowledge the rich variety of preferred sensory modalities of their students in their classrooms. Such knowledge impacts the selection of teaching style(s) employed with maximum effect. This understanding is of fundamental importance for developing appropriate curricula, pedagogy, and teaching materials in order to meet the diverse learning styles of *all* American children.

Other research finds a strong relationship between increased arts education and improved academic achievement. For example, an analysis of the U.S. Department of Education database of 25,000 students over a 10-year period found that students involved in music scored higher on standardized tests and reading proficiency exams. This achievement is regardless of socioeconomic background; in fact, the high level of participation in the arts makes a more significant difference to students from low-income backgrounds. Sustained involvement in music and theater are highly correlated with success in mathematics, reading, history, geography, and citizenship. Music students had higher grades, scored better on standardized tests, and had better attendance records (Caterall, Chapleau, & Iwanaga, 1999).

According to the Boston Foundation's *Boston Indicators Report 2002,*

> economic contraction combined with a sharp downturn in the stock market triggered declining state revenues. Cuts in the state's budget are affecting all sectors—particularly education reform, public health and the arts . . . particularly for low-income and vulnerable populations . . . in Boston.

Undoubtedly most of these conditions are typical of urban centers across the United States. Harsh economic conditions in the city of Boston and elsewhere have seriously impacted academic achievement and high school graduation rates for many children. Other socioeconomic factors contribute to the necessity for schools to address the urgent needs of their urban populations.

One way to address these issues is to infuse one or more domains of arts instruction into the curriculum. This often provides a significant avenue for success in school, improving student attendance and achievement. Unfortunately, elementary schools in urban Massachusetts typically only offer music once a week or visual art once a week, and there are numerous elementary schools with no regular art or music instruction by qualified, licensed teachers. Rarely do urban students have regular, organized instruction in dance or theater. With such limited exposure to the arts, it is not possible to achieve the learning standards of the Massachusetts Arts Curriculum Framework or the National Standards for Arts Education. Additionally, with the directive to improve student achievement by demonstrating adequate yearly progress through the Massachusetts Comprehensive Assessment System (MCAS) and No Child Left Behind guidelines, particularly in English Language Arts and Mathematics, urban classroom teachers typically do not consider arts integration to be a priority in their daily activities.

FOUNDING OF THE CONSERVATORY LAB CHARTER SCHOOL

These educational challenges formed the backdrop for the founding of the Conservatory Lab Charter School (CLCS) by four members of the faculty and staff of the New England Conservatory in 1998. Their intent was to develop an independent public school in downtown Boston that had music at the center of its curriculum. These four founders—Rhoda Bernard, Lyle Davidson, Larry Scripp, and Mary Street—designed a *Learning through Music* conceptual approach to address the achievement gap typical of urban schools. The CLCS opened its doors in September 1999, and since that time has served children grades K–five from the City of Boston. Its primary mission is "to engage all children by using the *Learning through Music* curriculum model to ensure every child's academic, creative, and social success, as validated by qualitative and quantitative measures." The school strives to (a) strengthen the place of the arts as a rigorous, standards-based core academic subject in the regular school curricula, (b) infuse music processes and fundamental concepts across all curricular subjects, and (c) have a positive effect on increased student achievement in other academic areas as well as in socialization and emotional skills.

The school is small, with a total of 132 children. Currently there are over 550 children waiting to enroll in the school. Students are chosen by lottery; there are no admission requirements or expectations of special academic or musical ability. Of the highly diverse student body, 80% are students of color, 73% qualify for free or reduced price lunch, 26% are special-needs students, and 18% are English-language learners.

In support of educational reform, the goal of CLCS is to create an innovative, effective Learning through Music model curriculum. As an overview, the Learning through Music model is based on three overarching principles:

1. *Five processes are intrinsic to learning music—listening, questioning, creating, performing, and reflecting.* These are applied across the school as a fundamental way for children to approach all learning. The five processes require the use of kinesthetic, auditory, and visual modalities of learning. Every child's preferred learning style is accessed while the weaker modalities are strengthened.
2. *Shared fundamental concepts—the natural, authentic, and meaningful ideas that music and academic subjects share—create connections for teachers and students to explore, with the goal of strengthening and enhancing student achievement.* These shared concepts form the links enabling the integration of music into academic subjects.
3. *Multiple literacies reinforce one another—learning another form of symbolic decoding—sight singing and writing music notation—helps give fluency to linguistic and numeric literacies.* Research indicates there is a strong correlation between music literacy and improved reading and mathematic achievement. (Gardiner, Fox, Knowles, & Jeffrey, 1996)

The three overarching principles described above are being used to build a strong and replicable Learning through Music curriculum model in the important ways that follow.

A Comprehensive Music Program

CLCS students in grades kindergarten through five are provided with daily music instruction via the Kodály concept to promote each child's creativity and natural love of music. Students in grades one through five take violin lessons twice a week with a modified Suzuki approach. All students have numerous performance opportunities throughout the year.

Unlike most public schools where students attend music classes infrequently, students at the CLCS have a 45-minute general music class each day. These classes build musical literacy through singing, movement, solfège, music reading, and rhythm/pitch studies. Application of musical knowledge and music literacy is applied to sight singing, the recorder, Orff percussion instruments, and computer notation programs. The program, based upon the Kodály concept, is highly sequential and is thoroughly aligned with the National Music Standards and the Massachusetts Arts Curriculum Framework.

The performing arts of dance, music, and theater often are treated as "recreating" arts in as much as previously created works are learned and then performed. The CLCS daily general music model provides the time, skill, and content knowledge to enable students to become *musically literate*, giving the necessary skills to create original musical compositions, to improvise, and to arrange music. This allows students to go far beyond only responding to or performing existing works. The process of gaining music literacy is critical not only for developing lifelong musical skills, but developing correlated skills in other subject areas as well. The CLCS intends eventually to investigate the notion that the ability to decode the sound of musical notation in one's mind, much the way an educated person reads a book silently, has a strong correlation with developing decoding skills in mathematics and language.

Starting in the first grade, students study the violin through a modified Suzuki approach in semiprivate lessons and in small group ensemble classes. The school provides every child with an appropriately sized violin. The use of a real (but technically difficult) instrument affords the opportunity for extensive musical learning, development of strong inner-hearing auditory skills, and social/emotional development as students learn to perform in groups, to practice, and to control their bodies in the complex ways needed to master the instrument. Through violin studies, children learn self-discipline (they are required to practice the violin at home each night), and gain a sense of community (they interact regularly in group lessons and group performances). At the CLCS, the Suzuki-based violin program helps students to develop refined musical intonation, as well as fine-motor skills, poise, focus, and positive behavior.

Students perform frequently throughout the academic year. Weekly assemblies showcase student achievement, and provide teachers and students with the opportunity to share what they have learned in their Learning through Music activities. In addition, students perform in winter and spring concerts held at the school or at New England Conservatory's renowned Jordan Hall. Multiple opportunities to perform help to build a positive school climate of accomplishment, respect, poise, and self-confidence. This intensive study of music not only meets, but also exceeds, the learning standards of the Massachusetts Arts Curriculum Framework and the National Standards for Arts Education in creating, performing, and responding to the arts.

Academic Enhancement Lessons (AELs) and Thematic Interdisciplinary Projects (TIPs)

Learning through Music is marked by collaborative planning and implementation of interdisciplinary lessons. This is organized in two ways. academic enhancement lessons (AELs) tend to be short-term, lasting one or two lessons. Thematic interdisciplinary projects (TIPs) are long-term, lasting as long as a full semester. Both explore and experiment with the many ways that music and other academic subjects stimulate one another and increase learning. These lessons and long-term projects feature concepts that are shared between music and academic subjects.

Sample interdisciplinary Learning through Music AELs:

- Math and music: Students learn addition and subtraction in math class, and then compare rhythmic patterns in four-beat musical phrases to count the number of sounds per pattern. Next, the students vary the patterns, either by adding or taking away sounds. Further extensions of this lesson would be to create rhythmic or melodic compositions to go with specific forms, and then to sing or play them on violin or recorder.
- Language arts and music: Students identify character and plot development in short stories they have read. In related music classes, they sing and learn about ballads—stories that are sung. Next, the students identify character and plot development within the ballads, and compare them with those found in the short stories.
- Science and music: Students classify the various plants they have been studying and then create their own classification scheme for various types of folk, classical, jazz, and popular musical idioms.
- Social studies and music: Students enliven the study of the American Revolution by learning and singing songs of the period. They also create their own lyrics for well-known revolutionary songs, such as "Yankee Doodle," that describe the facts of history they have studied.

Music and classroom teachers co-plan and coteach these interdisciplinary lessons, providing a cohesive context for the students' studies across the curriculum. This integration of subjects engages student interest by providing depth of analysis, and it amplifies student understanding by making important connections between disciplines.

Thematic interdisciplinary projects (TIPs) bring music together with a social studies topic and/or may include language arts, science, and math.

Sample interdisciplinary Learning through Music TIPs:

- Social studies: The third-grade class studies the Wampanoag tribe of Massachusetts. Students listen to and sing Native American lullabies and compose their own lullaby in music class. Together in a group, the students write the lyrics and music, and then play and sing the lullaby at a special performance.
- Science and math: The second-grade teacher uses recorders and flutes of different lengths. Students measure and play the instruments, discovering the relationship between an instrument's length and the range of pitches it produces. This project can be extended into the study of vibration and frequency in older grades, and children can record their observations in an essay or journal entry. Further extensions could include students making their own instruments of varying sizes, applying the mathematical and scientific lessons learned, and then composing an original piece of music to perform on the newly created instruments.

CLCS teachers love to teach in this school for a variety of reasons. Teachers comment that the "walls breathe music." Even classroom teachers who may not have formal musical training recognize that the music component gives the school a special feeling. The use of music as an integrated way of learning academics also challenges every teacher to be creative, try new things, and adapt and revise teaching strategies and approaches on a regular basis. The "laboratory" environment of the school encourages experimentation and gets the faculty's "creative juices" flowing! The collegial atmosphere, where classroom and music teachers co-plan and coteach integrated lessons, also contributes to the unique atmosphere of the school. The success of the school is due, in no small part, to the enthusiastic "buy-in" of the teaching staff to the Learning through Music component of the school.

Music Listening Program

Research suggests that music can be a powerful tool for social and emotional development. The school has a goal for students to listen to music daily. Students are also encouraged to select the music that they listen to for specific purposes and discuss the appropriateness of their choices. Teachers at the CLCS have experimented with a variety of ways to use music listening and include some of the following on a regular basis:

- Teachers use music to help students move from one task to another.
- Students listen to music and write reflections on what they have heard, both in the general classroom as well as music class.
- Both teachers and students design expressive movement to accompany some music listening. Often such expressive movement indicates the form or some other musical element that is present in the listening example.

With listening as one of the five processes at the core of the school, this program will continue to expand and be evaluated for its effectiveness.

To our knowledge, the CLCS is unique with the combination of three distinctive prongs in the Learning through Music program: (a) an elementary daily music model, grades kindergarten through five, (b) twice-weekly violin instruction, grades one through five, and (c) integrated learning, grades kindergarten through five, using music as an entry point for academic understanding, knowledge, and skills.

CHOICE OF MUSIC METHODOLOGIES

Two widely known methodologies are being used for the music components of this project. The daily general music component uses the Kodály concept of music education, named after Hungarian composer and educator Zoltán Kodály (1882–1967). This approach was chosen because it uses culturally relevant folk materials that are meaningful to the students. Using multicultural folk songs that represent students' cultural heritages is critical in validating our diverse student body. Kodály stressed the use of quality musical materials, beginning with folk songs, which he called the child's "musical mother tongue." The Kodály concept is based on the idea that "music is for everyone" and not just for the "talented." Therefore it stresses high expectations for learning musical skills and knowledge for all students. The highly sequential approach stresses hands-on, participatory music making through the human voice and body and gradually extracts melodic and rhythmic elements from the music, leading to musical literacy. Acute auditory skills and student skill development such as in-tune singing, beat and rhythm development, and the ability to sight sing and compose melodies are dramatic in Kodály-trained students. Such skills also increase the likelihood of success in instrumental music study. Additionally, the CLCS is fortunate that there is a nationally recognized Kodály training center within Boston, the Kodály

Music Institute (KMI), located at the New England Conservatory (NEC), which provides professional development and support.

While the Kodály approach has been used extensively throughout the United States since the mid-1960s, the usual model is typically once or twice-weekly instruction. In Hungary, it was originally conceived as a daily model, and the CLCS is replicating that model. It is a core belief of the school that the specific process of learning music through the Kodály approach, including the comprehensive development of specific musical knowledge and skills (especially the ability to sight-read music), has a profound effect on the cognitive development of children. Because reading and writing music is a complex language-decoding skill unto itself, it is believed that the effects of Kodály training on math, reading, and writing decoding skills are considerable.

Numerous scientific studies correlate Kodály-based music study with increased academic and social learning for students at the stage of education of the CLCS. In a study reported in *Nature*, grade-one and grade-two students from two elementary schools showed important gains in reading and still more striking gains in mathematics after Kodály training. Students in the experimental group caught up with or exceeded the "control" students, even though the test group had started considerably behind the "control" group in these skills. Researchers noted similar gains in classroom attitude and behavior ratings. In three similar studies, researchers noted comparable gains in mathematics skills and classroom behavior (Gardiner, Fox, Knowles, & Jeffrey, 1996; Gardiner & Olson, 1999; and Gardiner, 2000). Additionally, evidence was found suggesting that one specific musical skill emphasized in early Kodály training—singing on pitch—was especially related to progress in math. Rhythm skills were connected to both reading and math, with some other skills more closely related to progress in reading alone. Finally, in a study recently concluded in Bristol/Warren, Rhode Island, Gardiner found that Kodály training contributed to not only math skill, but also accelerated learning in math (2003a). It seems that pitch acquisition and rhythm skills both have a role in a math–music interrelationship. This study also found a strong association between musical learning and the learning and acceleration of the development of writing skills. This may be due to the interrelationship of language writing with the writing of rhythmic and melodic music notation. This last relationship also appeared in another study by Gardiner (2003b) done in the Cambridge, Massachusetts, public schools. Most of these studies have involved children who receive music instruction twice weekly. The CLCS program provides Kodály instruction on a daily basis, and it will be interesting to see if the effects noted in previous studies will become accelerated through planned research over the course of the next three years at the CLCS.

The Conservatory Lab Charter School uses a modified Suzuki approach for the twice-weekly violin component. This method was developed by Japanese violinist and educator Dr. Shinichi Suzuki (1898–1998). The CLCS chose violin instruction via Suzuki because it provides children with a "real musical instrument" that can be played as a solo or ensemble instrument and comes in a size appropriate to the size of each child. Playing the violin requires the development of fine-motor control, and this is important to children's overall development. Suzuki-based lessons insist upon strong auditory development, listening skills, and concentration, all of which coordinate easily with the Kodály approach.

Some of the ways that CLCS has modified the Suzuki approach include the following:

- Culturally appropriate folk materials have been added to the traditional Suzuki musical materials.
- Parental participation is not required during school hours (although the school does offer parent lessons in late afternoons or Saturdays to encourage their participation).
- Both group instruction and semiprivate lessons are offered.
- Music notation is introduced sooner than in the traditional Suzuki approach.
- Lessons do not start in our earliest grade (K) so the children will have general music classes for one year prior to commencing violin study.

Dr. Suzuki realized that children the world over learn to speak their native language with ease. He began to apply the basic principles of language acquisition to the learning of music, and, similar to Zoltán Kodály, called his method the "mother-tongue" approach. He believed that the early years are crucial for developing mental processes and muscle coordination. Since children learn words after hearing them spoken hundreds of times by others, listening to music every day is important, and this should begin at birth. Formal training may begin at age three or four, but it is never too late to begin. Constant repetition is essential in learning to play an instrument—children do not learn a word or piece of music and then discard it. They add it to their vocabulary or repertoire, gradually using it in new and more sophisticated ways.

Suzuki also felt children should learn an instrument together with other children. For this reason, children in the CLCS program participate in regular semiprivate and group lessons each week, as well as in regular Friday assemblies and other performances. Such experiences help children to learn from and be motivated by one another.

Graded repertoire is another important component. Children do not practice exercises to learn to talk, but use language for its natural purpose of communication and self-expression. Similarly, the Suzuki repertoire is designed to present technical problems in the context of the music rather than through dry technical exercises.

The Suzuki approach has been researched extensively. Using four- and five-year-old Suzuki violin students, a McMaster University research team assessed students using the Human Neural Plasticity Lab where researchers have determined that musical training does more than just enlarge the part of the brain called Heschl's gyrus. It also boosts the brain's response to music—in its activation of neurons (nerve cells) by music—especially when you hear the instrument on which you trained. Additionally, the development of the Suzuki children's sound-processing auditory cortexes was advanced by two to three years over those of nonmusic students (Shahin, Roberts, & Trainor, 2004).

Another important ingredient in the success of both the Kodály and Suzuki approaches is the development of "timing," the ability to maintain an even internal pulse. Several research studies have indicated that timing correlates with abilities in broader academic learning. Kuhlman and Schweinhart (1999) found that timing was not only fundamental to movement and dance, but it affected sports skills, musical performance, speech flow, and the performance of timed-motor tasks. In previous studies, timing was shown to be related to overall school achievement including math and reading (Weikart, Schweinhart, & Larner, 1987), self-control, and gross motor skills (Kiger, 1994; Mitchell, 1994). Other studies indicate that fewer than 10% of kindergarten children and fewer than 15% of first-grade children could independently feel and express the steady beat of recorded music. Even older children, who are developmentally more advanced, have difficulties: less than 50% of children in grades four through six could walk to the steady beat of a musical selection. Children's personal tempo has been found to correlate with achievement test scores in grades one and two, and gross motor skills and reading group level in grades one, three, and five. Some of the results of the timing study suggest that there is a correlation between timing and the ability to attend to a task over long periods of time, with academic achievement, and with parental income and education (Kuhlman and Schweinhart, 1999).

A LEARNING LABORATORY

With increasing national interest in the impact of music on children's capacity and readiness to learn, the CLCS is a singular environment where curriculum, best instructional practices, and assessment tools are being developed and implemented over time. A continual process of professional development involving teachers and outside specialists has resulted in the expansion of these materials along with the simultaneous evaluation of student performance. The CLCS is in a unique position to use the results of this groundbreaking work to build a new model for reforming public schools. This is especially critical as the school examines ways of closing the achievement gap typical of ethnically diverse and impoverished children in inner-city schools.

ASSESSMENT

The CLCS conducts intensive assessments throughout the year to evaluate the success of the program on student achievement. Children in grades three, four, and five regularly take the Massachusetts Comprehensive Assessment System (MCAS) state exams in March or May of each year in reading, writing, and mathematics. To date, CLCS students are achieving significantly higher in MCAS science than their counterparts in the Boston Public Schools, and sometimes higher in the MCAS English language arts and math. The school conducts internally developed measurements in math and writing four or more times annually, the Developmental Reading Assessment (DRA) three times yearly, and internally developed Essential Skills Tests in music and for violin. As the music program has strengthened and the staff has refined curriculum, the CLCS sees increased achievement not only in music, but in traditional academic areas as well. The school continues to have a strong attendance record, and it is clear that the music instruction and performance opportunities have instilled poise and self-confidence while developing presentation and socialization skills. The school anticipates that these trends will strengthen each year as the school constantly adapts and refines curricula, teaching strategies, and implementation of Learning through Music components. The school will soon begin its eighth year as a music-based charter public school. Its goal is to continue refining the Learning through Music curriculum model in order to enhance learning across academic disciplines.

REPLICATING THE LEARNING
THROUGH MUSIC MODEL

The Learning through Music (LTM) model of extensive music integration across all disciplines is replicable in other settings. The Conservatory Lab Charter School has been in existence for seven years and has spent considerable resources developing, refining, implementing, reexamining, and further refining the various components of the program. It has well-developed products, already in place, including documented academic enhancement lessons (AELs) and thematic interdisciplinary projects (TIPs), as well as curricula aligned to state frameworks and national learning standards. The school intends to further refine these materials during future years so that they may soon be shared with other schools.

RESEARCH STUDIES AT THE CLCS

As the Conservatory Lab Charter School has a high "at-risk" population from urban Boston that includes 73% of students at or below the poverty level, significant populations of special education students (26%), and a large number of English-language learners (18%), the school believes that the Learning through Music model will point to ways in which significant inroads may be made in closing the achievement gap so typical between inner-city children and their suburban counterparts. Beginning in the fall of 2005, a scientifically based research project at the school was begun by well-known university research centers in the Boston area. The study's focus is on preliteracy reading component subskills as correlated to music subskills, beginning with kindergarten children. The purposes of this study include the following:

- To examine the relationship (correlations) between skills across the musical and linguistic domains in kindergarten children, with a focus on preliteracy component subskills.
- To assess whether there are significant changes in the children's preliteracy component subskills after their participation in the CLCS kindergarten music curriculum.

It is expected that a detailed analysis of these subskills will enable the school to accurately diagnose potential reading problems early on. This analysis will guide the school in addressing student weaknesses not only with traditional academic remediation, but also with increased music learning. This work has the power to have a dramatic impact on our knowledge of how children learn, how music affects the development of specific skills, and how educators may use this knowledge to more effectively help all children to learn and reach high academic standards. Additional studies will be conducted by other area universities and researchers beginning in 2006–2007.

PARTNERING WITH AREA INSTITUTIONS

The CLCS has initiated extensive partnerships with state agencies and area institutions. The first two include the Massachusetts Cultural Council (MCC) and the Massachusetts Department of Education (MA DOE). Both of these state agencies are positioned and have the resources and connections for regional and national dissemination of curriculum, lesson plans/units, and project research findings, and they are partnering with the CLCS for several grants to further research and dissemination. The CLCS and the MCC will make presentations to state professional organization conventions and national conferences, and prepare articles for appropriate professional research and education publications.

Several Boston-area universities, colleges, and conservatories are also partnering with the CLCS. These include New England Conservatory, Boston University, Tufts University, Harvard University, Wheelock College, Berklee College of Music, and Wheaton College. Several of these colleges have developed a professional development relationship with the CLCS and frequently send student interns to observe or for student-teaching practicums at the school.

The CLCS is committed to becoming one of the finest elementary schools in the nation over the next few years. The school believes its unique Learning through Music program will be a trailblazer for educational reform, showing the importance of music and the arts in providing a quality education for all children. Instead of being a frill, music will be seen for what it really is: an essential, core-curricular subject that creates an environment of listening, questioning, creating, performing, and reflecting that has a profound effect on the academic, artistic, creative, and social development of children.

REFERENCES

A League Table of Disadvantage in Rich Nations. (2002). *Innocenti report card, 4, November 2002.* As retrieved July 2005, from www.unicef-icdc.org/publications/pdf/ repcard4e.pdf. Florence, Italy: United Nations Children's Fund, Innocenti Research Center.

Boston indicators report 2002. (2002). Boston: The Boston Foundation.

Caterall, J. S., Chapleau, R., & Iwanaga, J. (1999). Involvement in the arts and human development: General involvement and intensive involvement in music and theater arts. *The imagination project.* Los Angeles: UCLA Graduate School of Education and Information Studies.

Gardiner, M. F. (2000). Music, learning, and behavior: A case for mental stretching. *Journal for Learning through Music,* Summer 2000.

Gardiner, M. F. (2003a). Unpublished paper.

Gardiner, M. F. (2003b). Unpublished paper.

Gardiner, M. F., Fox, A., Knowles, F., & Jeffrey, D. (1996). Learning improved by arts training. *Nature,* 381, 284.

Gardiner, M. F., & Olson, E. (1999). Arts training and academic progress. Paper presented at the University of Maryland, Fowler.

Kiger, J. E. (1994). Relationship among the development of fundamental motor skills, basic timing, and academic performance in elementary school age children. Unpublished paper, University of Wisconsin-Whitewater.

Kuhlman, K., & Schweinhart, L. J (1999). Timing in child development. High/Scope Educational Research Foundation, as retrieved June 2003, from www.highscope.org/Research/TimingPaper/timingstudy.htm.

Mitchell, D. L. (1994). The relationship between rhythmic competency and academic performance in first grade children. (Doctoral dissertation, University of Central Florida Department of Exceptional and Physical Education.)

National Center for Education Studies. (2000). National assessment shows encouraging trends in mathematics performance. As retrieved July 2005, from nces.ed.gov/pressrelease/rel2000/8_24_00.asp. Washington, DC: National Center for Education Studies.

Park, C. C. (2001). Learning style preferences of Armenian, African, Hispanic, Hmong, Korean, Mexican, and Anglo students in American secondary schools. *Springer Science and Business Media B.V.*, 4(2), 175–191.

Parsing the achievement gap: Baselines for tracking progress. (2003). As retrieved July 2005, from www.ets.org/research/pic/parsing.pdf. Princeton, NJ: Education Testing Service.

Shade, B. J., & Jones, R. L. (Ed.). (1991). *African American patterns of cognition. Black psychology.* 3rd ed. Berkeley, CA: Cobb & Henry.

Shahin, A., Roberts, L. E., & Trainor, L. J. (2004). Enhancement of auditory cortical development by musical experience in children. *Neuroreport*, 15(12), 1917–1921.

Social Science Data Analysis Network (2000). As retrieved April 2005, from www.CensusScope.org/us/s25/rank_education_withouths_2000.html. University of Michigan: Social Science Data Analysis Network.

Weikart, P. S., Schweinhart, L. J., & Larner, M. (1987). Movement curriculum improves children's rhythmic competence. *High/Scope ReSource*, 6(1), 8–10.

IV

SCHOOL REFORM

16

Arts for All Sakes: Arts-Infused Curriculum as a School Reform Model

Susan Snyder

The arts are essential for students in urban schools. Music and the other arts can and should be at the center of school change, the core of arts-based schools. They allow teachers to tap into students' cultural backgrounds, provide diverse routes to learning, and enable new strategies for children who may not fit the stereotypical mold of "student." The arts are about empowering learners, and the social/emotional advantages of arts-infused learning are paramount to success in school and life. For disenfranchised students and teachers, this approach affords a new opportunity for success.

Our culture has changed, our demographics have changed, and if schools are to succeed, they too must change. School change must be a thoughtful, intentional process of problem solving that results in a transition from less effective practice to something different, and hopefully better. Although the idea of change is exciting, even invigorating, the act of making change requires shifts in mental and physical schema. Change can be threatening and will meet with resistance at some point from someone. There is no substitute for careful planning and goal setting before beginning.

Music educators have a responsibility to consider the role of music education in light of cultural changes. Imaginative and process-oriented music instruction that focuses on communicating in music through creating, performing, and responding is known to impact student learning in all disciplines (Fiske, 1999). It is the teaching of musical processes, rather than the teaching of the concepts and skills in other disciplines through music, that provides students with a foundation for all learning, and skills for living productive lives.

A FOUNDATIONAL THEORY

In the early 1970s, integrated curriculum models emerged within and outside the discipline of music. The Comprehensive Musicianship Project and other compositional approaches opened a door to music education that went beyond performance training. Project Zero added more rigorous standards and a model for critical thinking through self and peer assessment. Orff-Schulwerk and jazz education invited improvisation, and an interest in world music led to an exploration of alternate ways to receive, perform, and create music. The technological and media explosion made music experiences available anytime and anywhere.

Outside of music, the teaching of language arts was broadening first through whole language, then the writing process. Mathematics instruction focused on pattern and problem solving. Cooperative learning, constructivist and discovery learning, and portfolio assessment developed, based on emerging information about learning and the brain. By exploring their practice, educators began to construct guidelines for integrated curriculum. One such guideline, *Integrate with Integrity*, was published for music educators in 1996 (Snyder, 1996) and was featured in the *Music Educators Journal* in 2001 (Snyder, 2001). *Integrate with Integrity* developed out of good teaching practice and is based on a number of learning and process theories. These ideas are applicable to a variety of settings and situations, each with unique combinations of expectations, personalities, advantages, and constraints. They have served as a catalyst for change from the individual music or grade-level teacher to the systemic level, and have shown particular success in urban school settings. Our experiences suggest that quality integrated curricula:

- Are based on standards, best practices, and research;
- Honor the integrity of each discipline;
- Focus on deep learning and higher order thinking skills;
- Put student needs at the center of decision making, and include strategies for differentiated instruction, multiple learning modalities, and diversity;
- Are planned and implemented through collaborative teacher teams that may include community members and resources;
- Are responsive to site-specific needs and configurations;
- Include extensive, sequenced professional development and support over a sufficient period of time to assure sustainability; and
- Include formative and summative assessment from the outset.

Many years of developing integrated, arts-infused, and arts-based initiatives lead me to suggest that there is a range of possible choices for implementation. Choices start with individual music teachers integrating the music curriculum, and the widening ripples expand to include nonmusic teachers, entire school faculties, and eventually reform at the district level. Each type of implementation is rich and rewarding, challenging participants to think in new ways about their curriculum, teaching, and students. In this chapter we will explore the implications of arts-infused curriculum and arts-based schools from the perspectives of music educators, classroom teachers, district-level administrators, and policy makers. Reviewing aspects of various initiatives that have been implemented over several decades will provide models and suggestions at each level. Most importantly, the central goals of student-centered learning and excellence in music and arts education will remain paramount.

THE MUSIC TEACHER

Music is one of "the arts," which also include dance, drama, and visual arts. Each is taught toward national standards (Blakeslee, 1994), with some states and districts also providing learning benchmarks. As of the No Child Left Behind Act of 2000 (Bush, 2001), the arts are, by law, core academic disciplines. Because the arts are presented together in the national standards, they are often mistakenly considered one discipline rather than four. The discipline of music is multifaceted, with the artistic processes of creating, performing, and responding (CSDE, 2002, p. 21) developed through skills such as singing, playing, composing, analyzing, and evaluating across a learning sequence that builds understanding through preparation, development, and assessment. Building and delivering a strong and balanced music curriculum can be perceived as an integration effort in its own right.

Integration for the music teacher is not about using music in the service of other disciplines' concepts and skills. The skills and concepts we teach actively in a process-based music curriculum have a direct impact on students' achievement in other areas. Integration is about learning to use these processes in the music class, recognizing their connections across the curriculum, and sharing that connection with colleagues. Arts-infused curriculum design is an opportunity for the music teacher's voice to be heard and to strengthen and infuse music into every part of the school and students' lives. The music teacher is indispensable in informing, implementing, and assessing the process with integrity.

Developing powerful music instruction is particularly difficult in settings where students are infrequently scheduled, student and teacher turnover is high, discipline is an issue, resources are scarce, and assessment of music teaching is performed by a nonmusic educator whose expectations may have little to do with music achievement and growth. Advocacy is necessary to preserve and build music programs that educate rather than entertain, and while mainly the responsibility of the administrator, the teacher must be prepared with the "why" of music education as well as the "what" to provide information to parents, teachers, and administrators who may not understand. Teaching music is definitely a full-time job!

In addition to teaching music, the music educator is part of a larger school community. Once the music program is established and strong, it is possible and desirable to reach out to teachers of the other arts disciplines, or across subjects. With some thought and collaboration, music teachers will find that their lessons are already delivering many of the skills and concepts taught in other disciplines. With time to speak with the other teachers, all learn one another's concepts and skills and can find the parallels that will create rich student experiences.

As the school transitions to arts-infused curriculum, the role of music in other classrooms can range from a transitional activity, to delivering content in other disciplines, to providing a unique and powerful perspective on a theme. The music teacher must determine how to deliver the music curriculum in addition to addressing integrated themes, and communicate these choices calmly and clearly to grade-level colleagues. Requests for music in the service of classroom disciplines should include teaching and learning of music and other art activities. The music teacher then becomes a resource and advisor, and perhaps even a professional development provider to help build classroom teacher skills. By sharing music expertise, everyone will gain.

Integrated curriculum design is popular in the push for innovative change that will make learning meaningful. In practice, it is often implemented without regard for the music program. The decision may be made by administrators or a group of classroom teachers who inform the music teacher of the initiative after the fact. When nonmusic educators construct arts-based plans without music teacher input, decisions may be driven by misunderstandings. Understandably, the music teacher may feel threatened or frustrated as a result. Additional responsibilities in an already overfull schedule may feel impossible to assimilate. Funds may be diverted from music initiatives to provide the new program. There may be an expectation for leadership that the teacher is not prepared to assume. These and many more factors, real or imagined, can lead to negative feelings.

At the very least, decisions impacting the music program should be made in consultation with the professional charged with delivering the program. When the music teacher is at the decision-making table, whether initiating the conversation or responding to someone else's interest, careful decisions can diminish concerns. Choosing a consultant or guide who understands the arts curricula and issues is critical. Music teachers and other arts educators are as much learners as others being trained. It should not be assumed that any teacher has the understandings and skills to assume more responsibility than any other participant.

CLASSROOM TEACHERS AND THE ARTS

The classroom teacher's perspective is different from that of the music teacher, so it should be considered separately. Most teachers want to learn new activities and enter the process with a positive outlook, particularly if there is an emphasis on literacy or other direct links to classroom content. Unless a teacher has had an unsettling experience in the arts, there is usually a sense that the arts are important and can enhance teaching and learning.

Many classroom teachers, particularly in the primary grades, use arts activities during transitions or as a "break." Although they are aware that students are particularly involved when singing, moving, or drawing, they may not have discovered that arts-based strategies are actually engaging children's brains in complex ways of thinking. Rather than being a break from learning, music and the arts provide powerful routes to deep understanding.

While some classroom teachers are also musicians and/or artists, most do not think of themselves in that way, any more than most music teachers think of themselves as visual artists, dancers, or actors. A comfortable, safe environment must be established in which classroom teachers can share what they know, and learn in and about the arts. Teachers from all grade levels have different perceptions of what an arts-based curriculum entails. Quality professional development opportunities will deepen understandings and skills, while changing attitudes about the value and reason for music and the arts. If the music teacher is understanding and helpful, the classroom teacher will become increasingly willing to incorporate music strategies into classroom instruction.

Ultimately the goal is for the classroom teacher to understand that music and the arts are powerful vehicles for learning across the curriculum, and that this deep learning is the right of all children. Far from being a break from rigorous learning, music engages the child in higher order, highly active learning. In parallel, the goal for the music and other arts teachers is to understand the skills and understandings the classroom teacher is delivering, and to support these with a layered approach that addresses the music and other curriculum simultaneously. When curricular knowledge is shared, many links become obvious and the resulting instructional changes lead to deeper student understanding.

Stress may be heightened as teachers try out new strategies along with their prior strategies during an assimilation period. This stress is alleviated when the teacher realizes that the arts-based strategies deliver the content powerfully. Watching their students engage in model lessons where music and classroom content are simultaneously taught is a powerful experience for classroom and music teachers. The high level of attention and participation in music and arts classes increases the chances that a child will gain knowledge and skills. Teachers often do not believe the research when they hear it, nor are they willing to implement workshop-delivered strategies in the classroom, until they see it work with "their own kids."

MUSIC AND OTHER TEACHERS
IN COLLABORATION

Correlations occur when two or more teachers choose to work together, sharing a common material, activity, or topic; each teaching the content, skills, and processes within his or her respective discipline. For example, an elementary language arts or reading teacher may put a metered poem on a flip chart and focus on the nouns, verbs, rhyming words, or other reading characteristics. The music teacher, sharing this poem, focuses on steady beat, rhythm of the words, ostinato patterns taking from or related to the text, or highlights key words with different pitched or unpitched instrument tone colors. Through this experience, the student is led to understand that materials can be explored in many ways, opening the door to further and greater exploration. At this point students and teachers begin to enjoy the process of discovery and seek deeper links.

Integrated or arts-infused curriculum works best when it is planned, implemented, and assessed with others. A music teacher sometimes collaborates with the other arts teachers to develop a multimodal instructional unit. The participants identify the goals of this work in the context of each teacher's curriculum, finding meaningful parallels between concepts and skills. Just as a concert permits students, teachers, and the audience to assess student growth in music, multidisciplinary end product(s) will represent and measure the learning in each discipline.

The quality of the learning determines the depth of student benefit. If the focus is contrived to meet an extracurricular need, such as a sporting event, the gains are less likely to be academically powerful than an exploration of a topic that is integral to each discipline, such as "line" in music, visual art, dance, and drama. While community spirit is enhanced by music and the arts, precious instructional time must be carefully spent. It is likely that the end products of the "line unit" will yield excellent visual, aural, and kinesthetic products and performances for the community celebration; however, student learning is the goal.

While important in their own right, music and the other arts have also been shown to be powerful motivators and delivery tools for content in other disciplines (Deasy, 2002; Snyder, 2004). While there is no question that intrinsic learning in music is essential, applying that learning to facilitate other kinds of achievement is also a possible and viable educational goal, and particularly powerful with nontraditional learners in urban and other settings.

While the music teacher may think a certain art lesson will be the perfect exploration of line, the art teacher is the one who is trained to make this determination, and will most likely suggest a different path than the music teacher imagined. If a math teacher is included, the definition of line is refined because in mathematics a line stretches to infinity, and the short piece between two points is called a line segment. Additionally, while the art, music, and movement teachers are teaching students about straight and curved pathways or lines, the math teacher is using the label of *arc* for a curved line. While children are capable of using synonyms, when teachers know each other's vocabulary, they can choose to be consistent for the students' benefit. When teachers understand the concepts and skills that overlap between disciplines, then very rich learning environments can be created.

Another collaborative opportunity exists with local artists. Working with the PTA or local arts agencies, local artists can provide enrichment and support to music and other teachers. Teachers can become skeptical and threatened when they feel that their program is being overlooked or disrespected by visiting artists. However, with careful planning and teamwork, the relationship can be positive and productive from the beginning.

In addition to working with other arts teachers, a music teacher may collaborate with a grade-level team at the elementary school, or a teacher cluster in the middle or high school. Some guidelines for collaborating have emerged over multiple implementations:

- The music educator should be clear about the music curriculum goals. Particularly for a beginning teacher, consult with the district coordinator and the school principal.
- Responsibility to deliver the music curriculum will not change; therefore establish appropriate and manageable expectations.
- Collaborative endeavors are exciting and challenging, but they do require extra work. No one should be forced to participate. However, invite all potential parties to the table.
- Involve parent and/or community representatives in the planning process. Parents require understanding of the importance and rationale for arts-based activities to embrace and support the initiative. Community members and business leaders are impacted by the quality of area schools and can provide additional support.
- During meetings, listen more and speak less. Each participant listens from a unique perspective, so attend carefully to what others are really saying.

BUILDING TEACHER TEAMS

After enjoying carefully designed, developmentally appropriate experiences, teachers may be willing to commit to a deeper level of collaboration. Carefully planned steps, ideally with the help of an outside facilitator, allow teachers first to experience high-quality models, then dip their toes in and test the waters. Building collaborative teacher teams requires time. Quality professional development allows participants to express their perspectives and concerns, and become more comfortable with the idea in the process. A possible sequence of explorations over time might include:

- Information gathering that leads to meaningful goal setting by participants;
- Description and rationale for the arts and arts education, based on research;
- Experiences in each of the arts that
  - build teacher skills and model hands-on strategies; and
  - link to classroom disciplines such as language arts, math, science, social studies, etc.;
- Description and modeling of a learning sequence that guides a learner from experience through labeling, practice, application, and assessment;
- Model lessons that incorporate the above two points, taught to children at the specific site, with teacher observation forms, effective teacher preparation, and debriefing;
- Identification of levels of integration from the most superficial in which the arts function in the service of other disciplines to deep integration in which a broad theme is carefully chosen, overall and discipline-specific goals and objectives are crafted, and teachers each approach the theme and their standards simultaneously;
- Walk-through of model units through which teachers can deepen skills in their classrooms and begin shaping their collaborative team;
- Exploration of change theory as an introduction to short- and long-term goal setting;
- Designing integration plans with coaching, and introduction of action research opportunities.

The music teacher can take a leadership role in this process, helping to ensure careful decisions regarding music and the arts as the initiative moves forward. The scope of this teacher's power is limited, however, and support from superiors will be necessary when changes outside the music classroom begin to occur.

THE DISTRICT MUSIC OR ARTS
COORDINATOR AND PRINCIPAL

It takes a concerted effort to implement integrated curriculum, and it cannot succeed without the support of middle management. A music coordinator or principal may instigate the initiative, or may support an effort started by others. Regardless of who started the ball rolling, this individual is an indispensable problem solver.

After information outlining the rationale and particulars of developing an arts-infused initiative has been collected, the idea can be presented to groups including music teachers, all arts teachers, classroom teachers, principals, or district peers and superiors. When interest is built slowly, input from each group will help shape the details.

Acquiring funds may take a year or more of study, development, and fund-raising. Funding may be available as part of a district initiative, but frequently there is grant searching and proposal writing involved. Many grants stipulate a specific level of socioeconomic status and are targeted at urban districts to address the achievement gap. During this preparation time, short introductory workshops can prepare the staff so when the funding comes through there is an interested critical mass ready to begin training and implementation. Establishing a small pilot to collect some data and demonstrate how the initiative will work might keep interest alive as you build capacity for a larger program.

There is no one right way to structure change. As a leader, the music coordinator makes choices about the most fertile ground for planting the seed of integrated curriculum. Variations include working with music teachers only; working deeply with one school; bringing several schools together across the district or region to share vision, training, and ideas; or constructing a districtwide initiative. Teachers, principals, district coordinators, and parents should be brought to the table at various points in the process to help in shaping and implementing the initiative. Scheduling professional development, arranging schedules for teachers and assessment, and troubleshooting when issues arise, the district music coordinator becomes the protector of music education integrity while pushing the envelope for teachers who are ready for more. The range of teacher expertise is wide, and although student growth is the ultimate goal, teachers are also learners in this approach, and require adult learning strategies over time to remain open and risk-taking.

An obvious but often overlooked characteristic of implementation is that something must change for change to occur. Once the easy adjustments are made, the harder ones begin to lie across the path to success. Teachers will make the easy changes on their own, but the deeply meaningful, substantive changes must be facilitated by principals, district coordinators, and other leadership figures. If these are not confronted and addressed, the initiative will not move forward. The coordinator and/or principal should be proactive about territorial issues. These can include access to materials, room design, flexible scheduling, inclusion of the arts in the core curriculum, performance expectations ("informances," the end product of a carefully planned learning process, replace traditional performances), the role of visiting artists collaborating with arts educators and classroom teachers, coverage for team meeting time, and data collection throughout the initiative. Actions speak volumes, and the music supervisor's attitude and support, along with the principal's, sets the tone for the initiative. Either the teachers will be supported and grow, or they will be held back and frustrated. Middle managers are powerful advocates for change.

EDUCATIONAL LEADERS AND POLICY MAKERS

There are thousands of reasons why educational decisions are made—some political, some functional, some personal. The reason for including music and the arts in children's lives is that the arts are beneficial for children, the adolescents and adults they become, and therefore for society. A visionary district leader such as a superintendent or board of education member may be the one who brings the concept of arts-infused curriculum to the table. When a leader's goals aim for excellence and extraordinary education, the arts are a natural piece of the puzzle.

In a large implementation, it helps to have a facilitator and an administrator who work as an implementation team and are in constant communication with one another. The facilitator is more responsible to the teachers, and the administrator oversees the scheduling; interface with parents, school, and district administration; and publicity. One successful process is to focus on individuals first and then on institutions in carefully planned steps that scaffold teacher learning of new strategies and approaches, with high-quality models and participant-developed expectations and goals.

In one district, after a series of colloquia, meetings, study groups, and site visits, the board of education refined their mission of providing extraordinary learning for all students. Communication skills became central to this mission, guiding students to learn how to communicate visually, auditorally, and kinesthetically and to choose the appropriate modality for any given situation. Problem solving became a second foundational goal. Arts-based strategies were placed at the center of the curriculum to help accomplish this mission districtwide. It is possible for a school district to fund change if the decision makers have a strong commitment to it. Allocation of funds for new initiatives usually means cutting funds for something else, so the priorities must be clarified from the outset.

The teacher who initiates an arts-based initiative has to build support from the bottom up in a grassroots way until he or she convinces the decision makers. Similarly, the educational leader must make a compelling case to those in the field who will implement the vision. In both cases, team building across the range of stakeholders will mean relinquishing ownership to the larger group.

Many excellent initiatives develop without upper management support, or sometimes even knowledge. For the effort to be sustainable, however, it must be an explicit part of the school mission. The approval of decision makers will help move the initiative forward, and also provide a feather in the cap of the school or district.

MEASURING SUCCESS

Assessment and evaluation are critical components of any change effort. Without data collection, there is no way to measure success. Assessment also requires that goals and objectives be determined at the outset, assuring clear vision and direction.

Assessment will be shaped by the initiative's goals and objectives. Quantitative measures often include student achievement in language and mathematics, student attendance, teacher attendance, and number of disciplinary referrals to the office. Qualitative measures might include changes in teacher, parent, administrative and/or student attitude and teacher comfort level with arts-based teaching and learning. Formative assessment should be ongoing, informing the initiative at various intervals so changes can be made in the implementation. Documentation is essential and can be done through a combination of journals, plans, student responses, videotape, interviews and surveys, and analysis of school records such as attendance and grades. Summative assessment will provide the data that is reported to funders, stakeholders, media, and so on.

Many urban districts prefer to employ evaluators that service multiple initiatives, and like to involve the assessment personnel from the central administration. If the data is being used to document program success, it is best to use an objective, third-party evaluator. Many grants will make this a funding stipulation. There are evaluators who are expert at arts-based curriculum evaluation, and finding those who have expertise will increase the chances that a meaningful array of data is collected.

Historically, arts-based initiatives have not been assessed as rigorously as other school change components, and therefore are not taken as seriously. In urban integrated curriculum projects, the quality of the implementation will determine its ability to effect student gains. There is as much variation between the implementation done by trained teachers as there is between trained and untrained teachers (Snyder, 2005). As we look to the future, planning should include rigorous, gold-standard research design whenever possible, and those involved should share strategies and evaluation tools.

CONCLUSION AND AN AGENDA FOR THE FUTURE

When the arts are a catalyst for change in schools, the results touch every aspect of the school community. In urban schools where the need is greatest, the opportunities for success are enormous and bring vitality and hope to teachers and administrators as well as children and families. Without abandoning the rigor of standards-driven, research-based excellence, arts-infused curriculum meets the educational needs of urban communities by starting from where students are. Music is communal, and learning in and through music changes the way in which school business is conducted. Civility, discourse, problem solving, and social structure are all a part of music making.

The conversation is robust, and you are invited to join in. Everyone has perspectives and experiences to add to the conversation. Music teachers and administrators can become leaders in the school change movement by bringing the concept of arts-based curriculum to decision makers, then helping to facilitate the change by imagining a powerful role for the arts in student learning. Teachers can begin by exploring collaborations that honor student capacity to learn in rich, multidimensional environments.

Music administrators and principals can share the abundance of literature that supports high-quality, standards-based arts programs and arts-infused curriculum design, and then begin to plan a schoolwide or districtwide initiative. Educational leaders can empower those working for them by taking interest, becoming informed, and taking action by arranging opportunities for carefully crafted communication with decision makers. Universities should take seriously their responsibility to recruit a teaching force (generally, and specifically in music) that reflects the demographic makeup of our society. They should also model the collaborations we hope to foster in schools, infusing quality music and arts education strategies across the curriculum, and supporting research on the effectiveness of multidisciplinary and arts-based models.

School change is intense, and arts-infused curriculum has the added burden of establishing the arts as core curriculum. But the process is incredibly rewarding and ultimately has great possibility for changing the lives of students, teachers, schools, and systems. We started by focusing on children in urban schools, and we must remind ourselves once again that the effort is worthy because it is right for children throughout their educational experiences. It engages and motivates them, helps them learn more deeply, gives purpose to lives and interest to learning, and teaches processes and skills that are necessary to build safe and democratic communities—and to pass the test. Along the way, music education will most likely become more valued than it has been because it will offer a richer array of musical entry points. Performances will shine because children will have more musical skills; understand more about what and how they create, perform, and respond; and will be more independent musicians. Hopefully one day this "out of the box" way of working will become the mainstream of education, for the sake of students, teachers, decision makers, and society.

REFERENCES

Arts Education Partnership. (2003). *Creating quality integrated and interdisciplinary arts programs*. Washington, DC: Arts Education Partnership.

———. (2004). *The arts and education: New opportunities for research*. www.aep-arts.org.

Blakeslee, M. (Ed.). (1994). *National standards for arts education: What every young American should know and be able to do in the arts*. Reston, VA: Music Educators National Conference.

Bush, G. W., et al. (2001). *No Child Left Behind Act (NCLB)*. Washington, DC: U. S. Department of Education.

Connecticut State Department of Education (CSDE). (1999). *Connecticut common core of teaching*. Hartford: State Board of Education.

———. (2002) *The Arts: A guide to K–12 program development*. Hartford: State Board of Education.

Deasy, R. J. (Ed.). (2002). *Critical links: Learning in the arts and student academic and social development*. Washington, DC: Arts Education Partnership.

Fiske, E. B. (Ed.). (1999). *Champions of change: The impact of the arts on learning*. Washington, DC: Arts Education Partnership.

Snyder, S. (1996). *Integrate with integrity*. Norwalk, CT: IDEAS Press.

———. (2001, March). *Connection, correlation and integration*. Reston, VA: *Music Educators Journal*.

———, et al. (2005). How to measure a wildflower (videotaped panel discussion). Norwalk, CT: Arts education IDEAS. Retrieved August 15, 2005, from www.aeideas.com.

Wilson, B., and Corbett, H. D. (2001). *Listening to urban kids: School reform and the teachers they want*. New York: State University of New York Press.

SUGGESTED READING FOR ARTS-INFUSED CURRICULUM

Arts Education Partnership. (2003). *Creating quality integrated and interdisciplinary arts programs*. Washington, DC: Arts Education Partnership.

———. (2004). *The Arts and education: New opportunities for research.* www.aep-arts.org.

Corbett, H. D., et al. (2002). *Effort and excellence in urban classrooms: Expecting—and getting—success with all students.* New York: Teachers College Press.

Dietel, R. J., et al. (1991). What does research say about assessment? Oak Brook: North Central Regional Educational Laboratory. Retrieved August 15, 2005, from www.ncrel.org/sdrs/areas/stw_esys/4assess.htm.

Herbert, D. (2004, Winter). Finding the will and the way to make the arts a core subject: Thirty years of mixed progress. The State Education *Standard*, National Association of State Boards of Education. Retrieved August 15, 2005, from www.nasbe.org/Standard/15_Winter2004/Herbert.pdf.

McCarthy, K., et al. (2005). *Gift of the muse: Reframing the debate about the benefits of the arts.* Santa Monica, CA: Rand Distribution Services.

Meyer, Lori. (2004, Winter). The compete curriculum: Ensuring a place for the arts in America's schools. The State Education *Standard*, National Association of State Boards of Education.

National Governors Association. (2002). Issue brief: The impact of arts education on workforce preparation. Washington, DC: National Governor's Association.

New Jersey Department of Education. (2000). Standards for required professional development of teachers. Retrieved August 15, 2005, from www.state.nj.us/njded/profdev/standards.htm.

Wilson, B., and Corbett, H. D. (2001). *Listening to urban kids: School reform and the teachers they want.* Albany: State University of New York Press.

17

Music in Urban School Reform: Know the Law—Be Accountable!

Robert Morrison

The publication of this book comes on the heels of the fourth anniversary of the enactment of the No Child Left Behind Act (United States Congress, 2002), creating one of the most sweeping education reform agendas ever. You may love NCLB, or you may not. Some object to the law for good reason (more on this in a moment). At the very least, it has been a great topic for many people to complain about and an unending source of parody: No Child Left in Band, No Subject Left Behind, No Child Left in Public School, No Child Left Untested . . . you get the drift.

I have been mentored in my career to be a practicing realist. Here is the reality: No Child Left Behind is here to stay. Even if there was momentum to significantly change the law it would take another five years just to get something else in place. The changes occurring in education now will drive education policy for the next decade, or longer.

No, the NCLB law is not about to change. So, to be successful in our collective efforts to expand access to music education in our public schools, we need to begin to deal with it. More important, we need to examine the opportunities NCLB provides us to advance our collective goals.

I WILL USE NO CHILD LEFT BEHIND AS AN ADVANTAGE . . . NOT A SCAPEGOAT

Heresy, you may think, but it really isn't. I have seen all of the reports about cutbacks due to NCLB. The report *Academic Atrophy* (Council for Basic

Education, 2004) was the first document to show the negative impact of the implementation of NCLB on arts programs (*implementation* being the key word here). The findings in our report from the Music for All Foundation, *Sound of Silence* (Music for All, 2004), reinforced much of what was in the earlier commentaries.

What is most often overlooked is that NCLB actually provides some important advantages, particularly for urban education, that have been obscured by the testing mandates. Since *accountability* is the buzzword of this law, we must hold our policy makers accountable for all the provisions of this law. Here are just a few of the advantages to keep in mind (Arts Education Partnership, 2004):

- NCLB mandates the arts and music as a core subject—There is nothing in the law that states, suggests, or implies that music should be cut in the name of reading, math, or testing mandates. Programs have been reduced or eliminated due to uniformed decisions made by local interpretation of the law. So, if someone says we need to cut back the music program because of NCLB mandates, tactfully point out the error in his or her ways. The best way to do this is to use the letter sent to all school superintendents by then secretary of education Rod Paige (2004). In the letter he points out the dangers of the "narrow interpretation" of the law and hammers home the point that the arts are a core subject to be included in education reform. Indeed, the arts are an important part of any real reform agenda.
- Follow the money—that's right. There is money tied to the law, and you and your school district have the right to apply for it. Title I provides funds for states to use as part of comprehensive reform plans, including the arts. Title I also provides funds that may be used to support music programs for disadvantaged students. Title II provides funds for teacher training, including music. Title IV provides funds for after-school programs (including music), and Title V provides money to support model programs, as well as grants for professional development.
- State plans: where the real action is—State education policy and planning is where the rubber meets the road. Making the connection to your local program is the key. Music and arts education groups in every state should be at the table when developing the state plans. Define the arts as a core subject. Have state standards in place. Encourage the inclusion of the arts as part of the state accountability systems through state or local assessments. In your local community, be sure your own curriculum is aligned with state standards. Provide ways to assess the music programs (how many people feel that a district festival is a performance assessment!).
- Highly qualified teachers—By the end of the 2005–2006 school year all

teachers of core academic subjects must be highly qualified. Since we know that music and arts education are considered core subjects, all music teachers must be highly qualified by the end of the 2005–2006 school year.

- In an era of accountability . . . be accountable—OK everyone, repeat after me: "Data is my friend. Data is my friend. . . ." It really is. The problem we have had in the music education community (and the arts, in general, for that matter) is that we have not gathered data on our programs in any meaningful way. Now, I am certain some of you do, but most places I have visited in my travels do not.

Some data gathering ideas for your consideration that may help support your program:

- Number of students enrolled in each arts discipline—total and by grade, by school, and, ideally, by district (we will call these "arts" students).
- Percentage of students enrolled in each art form by grade, by school, and districtwide.
- School attendance rate of these students vs. nonarts students.
- Dropout rate of these students vs. nonarts students.
- Average standardized test scores, arts vs. nonarts.
- Impact of arts students on AYP scores vs. nonarts students (AYP is NCLB lingo for adequate yearly progress. This is the number you hear everyone yelling about when they dub a school "low performing").

By gathering and providing this kind of information we are able to make a compelling case for the impact our music and arts programs have on children, schools, and communities. Embrace NCLB and use the facts of the law to your advantage. By being informed about the law you will be empowered to use NCLB as a tool to strengthen your own programs and expand access to music for all of our children.

REFERENCES

Arts Education Partnership. (2004). *No subject left behind.* Washington, DC: Author. Retrieved on September 1, 2005, from aep-arts.org/PDF%20Files/NoSubjectLeft Behind.pdf.

Council for Basic Education. (2004). *Academic atrophy.* Washington, DC: Author. Retrieved September 1, 2005, from music-for-all.org/documents/cbe_principal_ Report.pdf.

Music for All Foundation. (2004). *Sound of silence—The unprecedented decline of music education in California's public schools.* Warren, NJ: Author. Retrieved on September 1, 2005, from www.music-for-all.org/sos.html.

Paige, R. (2004, July). *Letter to superintendents from U.S. Secretary of Education Rod Paige* [letter]. Retrieved on September 1, 2005, from www.ed.gov/policy/elsec/guid/secletter/040701.html.

United States Congress. (2004). *No Child Left Behind Act of 2002.* Washington, DC: Author.

Conclusion

Music Educators in the Urban School Reform Conversation

Carol Frierson-Campbell

MUSIC IN URBAN SCHOOL REFORM

Urban schools have been a critical part of the school reform conversation since the turn of the last century. Whether as the "crucible" to begin the process of assimilation, the training place for workers in the nation's industries and armies, or the last bastion of hope for the nation's impoverished children, schools in America's cities have long held the attention of educational policy makers and reformers. Since the beginning of this conversation, many have indicated that music is a worthwhile discipline for study in urban schools. If this were universally accepted, however, we would not need this chapter, or this book. Music teachers, who believe passionately in the power of music to change student lives, struggle daily to find a place in the school reform efforts that have, for better or worse, come to define *urban schooling* in the United States.

Part of this conversation concerns the role of teachers in the school reform process. Recent case studies of successful school reform efforts indicate that "reform-minded" teachers have a prominent role as

> the protagonists of change mindful of and responsive to the needs of their students and those conditions that create the best opportunities for the development of their students, classrooms, and school. As reforms evolve, their voices are heard, their choices recognized, their knowledge sought and interrogated, and their changes engaged and extended. (Thiessen & Barrett, 2002, p. 766)

215

Similarly, many school districts and educational administration programs are changing their emphasis from a traditional "top-down" management style to a collective kind of leadership in which all educational professionals, from paraprofessionals to grade-level teachers to special area teachers to building administrators, participate with the principal serving as a "leader of leaders." This involves a commitment on the part of all to lead as experts in their subject area, their classrooms, and in the vision and mission of the school/district. "Teacher leadership" is a common label for this arrangement.

Wynne (2001) notes the following commonalities in the literature: Teacher leaders are expert teachers who "are consistently on a professional learning curve" (p. 5) and willingly share their knowledge with others. They are reflective practitioners who constantly seek what is best for children and use action research to test their own effectiveness. They "collaborate with their peers, parents, and communities, engaging them in dialogues of open inquiry/action/ assessment models of change" (p. 5). Finally, they are "risk-takers" who are active at the building level as leaders and mentors, and who work with colleges in the preparation of new teachers.

Spillane, Hallett, and Diamond, three researchers who study the ways teachers impact school reform efforts, have found that teacher leaders are "fundamental in efforts to change instructional practices" (2003). Thiessen and Barrett (2002) apply this concept to "reform-minded music teachers," suggesting that they have "the capacity . . . to act as savvy, informed change agents" (p. 759). They assert that "right from the outset of and continuing throughout their careers, the professional work of teachers encompasses an intricate web of responsibilities" (p. 761) that includes music classrooms, the school corridors, and the community beyond the school. My research, however, indicates that music teachers may not have opportunities for this kind of leadership, particularly in urban settings.

THE SOUND WAYS OF
LEARNING PARTNERSHIP

In 1999, the College of Education at William Paterson University joined two other New Jersey universities to form the New Jersey State Teacher Quality Enhancement Consortium. The coalition was created to implement a five-year Federal Teacher Quality Enhancement grant that was awarded to a number of university coalitions across the country to support efforts to develop school reform partnerships between colleges of education and high-needs, culturally diverse urban schools in the region served by each consortium. While our partnership was begun under the guise of developing a professional development school (PDS) relationship, these findings relate to music educators working in any kind of school reform effort.

Initially, our College of Education (COE) chose five schools from three city school districts in New Jersey as preliminary sites. COE faculty members were recruited to serve as liaisons between each PDS site and the university and to plan and coordinate partnership activities at their site. The grant required the involvement of arts and science faculty from the university but did not stipulate a specific role for their participation.

Preplanning

The grant application process provided the initial direction for the partnership, as it required clear goals with measurable outcomes that had the capacity to impact urban education at the local, regional, and state level. This forced us to expand our vision from serving teachers at the local level to impacting the music education community on a broader level. It is impossible to overemphasize the importance of these goals to the overall project; they provided benchmarks throughout the duration of the project. In addition to the partnership goals, I established "navigational points" and "unacceptable rationales" for the project prior to getting involved.

Navigational Points

- Belief in importance of music as a discipline for students of all ages and cultures.
- Desire to become involved in urban music education as researcher and colleague.
- Belief in interdisciplinary education that is true to all disciplines, both in a discrete and a multidisciplinary sense.

Unacceptable Rationales

- The idea that music education is purely for "relaxation" or "enjoyment" without a disciplinary or skills base in the curriculum.
- The idea that the purpose of music education is to enrich other academic subjects without recognition of the academic nature of musical skill and knowledge.

Method

As the coordinator of the music partnership, I was determined to focus on the needs of the music teachers from the partner schools rather than those noted by their administrators, the grant directors, or even my own perceptions. For this reason I began to collect data related to the participants' needs from the outset of the project. The nature of the study evolved as the partnership developed. Eventually the data that comprise this study came from three types of interactions:

1. On-site interviews and observations of a small number of music teachers and administrators make up the first year's data.
2. Data from the second year consist of field notes from a series of meetings on the WPU campus with a somewhat larger group (n = 9) of music teachers who became the advisory group for the fledgling music partnership.
3. The third year's data reflect the results of a formal needs assessment administered to all music teachers from the three districts served by the COE partnership (n = 76). While it was not planned beforehand, our interactions fell naturally into stages marked by the school year.

Who Are You and What Do You Want?

The process of building the partnership began with a series of unstructured interviews and observations. This involved making "cold calls" to administrators and music teachers in each of the COE's partner schools. It took a few attempts before I realized the hierarchies in these districts. I learned to speak to building administrators in order to gain access to music teachers, and eventually I was able to visit the administrator and music teacher at each partner school. None of the music teachers was aware of their school's participation in the partnership.

I have previously referred to this stage of our relationship as the "who are you and what do you want?" stage (Frierson-Campbell, 2003). It is uncomfortable, particularly after committing to action and being provided with resources, but it seems to be a necessary part of any successful partnership. Robinson (2000) mentions similar stages in his review of the arts partnership literature. My journal during the first year of the partnership reflects a growing understanding that Title I schools that had also been designated "Abbott" (New Jersey's "failing school" designation) provided few opportunities for music teachers to participate in the school reform efforts that each of their schools was required to undertake.

Forming the Core

Research indicates that activities rather than goals propel partnerships through their initial stages (Robinson, 2000). With this in mind we invited the PDS music teachers to come to the university to move the music partnership forward. Planning for this meeting began on September 11, 2001; the events of that sad day meant that it was not until February of 2002 that we actually met. Since the COE partnership had expanded to five schools by year two, a total of 11 teachers were invited to attend a professional development session at the university. The agenda consisted of explaining the basic goals of the partnership and leading participants to brainstorm about ways we could meet their instructional needs. The participants were enthusiastic, and the meeting concluded with an ambitious list of needs to be met, primarily related to materials, professional development, and recognition. While more concrete issues (materials and training) are the easiest to address in a partnership relationship, notes from the first meeting indicate the greatest interest in the area of professional recognition: *There is a strong sense among these attendees that they need a collective voice that has the power to speak about the needs of urban music teachers in a more public forum. . . .*

The group met a total of three times before the end of the school year. During the second meeting, based on a strong sense that conveying the importance of music in urban schools to state leaders would bring them more recognition in their day-to-day work, the group decided to focus most of their energy on the creation of a mission statement. A third meeting was called for that purpose, and at that meeting the group decided that involving all of their colleagues—all of the music teachers from the three urban districts in the partnership—would help them create a stronger mission statement. This idea propelled us into year three of our relationship.

The Formal Needs Assessment

Reaching out to all of the music teachers from the three partner districts changed the direction and scale of the music partnership. Instead of planning activities at individual schools to respond to the needs of specific music teachers, we began to analyze music teacher need from a broader perspective. Although we continue into the present to define our model as the professional development school, in many ways this activity launched our partnership into a more traditional "arts partnership" role, one with less interaction between partners, where the university provides content designed to meet the professional development needs of its partners.

Our needs assessment was scheduled in September of 2002 as a full-day in-service workshop for all music teachers from the three partnership districts. The president of the state Music Educators Association (MEA) and members of its Multicultural Awareness Committee were also invited to speak and participate in the event. The formal needs assessment followed the three-phase model suggested by Altschuld and Witkin (1995). Briefly, during the *pre-assessment* stage a committee is formed to decide whether there are needs to be met. The advisory group from the second year served as this committee. The *assessment* stage involves formal assessment of a constituent group for the purpose of understanding and prioritizing the perceived needs of the participants. Our in-service day provided quantitative data for the needs assessment; qualitative data including observations and unstructured interviews were held with the advisory group. The *post-assessment* stage involves identifying and selecting solution strategies; we began this stage in the spring of 2002 with a second full-scale event, this time focusing on the professional development needs that were indicated by the participating teachers.

The needs assessment was based on the question: *"What is needed to take urban music education from where it is now to where it could be?"* The day was structured to direct participants to construct and then prioritize their professional needs both as individuals and as a group, to give focus to our mission statement and to the partnership. Participants were organized by specialty (general music, band, or chorus) and then divided into focus-type groups of approximately nine people. Each focus group was facilitated by one of the CMTs. The process began with a dialoguing exercise that served to prepare the participants for the in-depth conversations that would comprise most of the day's activities. In the next activity, individual participants created "mind-maps" around the question of the day. They shared their maps with a partner and later with their groups. Each group then created a prioritized list of professional need based on the lists created by each individual. In a final presentation, each group presented their 8–10 priorities to all of the teachers in attendance. The priorities listed by two or more groups included the following:

- Facilities   8
- Supplies/Instruments   7
- Administrative/Collegial (nonmusic) support   5
- Funding   4
- Scheduling   4
- Discipline   3
- In-District Networking/Staff Development   2

Participants were also asked to complete an open-ended questionnaire to further define and strengthen the data related to their professional needs. The questionnaire, based on a survey by Fiese and Decarbo (1995), was returned by 52 out of the 76 music teachers in attendance at the workshop. Not every respondent answered every question. Still, answers provided by those who did respond provide interesting insights about music educators in these three districts' school reform efforts. Respondents' answers were categorized post hoc.

The first question had two parts: "Did your undergraduate/graduate education courses prepare you to teach in the urban setting? If yes, what specific areas in your education prepared you? If no, what areas would you suggest need to be included?" A majority of respondents (66.7%) indicated that their undergraduate preparation had not prepared them for teaching in an urban setting. Fifty-seven percent responded that *experience teaching in the urban environment* should be part of undergraduate training. *Navigating the school culture* (dealing with administrators, getting by with limited resources, understanding that the system breaks down sometimes) was mentioned by an additional 16%. *Discipline specific training, educational issues* (primarily having to do with overcoming language barriers) and *musical/cultural issues* (music for diverse cultures of students) rounded out the lot.

Fiese and DeCarbo (1995) surveyed 20 urban music teachers who were recognized by state-level MEA presidents as highly successful. Their responses to this question—published almost seven years before our survey—were almost identical. Responses to Fowler's 1970 interviews of music teachers from urban schools are also strikingly similar, stressing the need for teacher education programs to provide a realistic picture of urban education, use culturally relevant curricula, emphasize general music as well as performance, emphasize a broader spectrum of musical genres, and provide "in-depth cultural, sociological, and psychological understanding of the students" (p. 83).

The second question asked participants about their practice: "Can you describe one or two specific teaching techniques, strategies, or approaches that you have found to be particularly effective for teaching music in the urban situation?" Specific musical approaches (i.e., the Kodály method) or teaching approaches (i.e., Gardner's Project Approach) were recommended by 11% of the respondents. Forty-one percent responded with either a *general teaching approach* (present content in small doses in an organized way) and another 41% with a *general musical approach* (use movement to keep students interested; relate concepts to music the students are familiar with).

The answers from the successful teachers surveyed by Fiese and DeCarbo were somewhat different, implying a broader sense of curriculum than most of the answers in the current survey. Many of those respondents indicated the importance of having "the respect of the students and control of the teaching/learning environment," being a master of the subject, understanding technology, and finding "a way to relate to the students initially and then adapt the curriculum with that in mind" (p. 28). They also mentioned group work, cooperative learning, and peer teaching as techniques that involved students in their own learning.

The third question asked teachers, "What factors have most contributed to your personal success as a music teacher in the urban setting?" Most responses fell into two categories: *personal traits* (flexibility, love of music teaching and/or children, patience, and stubbornness) and *professional traits and knowledge: teacher-ship* (ability to relate to students, having and communicating high standards, putting in extra effort, and being involved in the school community). A notable number of responses fell into the category of *professional traits and knowledge: musicianship* (knowledge of piano, knowing what students listen to). Other categories revealed in this question include *professional opportunities* (workshops, seminars, and earning a paycheck), *school environment* (mentioned by only four participants), and *prior experience* (having primarily to do with growing up in an urban environment). A few teachers (four out of 46) mentioned that administrator support and school size were important aspects of their success.

Fiese and DeCarbo's respondents indicated that support networks ("teachers, supervisors, mentors, and others") were very important to them. It is clear from their responses that going "beyond the classroom" to take classes, attend conferences, and contribute to the school community both inside and outside the building were factors that they considered key to their success (p. 29).

The next questions asked respondents for their opinions: "What general comments do you have related to improving music education in the urban schools?" A third of the respondents indicated that *facilities/supplies/ funding* was their greatest need. Seventeen percent indicated a need for *professional development,* including understanding music in context of culture; eliminating bias against non-Eurocentric music; integrating music across the curriculum; having higher standards for students. *Support from administration and school community* was mentioned by 13% of respondents. Thirteen percent of respondents mentioned *scheduling* while 11% mentioned *class size* and another 11% suggested *coordination of the music teacher agenda* (networking and sharing ideas, centralizing supplies, maintaining high hiring standards, seeking a state mandate for music). Responses to this question were markedly similar to those of the focus groups discussed earlier.

While many of the responses from our participants indicated needs that were beyond themselves, the majority of suggestions from Fiese and DeCarbo's respondents were more personal. They noted the need for relevant training by qualified trainers in the area of management skills, repertoire choices, multicultural education, and "the psychology of urban students" (p. 29). Some suggested that they needed a greater understanding of how to reach low-income students, and that such understanding needed to be integrated schoolwide. Finally, they noted the importance of relationships "among music teachers, administrators, and music supervisors." As Fiese and Decarbo note, "Having all of the constituencies involved in dialogue, rather than parallel monologues, for the advancement of the students' music education is perhaps one of the central features of successful urban school music programs, according to the respondents" (p. 30).

Two questions specific to this project asked participants for their opinions about the needs assessment and about future professional development opportunities. When asked, "Which of today's activities was most valuable for you?" 50% responded that *networking (getting out of school—being with colleagues; talking to the person next to me, who does a job similar to mine, but on the other side of town*) was the most valuable part of the day. Other activities (*the jazz workshop, the mind-mapping exercises, the setting of priorities,* even *venting*) were also mentioned. It is notable that simply having an opportunity to interact with discipline-specific teaching peers was the activity these music teachers found to be the most useful. When asked, "What issues do you suggest we target for our next workshop?" the majority of respondents mentioned issues that implied action beyond the classroom. These included *policy issues* (bringing our needs to the larger educational community; state mandates; getting teachers to agree on a plan of action), *district-level issues* (educating administration as to the viability of music and its relation to education), and *building-level issues* (convincing and educating administrators and building-level peers, improving scheduling and facilities).

In New Jersey, schools that receive Title I funding or have acquired Abbott status are required to be involved in one of the whole school reform (WSR) models. Each of these models stresses the importance of teacher involvement in the reform process. A common feature of these models is site-based management, in which a small advisory team of teachers assists in the governance of the school. Each member of the advisory team creates a secondary team and all members of the school's faculty are required to serve on one of these teams. Collaborative planning is another feature of most school reform models. To investigate the kinds of opportunities these music teachers had for collegiality in and outside their buildings, four additional questions were posed:

1. How much planning time do you have in the school day?
2. How does this compare to the time given other teachers in your building?
3. How much time do you have time to plan/collaborate with music teaching colleagues? With grade-level colleagues?
4. How does this compare to the time given other teachers in your building?

Participants who responded to these questions indicated that while "prep time" is roughly equal for music teachers and grade-level teachers (one "prep" each day), it is not *equitable* in many of the buildings where they teach. Roughly half (15 out of 27 respondents) indicated that they had no time to collaborate with other teachers in their buildings (nine of the 27 indicated one collaborative planning period each week; an additional three indicated one period each month), and a large majority, 39 out of 47 respondents, indicated that they had no opportunities for collaboration with other music teachers during their work time. This is in stark contrast to grade-level teachers who have both daily "prep time" and weekly "grade-level" meetings for the purpose of collaboration.

An interesting example of the role special area teachers play in the WSR process was revealed in an earlier interview with a member of the advisory group. This is how one music teacher describes his involvement in his school's "special" teachers school reform team:

> *see, what they do, in here, is that they put together the music teachers, the art teachers, and the gym teachers, and we all sit together and say "what are we doing here" and we write down some issues that nobody reads. You know . . . and that's not right.*

Thiessen and Barrett (2002) suggest a very different reality; one in which reform-minded music teachers have opportunities to "work with colleagues and other stakeholders . . . in ways that

- Build their capacity for joint work;
- Focus on school-based, collaborative, and inquiry-oriented professional learning;
- Create a balance and connection between disciplinary and interdisciplinary curriculum practices; and
- Expand their involvement in and commitment to making shared decisions about classroom and school improvement." (p. 770)

DIRECTION FOR THE FUTURE

The results of the two stages of needs assessment used to provide direction for our partnership have implications well beyond this project. Our experience and the results of our needs assessment suggest that it is possible to create a partnership to meet the professional needs of music teachers from urban schools involved in whole school reform, but they also suggest that the definition of *need* and the role of music teachers in the reform process should be explored further by music teachers, teacher educators, and others who have a stake in urban education.

Sociologists use the term *capital* to describe the often intangible human resources that make people successful in their jobs and daily lives. Forms of capital include *human capital* (skills, knowledge, and expertise), *cultural capital* (ways of being), *social capital* (networks and relations of trust), and *economic* or *physical capital* (material resources). James Coleman (1988) is credited with the first application of this concept to education. He explains it this way:

Social capital . . . comes about through changes in the relations among persons that facilitate action. If physical capital is wholly tangible, being embodied in observable material form, and human capital is less tangible, being embodied in the skills and knowledge acquired by an individual, social capital is less tangible yet, for it exists in the *relations* among persons. Just as physical capital and human capital facilitate productive activity, social capital does as well. For example, a group within which there is extensive trustworthiness and extensive trust is able to accomplish much more than a comparable group without that trustworthiness and trust. (pp. S100–S101, emphasis in original)

Spillane, Hallett, and Diamond (2003) studied the relationships between educators in eight Chicago public elementary schools to understand how capital and teacher leadership impact reform in urban schools. While school administrators in their study were considered leaders on the basis of who they were (their cultural capital), certain teachers were also considered by their peers to be leaders in the reform process. The researchers found that teachers were "more likely to be constructed as leaders on the basis of their human capital" (pp. 10–11), or the skills and knowledge they exhibited to their peers. As they describe it, "the social capital among teachers is a basis for the construction of leadership. The teachers in this group constructed each other as leaders on the basis of this social capital, facilitating the dissemination of human capital" (pp. 8–9). "Specialist" teachers were not seen by "ordinary" (i.e., grade-level) teachers as leaders because grade-level teachers defined leadership as the capacity to help them "learn about and change their teaching practices" (p. 11).

The majority of needs stated by the music teachers involved in this project (primarily facilities and supplies) are examples of *economic capital*. While these are very real needs, economic capital was not seen by the urban teachers in Spillane's study as indicative of leadership. Instead, teachers constructed those who shared educational insights and expertise as leaders. In sociological terms, the grade-level teachers from the Chicago schools constructed their peers "as leaders on the basis of their human capital" (p. 11), and the development of human capital was facilitated by social capital such as grade level meetings (p. 9). The music teacher responses to the *Sound Ways of Learning* questionnaire noted a desire for further opportunities to develop social capital—expressing that the most valuable part of the formal needs assessment for them was networking—but it is clear from their responses that they have little or no opportunity to develop the kinds of teacher-leadership skills that support the reform process.

Michelle Zederayko (2000), a researcher and art education professor from Toronto, Canada, had different but related results. She studied an urban high school in Canada where arts educators were credited with turning the school climate from one of failure to one of success. This school had not adopted a formal arts-based-reform model; it had simply made a decision to support the arts and arts participation for all students. The arts teachers responded by building strong programs that met the needs of as many students as possible.

Zederayko found that the music and visual art teachers in the school who were the catalysts for the successful reform effort *and were credited by their administrators as such*, did not see their efforts as teacher leadership. As Spillane and his colleagues note (2003): "The construction of leadership does not presume intent by leaders. . . . People are often unwitting leaders, and it is not surprising that when followers label someone a leader, the leader may respond by saying, "I am?" (p. 9). Zederayko warns that this difference in the definition of *leadership* as understood by administrators and arts teachers could undermine communication between these two groups. It was beyond the scope of our assessment to explore differences between administrators' and music teachers' perceptions of leadership, but the fact that more than half of the focus groups in our formal needs assessment mentioned administrative support as a concern, and that this concern was reiterated in individuals' responses to the questionnaire, suggests that communication between the music teachers and administrators in our partner districts may be a concern.

CONCLUSION

This discussion does not intend to play down the importance of materials, supplies, facilities, or program funds to urban music educators. All of those things are certainly critical for high-quality music programs. It does suggest, however, that "need" on the part of music educators involved in urban school reform encompasses several issues beyond the usual trappings of the music room. Coleman (1988) noted that *social capital* is a resource that people "can use to achieve their interests" (p. S101). But opportunities for building social capital, such as formal and informal interactions between music teachers with teachers and administrators at the building level, and with the larger educational enterprise, are almost entirely absent from the professional lives of these music teachers.

Thiessen and Barrett (2002) cite an idealized (and fictional) middle-school music teacher who has jumped into her school's reform efforts with both feet. Her professional life is strikingly different from the reality described by our participants. As she tells it:

> My life in school is very different now that my school has agreed to participate in a school reform network. The nature of my work includes more time with colleagues, more involvement in school-level decisions, more contact, and even

partnerships with more people outside the school . . . all of which enrich and extend the professional role I play." (p. 767)

This kind of participation was not expected by, required of, or available to most of the music teacher participants in our assessment.

If music education is to become a critical piece of the urban school reform conversation, then the role of music educator in schools, urban and otherwise, must expand beyond the music classroom to include the corridors and community on both a micro and macro scale. Emphasizing *only* the classroom work of music teachers "fails to adequately acknowledge the work of teachers in other contexts and, consequently, underplays the inter-dependence of what teachers do inside and outside the classroom" (Thiessen & Barrett, p. 761). As Zederayko noted, the skills that many arts teachers use in their daily work have the capacity to make a positive difference in the climate of a school. But this will not happen if music educators do not have and do not take opportunities in their work lives to join the conversation.

The William Paterson Sound Ways of Learning partnership began with a generous grant from the New Jersey State Teacher Enhancement Consortium. The outreach part of the project continues to be supported by a grant from William Paterson University's Provost's Incentive Fund, while related research is supported by an Assigned Release Time Award. The author is grateful for this support.

REFERENCES

Altschuld, J. W., & Witkin, B. R. (2000). *From needs assessment to action: Transforming needs into solution strategies*. Thousand Oaks, CA: Sage.

Coleman, J. S. (1988). Social capital in the creation of human capital. *American Journal of Sociology, 94* (supplement), S95–S120.

Conkling, S. W., & Henry, W. (1999). Professional development partnerships: A new model for music teacher preparation. *Arts Education Policy Review*, 100 (4), 19–23. Retrieved February 8, 2003 from www.hwwilsonweb.com.

Fiese, R. K., & DeCarbo, N. J. (1995). Urban music education: The teachers' perspective. *Music Educators Journal*, 81(6), 27–31.

Fowler, C. (1970). Teacher education: Stop sending innocents into battle unarmed. *Music Educators Journal, Special Issue*.

Parsons, M. (1995). A PDS network of teachers: The case of art. In M. Johnston, P. Brosnan, D. Cramer, & T. Dove (Eds.), *Collaborative reform and other improbable dreams* (pp. 223–231). Albany: State University of New York Press.

Robinson, M. (2000). A theory of collaborative music education between higher education and urban public schools (unpublished doctoral dissertation, Eastman School of Music of the University of Rochester).

Spillane, J. P., Hallett, T., & Diamond, J. B. (2003). Forms of capital and the construction of leadership: Instructional leadership in urban elementary schools. *Sociology of Education*, 76, 1–17.

Thiessen, D., & Barrett, J. R. (2002). Reform-minded music teachers: A more comprehensive image of teaching for music teacher education. In R. Colwell and C. Richardson (Eds.), *The new handbook of research on music teaching and learning* (pp. 759–785). New York: Oxford.

Wynne, J. (2001). *Teachers as leaders in education reform. ERIC digest* (ERIC Document Reproduction Service No. ED462376).

Zederayko, M. W. (2000). The impact of administrator and teacher leadership on the development of an exemplary arts program and its role in school reform: A case study. *Dissertation Abstracts International*, 61, 04A (UMI number 9971274).

About the Contributors

Randall Everett Allsup, Ed.D., is assistant professor of music and music education at Teachers College, Columbia University, New York, New York. **Amylia C. Barnett** and **Emily J. Katz** earned the degree Master of Arts from Teachers College. Katz and Barnett teach public school music in New York City.

Cindy L. Bell is assistant professor of Music at the Aaron Copland School of Music, Queens College, City University of New York, where she teaches undergraduate and graduate music education. Dr. Bell is a specialist in choral music education and guest conducts festival choirs of all ages. Recent articles appear in the *International Journal of Research in Choral Singing* (www .choralresearch.com), *Bulletin of the Council for Research in Music Education*, *Journal of Music Teacher Education*, and the *Music Educators Journal*.

Donna T. Emmanuel, currently an assistant professor at the University of North Texas, holds degrees from the University of Michigan and Michigan State University. She has taught in inner-city schools in Florida and Michigan, and worked extensively with the Detroit School District. She worked as a research associate with Dr. Hal Abeles in evaluating arts-centered education programs in Detroit, and was a research assistant for Dr. Richard Colwell on the second edition of *The New Handbook of Research on Music Teaching and Learning*.

Fred P. Eyrich Jr. is the director of Instrumental Music at Abraham Lincoln High School in Philadelphia, Pennsylvania, where he directs the instrumental ensembles and teaches instrumental music, music appreciation, and music technology classes. He has been a teacher of vocal and instrumental music at all grade levels within the School District of Philadelphia for 18 years. Mr.

Eyrich has a bachelor's degree in Music Education from Temple University. He is a member of the Pennsylvania Music Educators Association (PMEA), MENC, and the Technology Institute for Music Educators (TI:ME), and is active as a professional musician in the Philadelphia area.

Michele A. Flagg has been teaching general and vocal music to urban students since 1992. She currently teaches at School No. 25 in Paterson, New Jersey. She holds a BA in Music Education from Fairleigh Dickinson University, an M.Ed. from Seton Hall University, and is currently working on an M.Ed. in Educational Leadership from William Paterson University.

Carol Frierson-Campbell, assistant professor of Music Education at William Paterson University, holds degrees from Tennessee Technological University, Ithaca College, and the Eastman School of Music. An active member of the William Paterson faculty, she teaches courses in music education and graduate research. Carol's professional activities focus on improving curricula and support for music education in urban settings.

Elizabeth N. Hazelette is senior coordinator of Music Education for Norfolk Public Schools in Norfolk, Virginia. She holds a BS and MS in Music Education from Old Dominion University and an Endorsement in Public School Supervision and Administration from the University of Virginia. She is past president of the Virginia Association of Music Education Administrators and currently serves as the supervisor representative on the Editorial Board for Virginia's *Notes, Music Educator's Journal.*

Al D. Holcomb is assistant professor and coordinator of music education at the University of Central Florida in Orlando. He is actively engaged as a researcher and presenter in the areas of professional development for urban music teachers, music assessment, and musicianship skill development. Dr. Holcomb received his degrees from Texas Christian University and the Hartt School, University of Hartford.

Patrick M. Jones, Ph.D., is associate professor, assistant director of the School of Music, and head of the Music Education Division at the University of the Arts in Philadelphia, Pennsylvania. In addition to his academic career, he is a lieutenant colonel and chief of Air National Guard Bands, where he is responsible for over 400 personnel in 11 bands across the United States. Dr. Jones is the chair of PMEA-SMTE, a board member of Philadelphia Academies Incorporated, an author, and a presenter on a variety of topics related to instrumental music education and bands, and is active as a guest conductor for honor bands in the United States and Europe.

Marsha Kindall-Smith is faculty associate in Music Education at the University of Wisconsin-Milwaukee and vice president for the Southeast District of the Wisconsin Music Educators Association (WMEA), and she served on the MENC Minority Task Force. She earned degrees from Oberlin College, Ohio State University, and Boston University. Awards include the UMW 2003–2004 Distinguished Undergraduate Teaching Award and the Minnesota Music Educators Association (MMEA) Lowell Mason Award for outstanding contributions to music education.

Herbert D. Marshall holds a Ph.D. in Music Education from Temple University and is assistant professor in Music Education at the University of Michigan. His work in teacher preparation is informed by over 20 years with learners from infants to adults in rural, suburban, and urban settings.

Corinne Mills is the district music coach for the Hartford Public Schools, responsible for a staff of 60 music teachers serving 24,000 students at 36 public and magnet schools. During her tenure she has developed and continues to explore innovative programming for city kids both site based and district wide. Ms. Mills has two college-age daughters and is a professional cellist, with over 100 performances annually throughout the greater Connecticut area.

Robert Morrison is the chairman and CEO of the Music for All Foundation, a national organization dedicated to expanding access to music and arts education in our schools and communities. He is a nationally known leader in the arts education and advocacy fields. His philanthropic work has led to more than $40 million being invested to support music education.

Jonathan C. Rappaport is the head of school of the Conservatory Lab Charter School in Boston, Massachusetts, and was formerly the performing arts liaison for the Worcester (MA) Public Schools. Additionally, Mr. Rappaport is the codirector of the Kodály Music Institute at New England Conservatory in Boston. He is a composer, author, conductor, and a contributor to the Massachusetts Arts Curriculum Framework, and has received awards from the Massachusetts Music Educators Association, the Massachusetts Alliance for Arts Education, and the New England Theatre Conference.

Mitchell Robinson is an assistant professor of music education at Michigan State University, where he teaches graduate and undergraduate courses and coordinates the music student teaching program. Dr. Robinson holds degrees from SUNY Buffalo, the Hartt School of Music, and the Eastman School of Music, and has studied music education and conducting at Northwestern University. Robinson was awarded the 1997 Reston Prize from Arts

Education Policy Review, the 1999 Research Award from the International Network of Performing & Visual Arts Schools, and is a coauthor of *Great Beginnings for Music Educators: Mentoring and Supporting New Teachers*, published by MENC.

Nathalie G. Robinson is associate professor and chair of the Undergraduate and Graduate Music Education Programs at Hofstra University, Hempstead, New York. Dr. Robinson is active as a clinician and guest speaker at local, state, and national music conferences. Prior to her work at Hofstra, Dr. Robinson served as the project administrator for the Creative Arts Laboratory at Teachers College, Columbia University, and as a visiting professor at the Cultural University in Taipei, Taiwan.

Susan Snyder is a consultant, author, teacher, policy advisor, and mentor focusing on arts-based and integrated curriculum design in education and media. She is president of arts education IDEAS, a company devoted to educational excellence in and through the arts. She has taught at every level from pre-K through postgraduate studies, and enjoys travel and photography.

Patrice Madura Ward-Steinman is an associate professor and chair of the Music Education Department at the Indiana University School of Music. Other research interests include vocal jazz, creative thinking, and the Big Band era, and she has published articles in the *JRME, ISME, JHRME, PMER, CRME, Psychology of Music,* and *Teaching Music.* Dr. Madura's book, *Getting Started with Vocal Improvisation*, is published by MENC, and she regularly presents workshops and papers on improvisation at national and international conferences.

Jill Warzer holds degrees in music education from the University of Vermont and Holy Names College. After teaching music in the public schools of Vermont and California for 13 years, she became the education program director for the Onion River Arts Council (Vermont) and the South Carolina Arts Commission, working with artists, teachers, administrators, and students to develop and implement programs that integrate the arts and other curricula. For the past eight years, Ms. Warzer has served as music and arts curriculum specialist, grades pre-K–12 for the Baltimore City Public School System.

Michelle Wiebe Zederayko is an art educator who has taught in several cities in Canada. She has acted as a curriculum leader in a Fine Arts department and observed teacher leadership in action. Currently Michelle is on Faculty at the School of Design, George Brown College in Toronto, Canada.